FIAT & ABARTH 500 600

Also from Veloce Publishing

Speedpro Series

4-Cylinder Engine Short Block High-Performance Manual (Hammill)
Alfa Romeo DOHC High-performance Manual (Kartalamakis)
Alfa Romeo V6 Engine High-performance Manual (Kartalamakis)
BMC 998cc A-series Engine, How to Power Tune (Hammill)
1275cc A-series High-performance Manual (Hammill)
Camshafts – How to Choose & Time Them For Maximum Power (Hammill)
Competition Car Datalogging Manual, The (Templeman)
Cylinder Heads, How to Build, Modify & Power Tune (Burgess & Gollan)
Distributor-type Ignition Systems, How to Build & Power Tune (Hammill)
Fast Road Car, How to Plan and Build – (Stapleton)
Ford SOHC 'Pinto' & Sierra Cosworth DOHC Engines, How to Power Tune (Hammill)
Ford V8, How to Power Tune Small Block Engines (Hammill)
Harley-Davidson Evolution Engines, How to Build & Power Tune (Hammill)
Holley Carburetors, How to Build & Power Tune (Hammill)
Honda Civic Type R High-Performance Manual, The (Cowland & Clifford)
Jaguar XK Engines, How to Power Tune (Hammill)
Land Rover Discovery, Defender & Range Rover – How to Modify Coil Sprung Models for High Performance & Off-Road Action (Hosier)
MG Midget & Austin-Healey Sprite, How to Power Tune (Stapleton)
MGB 4-cylinder Engine, How to Power Tune (Burgess)
MGB V8 Power, How to Give Your (Williams)
MGB, MGC & MGB V8, How to Improve – (Williams)
Mini Engines, How to Power Tune On a Small Budget (Hammill)
Motorcycle-engined Racing Car, How to Build (Pashley)
Motorsport, Getting Started in (Collins)
Nissan GT-R High-performance Manual, The (Gorodji)
Nitrous Oxide High-performance Manual, The (Langfield)
Race & Trackday Driving Techniques (Hornsey)
Retro or classic car for high performance, How to modify your (Stapleton)
Rover V8 Engines, How to Power Tune (Hammill)
Secrets of Speed – Today's techniques for 4-stroke engine blueprinting & tuning (Swager)
Sportscar & Kitcar Suspension & Brakes, How to Build & Modify (Hammill)
SU Carburettor High-performance Manual (Hammill)
Successful Low-Cost Rally Car, How to Build a (Young)
Suzuki 4x4, How to Modify For Serious Off-road Action (Richardson)
Tiger Avon Sportscar, How to Build Your Own (Dudley)
TR2, 3 & TR4, How to Improve (Williams)
TR5, 250 & TR6, How to Improve (Williams)
TR7 & TR8, How to Improve (Williams)
V8 Engine, How to Build a Short Block For High Performance (Hammill)
Volkswagen Beetle Suspension, Brakes & Chassis, How to Modify For High Performance (Hale)
Volkswagen Bus Suspension, Brakes & Chassis for High Performance, How to Modify (Hale)
Weber DCOE, & Dellorto DHLA Carburetors, How to Build & Power Tune(Hammill)

Enthusiast's Restoration Manual Series

Citroën 2CV, How to Restore (Porter)
Classic Car Bodywork, How to Restore (Thaddeus)
Classic British Car Electrical Systems (Astley)
Classic Car Electrics (Thaddeus)
Classic Cars, How to Paint (Thaddeus)
Jaguar E-type (Crespin)
Reliant Regal, How to Restore (Payne)
Triumph TR2, 3, 3A, 4 & 4A, How to Restore (Williams)
Triumph TR5/250 & 6, How to Restore (Williams)
Triumph TR7/8, How to Restore (Williams)
Triumph Trident T150/T160 & BSA Rocket III, How to Restore (Rooke)
Ultimate Mini Restoration Manual, The (Ayre & Webber)
Volkswagen Beetle, How to Restore (Tyler)
VW Bay Window Bus (Paxton)

Expert Guides

Land Rover Series I-III – Your expert guide to common problems & how to fix them (Thurman)
MG Midget & A-H Sprite – Your expert guide to common problems & how to fix them (Horler)

Those Were The Days ... Series

Alpine Trials & Rallies 1910-1973 (Pfundner)
American 'Independent' Automakers – AMC to Willys 1945 to 1960 (Mort)
American Station Wagons – The Golden Era 1950-1975 (Mort)
American Trucks of the 1950s (Mort)
American Trucks of the 1960s (Mort)
American Woodies 1928-1953 (Mort)
Anglo-American Cars from the 1930s to the 1970s (Mort)
Austerity Motoring (Bobbitt)
Austins, The last real (Peck)
Brighton National Speed Trials (Gardiner)
British and European Trucks of the 1970s (Peck)
British Drag Racing – The early years (Pettitt)
British Lorries of the 1950s (Bobbitt)
British Lorries of the 1960s (Bobbitt)
British Touring Car Racing (Collins)
British Police Cars (Walker)
British Woodies (Peck)
Café Racer Phenomenon, The (Walker)
Don Hayter's MGB Story – The birth of the MGB in MG's Abingdon Design & Development Office (Hayter)
Drag Bike Racing in Britain – From the mid '60s to the mid '80s (Lee)
Dune Buggy Phenomenon, The (Hale)
Dune Buggy Phenomenon Volume 2, The (Hale)
Endurance Racing at Silverstone in the 1970s & 1980s (Parker)
Hot Rod & Stock Car Racing in Britain in the 1980s (Neil)
Last Real Austins 1946-1959, The (Peck)
Mercedes-Benz Trucks (Peck)
MG's Abingdon Factory (Moylan)
Motor Racing at Brands Hatch in the Seventies (Parker)
Motor Racing at Brands Hatch in the Eighties (Parker)
Motor Racing at Crystal Palace (Collins)
Motor Racing at Goodwood in the Sixties (Gardiner)
Motor Racing at Nassau in the 1950s & 1960s (O'Neil)
Motor Racing at Oulton Park in the 1960s (McFadyen)
Motor Racing at Oulton Park in the 1970s (McFadyen)
Motor Racing at Thruxton in the 1970s (Grant-Braham)
Motor Racing at Thruxton in the 1980s (Grant-Braham)
Superprix – The Story of Birmingham Motor Race (Page & Collins)
Three Wheelers (Bobbitt)

Great Cars

Austin-Healey – A celebration of the fabulous 'Big' Healey (Piggott)
Triumph TR - TR2 to 6: The last of the traditional sports cars (Piggott)

Rally Giants Series

Audi Quattro (Robson)
Austin Healey 100-6 & 3000 (Robson)
Fiat 131 Abarth (Robson)
Ford Escort Mkl (Robson)
Ford Escort RS Cosworth & World Rally Car (Robson)
Ford Escort RS1800 (Robson)
Lancia Delta 4WD/Integrale (Robson)
Lancia Stratos (Robson)
Mini Cooper/Mini Cooper S (Robson)
Peugeot 205 T16 (Robson)
Saab 96 & V4 (Robson)
Subaru Impreza (Robson)
Toyota Celica GT4 (Robson)

WSC Giants

Audi R8 (Wagstaff)
Ferrari 312P & 312PB (Collins & McDonough)
Gulf-Mirage 1967 to 1982 (McDonough)
Matra Sports Cars – MS620, 630, 650, 660 & 670 – 1966 to 1974 (McDonough)

Biographies

A Chequered Life – Graham Warner and the Chequered Flag (Hesletine)
A Life Awheel – The 'auto' biography of W de Forte (Skelton)
Amédée Gordini ... a true racing legend (Smith)
André Lefebvre, and the cars he created at Voisin and Citroën (Beck)
Cliff Allison, The Official Biography of – From the Fells to Ferrari (Gauld)
Driven by Desire – The Desiré Wilson Story
First Principles – The Official Biography of Keith Duckworth (Burr)
Inspired to Design – F1 cars, Indycars & racing tyres: the autobiography of Nigel Bennett (Bennett)
Jack Sears, The Official Biography of – Gentleman Jack (Gauld)
John Chatham – 'Mr Big Healey' – The Official Biography (Burr)
The Lee Noble Story (Wilkins)
Mason's Motoring Mayhem – Tony Mason's hectic life in motorsport and television (Mason)
Raymond Mays' Magnificent Obsession (Apps)
Pat Moss Carlsson Story, The – Harnessing Horsepower (Turner)
Tony Robinson – The biography of a race mechanic (Wagstaff)
Virgil Exner – Visioneer: The Official Biography of Virgil M Exner Designer Extraordinaire (Grist)

General

1½-litre GP Racing 1961-1965 (Whitelock)
AC Two-litre Saloons & Buckland Sportscars (Archibald)
Alfa Romeo 155/156/147 Competition Touring Cars (Collins)
Alfa Romeo Giulia Coupé GT & GTA (Tipler)
Alfa Romeo Montreal – The dream car that came true (Taylor)
Alfa Romeo Montreal – The Essential Companion (Classic Reprint of 500 copies) (Taylor)
Alfa Tipo 33 (McDonough & Collins)
Alpine & Renault – The Development of the Revolutionary Turbo F1 Car 1968 to 1979 (Smith)
Alpine & Renault – The Sports Prototypes 1963 to 1969 (Smith)
Alpine & Renault – The Sports Prototypes 1973 to 1978 (Smith)
Anatomy of the Classic Mini (Huthert & Ely)
Anatomy of the Works Minis (Moylan)
Armstrong-Siddeley (Smith)
Art Deco and British Car Design (Down)
Autodrome (Collins & Ireland)
Autodrome 2 (Collins & Ireland)
Automotive A-Z, Lane's Dictionary of Automotive Terms (Lane)
Automotive Mascots (Kay & Springate)
Bahamas Speed Weeks, The (O'Neil)
Bentley Continental, Corniche and Azure (Bennett)
Bentley MkVI, Rolls-Royce Silver Wraith, Dawn & Cloud/Bentley R & S-Series (Nutland)
Bluebird CN7 (Stevens)
BMC Competitions Department Secrets (Turner, Chambers & Browning)
BMW 5-Series (Cranswick)
BMW Z-Cars (Taylor)
BMW – The Power of M (Vivian)
British at Indianapolis, The (Wagstaff)
British Cars, The Complete Catalogue of, 1895-1975 (Culshaw & Horrobin)
BRM – A Mechanic's Tale (Salmon)
BRM V16 (Ludvigsen)
Bugatti Type 40 (Price)
Bugatti 46/50 Updated Edition (Price & Arbey)
Bugatti T44 & T49 (Price & Arbey)
Bugatti 57 2nd Edition (Price)
Bugatti Type 57 Grand Prix – A Celebration (Tomlinson)
Caravan, Improve & Modify Your (Porter)
Caravans, The Illustrated History 1919-1959 (Jenkinson)
Caravans, The Illustrated History From 1960 (Jenkinson)
Carrera Panamericana, La (Tipler)
Chrysler 300 – America's Most Powerful Car 2nd Edition (Ackerson)
Chrysler PT Cruiser (Ackerson)
Citroën DS (Bobbitt)
Classic British Car Electrical Systems (Astley)
Cobra – The Real Thing! (Legate)
Competition Car Aerodynamics 3rd Edition (McBeath)
Competition Car Composites A Practical Handbook (Revised 2nd Edition) (McBeath)
Concept Cars, How to illustrate and design (Dewey)
Cortina – Ford's Bestseller (Robson)
Coventry Climax Racing Engines (Hammill)
Daily Mirror 1970 World Cup Rally 40, The (Robson)
Daimler SP250 New Edition (Long)
Datsun Fairlady Roadster to 280ZX – The Z-Car Story (Long)
Dino – The V6 Ferrari (Long)
Dodge Challenger & Plymouth Barracuda (Grist)
Dodge Charger – Enduring Thunder (Ackerson)
Dodge Dynamite! (Grist)
Dorset from the Sea – The Jurassic Coast from Lyme Regis to Old Harry Rocks photographed from its best viewpoint (Belasco)
Draw & Paint Cars – How to (Gardiner)
Drive on the Wild Side, A – 20 Extreme Driving Adventures From Around the World (Weaver)
Dune Buggy, Building A – The Essential Manual (Shakespeare)
Dune Buggy Files (Hale)
Dune Buggy Handbook (Hale)
East German Motor Vehicles in Pictures (Suhr/Weinreich)
Fast Ladies – Female Racing Drivers 1888 to 1970 (Bouzanquet)
Fate of the Sleeping Beauties, The (op de Weegh/Hottendorff/op de Weegh)
Ferrari 288 GTO, The Book of the (Sackey)
Ferrari 333 SP (O'Neil)
Fiat & Abarth 124 Spider & Coupé (Tipler)
Fiat & Abarth 500 & 600 – 2nd Edition (Bobbitt)
Fiats, Great Small (Ward)
Ford Cleveland 335-Series V8 engine 1970 to 1982 – The Essential Source Book (Hammill)
Ford F100/F150 Pick-up 1948-1996 (Ackerson)
Ford F150 Pick-up 1997-2005 (Ackerson)
Ford GT – Then, and Now (Streather)
Ford GT40 (Legate)
Ford Midsize Muscle – Fairlane, Torino & Ranchero (Cranswick)
Ford Model Y (Roberts)
Ford Small Block V8 Racing Engines 1962-1970 – The Essential Source Book (Hammill)
Ford Thunderbird From 1954, The Book of the (Long)
Formula 5000 Motor Racing, Back then ... and back now (Lawson)
Forza Minardi! (Vigar)
France: the essential guide for car enthusiasts – 200 things for the car enthusiast to see and do (Parish)
Grand Prix Ferrari – The Years of Enzo Ferrari's Power, 1948-1980 (Pritchard)
Grand Prix Ford – DFV-powered Formula 1 Cars (Robson)
GT – The World's Best GT Cars 1953-73 (Dawson)
Hillclimbing & Sprinting – The Essential Manual (Short & Wilkinson)
Honda NSX (Long)
Inside the Rolls-Royce & Bentley Styling Department – 1971 to 2001 (Hull)
Intermeccanica – The Story of the Prancing Bull (McCredie & Reisner)
Jaguar, The Rise of (Price)
Jaguar XJ 220 – The Inside Story (Moreton)
Jaguar XJ-S, The Book of the (Long)
Jeep Wrangler (Ackerson)
The Jowett Jupiter - The car that leaped to fame (Nankivell)
Karmann-Ghia Coupé & Convertible (Bobbitt)
Kris Meeke – Intercontinental Rally Challenge Champion (McBride)
Lamborghini Miura Bible, The (Sackey)
Lamborghini Urraco, The Book of the (Landsem)
Lancia 037 (Collins)
Lancia Delta HF Integrale (Blaettel & Wagner)
Land Rover Series III Reborn (Porter)
Land Rover, The Half-ton Military (Cook)
Lea-Francis Story, The (Price)
Le Mans Panoramic (Ireland)
Lexus Story, The (Long)
Little book of microcars, the (Quellin)
Little book of smart, the – New Edition (Jackson)
Little book of trikes, the (Quellin)
Lola – The Illustrated History (1957-1977) (Starkey)
Lola – All the Sports Racing & Single-seater Racing Cars 1978-1997 (Starkey)
Lola T70 – The Racing History & Individual Chassis Record – 4th Edition (Starkey)
Lotus 18 Colin Chapman's U-turn (Whitelock)
Lotus 49 (Oliver)
Marketingmobiles, The Wonderful Wacky World of (Hale)
Maserati 250F In Focus (Pritchard)
Mazda MX-5/Miata 1.6 Enthusiast's Workshop Manual (Grainger & Shoemark)
Mazda MX-5/Miata 1.8 Enthusiast's Workshop Manual (Grainger & Shoemark)
Mazda MX-5 Miata, The book of the – The 'Mk1' NA-series 1988 to 1997 (Long)
Mazda MX-5 Miata Roadster (Long)
Mazda Rotary-engined Cars (Cranswick)
Maximum Mini (Booij)
Meet the English (Bowie)
Mercedes-Benz SL – R230 series 2001 to 2011 (Long)
Mercedes-Benz SL – W113-series 1963-1971 (Long)
Mercedes-Benz SL & SLC – 107-series 1971-1989 (Long)
Mercedes-Benz SLK – R170 series 1996-2004 (Long)
Mercedes-Benz SLK – R171 series 2004-2011 (Long)
Mercedes-Benz W123-series – All models 1976 to 1986 (Long)
Mercedes G-Wagen (Long)
MGA (Price Williams)
MGB & MGB GT– Expert Guide (Auto-doc Series) (Williams)
MGB Electrical Systems Updated & Revised Edition (Astley)
Micro Caravans (Jenkinson)
Micro Trucks (Mort)
Microcars at Large! (Quellin)
Mini Cooper – The Real Thing! (Tipler)
Mini Minor to Asia Minor (West)
Mitsubishi Lancer Evo, The Road Car & WRC Story (Long)
Montlhéry, The Story of the Paris Autodrome (Boddy)
Morgan Maverick (Lawrence)
Morgan 3 Wheeler – back to the future!, The (Dron)
Morris Minor, 60 Years on the Road (Newell)
Motor Movies – The Posters! (Veysey)
Motor Racing – Reflections of a Lost Era (Carter)
Motor Racing – The Pursuit of Victory 1930-1962 (Carter)
Motor Racing – The Pursuit of Victory 1963-1972 (Wyatt/Sears)
Motor Racing Heroes – The Stories of 100 Greats (Newman)
Motorsport In colour, 1950s (Wainwright)
N.A.R.T. – A concise history of the North American Racing Team 1957 to 1983 (O'Neil)
Nissan 300ZX & 350Z – The Z-Car Story (Long)
Nissan GT-R Supercar: Born to race (Gorodji)
Northeast American Sports Car Races 1950-1959 (O'Neil)
Nothing Runs – Misadventures in the Classic, Collectable & Exotic Car Biz (Slutsky)
Pass the Theory and Practical Driving Tests (Gibson & Hoole)
Peking to Paris 2007 (Young)
Pontiac Firebird (Cranswick)
Porsche Boxster (Long)
Porsche 356 (2nd Edition) (Long)
Porsche 908 (Födisch, Neßhöver, Roßbach, Schwarz & Roßbach)
Porsche 911 Carrera – The Last of the Evolution (Corlett)
Porsche 911R, RS & RSR, 4th Edition (Starkey)
Porsche 911, The Book of the (Long)
Porsche 911 – The Definitive History 2004-2012 (Long)
Porsche – The Racing 914s (Smith)
Porsche 911SC 'Super Carrera' – The Essential Companion (Streather)
Porsche 914 & 914-6: The Definitive History of the Road & Competition Cars (Long)
Porsche 924 (Long)
The Porsche 924 Carreras – evolution to excellence (Smith)
Porsche 928 (Long)
Porsche 944 (Long)
Porsche 964, 993 & 996 Data Plate Code Breaker (Streather)
Porsche 993 'King Of Porsche' – The Essential Companion (Streather)
Porsche 996 'Supreme Porsche' – The Essential Companion (Streather)
Porsche 997 2004-2012 – Porsche Excellence (Streather)
Porsche Racing Cars – 1953 to 1975 (Long)
Porsche Racing Cars – 1976 to 2005 (Long)
Porsche – The Rally Story (Meredith)
Porsche: Three Generations of Genius (Meredith)
Preston Tucker & Others (Linde)
RAC Rally Action! (Gardiner)
RACING COLOURS – MOTOR RACING COMPOSITIONS 1908-2009 (Newman)
Rallye Sport Fords: The Inside Story (Moreton)
Renewable Energy Home Handbook, The (Porter)
Roads with a View – England's greatest views and how to find them by road (Corfield)
Rolls-Royce Silver Shadow/Bentley T Series Corniche & Camargue – Revised & Enlarged Edition (Bobbitt)
Rolls-Royce Silver Spirit, Silver Spur & Bentley Mulsanne 2nd Edition (Bobbitt)
Rover P4 (Bobbitt)
Runways & Racers (O'Neil)
Russian Motor Vehicles – Soviet Limousines 1930-2003 (Kelly)
Russian Motor Vehicles – The Czarist Period 1784 to 1917 (Kelly)
RX-7 – Mazda's Rotary Engine Sportscar (Updated & Revised New Edition) (Long)
Scooters & Microcars, The A-Z of Popular (Dan)
Scooter Lifestyle (Grainger)
SCOOTER MANIA! – Recollections of the Isle of Man International Scooter Rally (Jackson)
Singer Story: Cars, Commercial Vehicles, Bicycles & Motorcycle (Atkinson)
Sleeping Beauties USA – abandoned classic cars & trucks (Marek)
SM – Citroën's Maserati-engined Supercar (Long & Claverol)
Speedway – Auto racing's ghost tracks (Collins & Ireland)
Standard Motor Company, The Book of the (Robson)
Steve Hole's Kit Car Cornucopia – Cars, Companies, Stories, Facts & Figures: the UK's kit car scene since 1949 (Hole)
Subaru Impreza: The Road Car And WRC Story (Long)
Supercar, How to Build your own (Thompson)
Tales from the Toolbox (Oliver)
Tatra – The Legacy of Hans Ledwinka, Updated & Enlarged Collector's Edition of 1500 copies (Margolius & Henry)
Taxi! The Story of the 'London' Taxicab (Bobbitt)
Toleman Story, The (Hilton)
Toyota Celica & Supra, The Book of Toyota's Sports Coupés (Long)
Toyota MR2 Coupés & Spyders (Long)
Triumph TR6 (Kimberley)
TT Talking – The TT's most exciting era – As seen by Manx Radio TT's lead commentator 2004-2012 (Lambert)
Two Summers – The Mercedes-Benz W196R Racing Car (Ackerson)
TWR Story, The – Group A (Hughes & Scott)
Unraced (Collins)
Volkswagen Bus Book, The (Bobbitt)
Volkswagen Bus or Van to Camper, How to Convert (Porter)
Volkswagens of the World (Glen)
VW Beetle Cabriolet – The full story of the convertible Beetle (Bobbitt)
VW Beetle – The Car of the 20th Century (Copping)
VW Bus – 40 Years of Splitties, Bays & Wedges (Copping)
VW Bus Book, The (Bobbitt)
VW Golf: Five Generations of Fun (Copping & Cservenka)
VW – The Air-cooled Era (Copping)
VW T5 Camper Conversion Manual (Porter)
VW Campers (Copping)
You & Your Jaguar XK8/XKR – Buying, Enjoying, Maintaining, Modifying – New Edition (Thorley)
Which Oil? – Choosing the right oils & greases for your antique, vintage, veteran, classic or collector car (Michell)
Works Minis, The Last (Purves & Brenchley)
Works Rally Mechanic (Moylan)

Veloce's other imprints:

BATTLE CRY!

Hubble & Hattie

www.veloce.co.uk

Also available ... Apps Download now from www.digital.veloce.co.uk

Also available ... eBook Download now from www.digital.veloce.co.uk

For post publication news, updates and amendments relating to this book please visit www.veloce.co.uk/books/V4998

First published in 1993 by Veloce Publishing Limited, Veloce House, Parkway Farm Business Park, Middle Farm Way, Poundbury, Dorchester DT1 3AR, England. Fax 01305 268864 / e-mail info@veloce.co.uk / web www.veloce.co.uk or www.velocebooks.com. Reprinted July 2016. ISBN 978-1-845849-98-6; UPC: 6-36847-04998-0.
© 1993 and 2016 Malcolm Bobbitt and Veloce Publishing. All rights reserved. With the exception of quoting brief passages for the purpose of review, no part of this publication may be recorded, reproduced or transmitted by any means, including photocopying, without the written permission of Veloce Publishing Ltd. Throughout this book logos, model names and designations, etc, have been used for the purposes of identification, illustration and decoration. Such names are the property of the trademark holder as this is not an official publication. Readers with ideas for automotive books, or books on other transport or related hobby subjects, are invited to write to the editorial director of Veloce Publishing at the above address.
British Library Cataloguing in Publication Data – A catalogue record for this book is available from the British Library. Typesetting, design and page make-up all by Veloce Publishing Ltd on Apple Mac. Printed and bound by CPI Group (UK) Ltd, Croydon, CR0 4YY.

Veloce *Classic Reprint* Series

FIAT & ABARTH 500 600

Malcolm Bobbitt

VELOCE PUBLISHING
THE PUBLISHER OF FINE AUTOMOTIVE BOOKS

ACKNOWLEDGEMENTS

Books such as this do not just happen; researching material has led me to a number of people who have gone out of their way to contribute information and illustrations, all of which is very much appreciated.

In particular I wish to thank Annice Collett and Paul Beard of the National Motor Museum Library who have so patiently suffered my never-ending requests and questions while searching the archives; also Liz English, archivist at Haymarket Publishing for helping to research photographs. Thanks also to Maria Cairnie who, apart from delving into photographs from family days in Italy, has assisted with translation. Special thanks are extended to Fiat Auto (UK) and Fiat SPA Limited who have provided many of the photographs; in this respect I appreciate the help of Giulietta Calabrese who has so patiently dealt with my numerous letters and telephone calls and has been the link with Centro Storico in Turin.

Special appreciation goes to Wally Pratt who, having imparted his knowledge of the Fiat 600, has also kindly provided photographs of his earlier racing days. My thanks to Abarth specialist Tony Castle-Miller of Middle Barton Garage, Oxfordshire, who has given up a lot of his time and allowed me to search his photographic collection. I am appreciative of the assistance given by Larry Collyer, Clifford Peters and Andrew Minney who have read through the text and offered valuable comments. I am further indebted to Andrew who has located a number of brochures in his visits to car meets and autojumbles. Fred Watts has provided both encouragement and information concerning the Topolino, likewise Tony Spillane who has helped with material on the Multipla models. I am also very appreciative of the help given by Jan and Jimmy Di Carlo of the Fiat 500 Club, also for the enthusiastic advice of Simon Martin and Allan McIntosh of Modena Classics.

I am indebted to the following who have lent me photographs or allowed me to photograph their cars: Malcolm Elder, Jill Forde, Terrence Goad, Daniel Hammond, Mike Marczynski and Claire Scott. Thanks also to Rod and Judith of Veloce for their support and help with the book.

Last but not least, my special thanks to Jean, my wife, for her continuing support and encouragement, even though she often suffered being rushed off to look at some interesting aspect of a particular Fiat.

For this second edition, it has been a pleasure to renew my acquaintance with the Fiat 500 and 600 and those enthusiastic owners who provided so much in the way of help when the first edition of this book was published. In the preparation of this revised edition – which is enlarged to provide buying and ownership advice on all aspects of Fiat's baby cars, as well as encompassing the Cinquecento – I'm grateful for the assistance and advice so freely given by a number of individuals: Simon Lynes of Autotoys, Janet Westcott of the Fiat 500 Owners Club, Donato Pepe of DP Motors, Jan and Jimmy Di Carlo of Ital Corsa, Tony Castle-Miller, Anthony Taylor, Jim and Sheila Ellis and Giulietta Calabrese of Fiat Auto (UK) Ltd.

Malcolm Bobbitt

CONTENTS

Acknowledgements	4
Introduction	6

Chapter I AFTER ZERO — 8
- Geneva 1955 — 8
- The Fiat Story — 11
- Giacosa and the Topolino — 14

Chapter II DESIGN AND DEVELOPMENT — 20
- The background — 20
- Concept — 20
- Tipo 100 — 22
- Getting closer … — 23
- Problems … — 25
- Acceptance — 27

Chapter III CHALLENGE FROM ITALY — 30
- Small, but stamina, too... — 30
- A threat to Britain — 31
- More for less — 32
- On the road — 35
- The engine — 37
- Carozzeria creations — 40

Chapter IV EVOLUTION AND BEYOND — 44
- New worlds — 44
- The Multipla — 46
- Fiat v. Dauphine — 46
- 1957 — 49
- 1958 & 1959 — 49
- 600D — 51
- Safer doors — 55
- 600: the Universal car — 57
- Motorsport — 58

COLOUR GALLERY — 65

Chapter V A NEW TOPOLINO — 68
- The micro-car era — 69
- Genesis — 69
- Defining the details — 72
- The green light — 78
- Great launch but cool reaction — 78

Chapter VI SMALL IS BEAUTIFUL — 82
- A real baby car — 82
- On the road — 84
- Engine — 87
- Getting it right — 88
- The 500 Sport — 88
- Gardiniera — 90
- 500D — 93
- 1961 — 95
- 500F — 96
- 1968 — 98
- 500R — 98
- Coachbuilt variants — 102

Chapter VII THE VARIANTS — 104
- Abarth and the sporting Fiats — 104
- 600 becomes Fiat Abarth 750 — 105
- Fiat Abarth 750 Zagato — 105
- Zagato Series II & III — 105
- Abarth and the Nuova 500 — 106
- Record breakers — 106
- Abarth TC — 107
- 850TC Nürburgring Corsa — 107
- Fiat Abarth 1000TC — 107
- 1000TC Radiale — 109
- Abarth 595 — 110
- Abarth 695 — 110
- Bertone and Boano Spyders, Viotti Coupé — 110
- Bialbero and Monomille — 110
- Steyr-Puch — 111
- 600 Multipla — 112
- Neckar and NSU-Fiat — 116
- Autobianchi — 118
- Vignale — 122
- Ghia — 122
- SEAT — 124
- Siata — 124
- Zastava — 124
- Motor Holdings, New Zealand — 124

Chapter VIII THE END OF AN ERA — 126
- Enter the 850 — 126
- Fiat 127 and Panda — 128
- Fiat 126 — 129
- Cinquecento — 132
- Seicento — 136

Chapter IX LIVING WITH A BABY FIAT — 137
- Topolino — 138
- 600 and Multipla — 140
- 500 Nuova — 144
- Fiat 126 — 152
- Cinquecento — 153

Appendices — 155
- Clubs, specialists & suppliers — 155
- Production figures — 156
- Specifications — 157
- Bibliography — 159

Index — 160

INTRODUCTION

Small economical cars have never been far from the top of the popularity stakes. From the early days of motoring the advent of cycle cars meant increased motor vehicle ownership, resulting in a new-found independence for many. During the inter-war years the light car followed in the wake of the cycle car, and the arrival of such delightful machines as the Austin Seven, Opel Laubfrosch, 5CV Citroën, Morris Eight and Ford Y type made ownership ever more attainable. Mass-production arrived in Italy in 1919 with the Fiat 501. Although highly popular, the car did not enjoy the same huge following as one of the world's most famous little cars, the 1936 Fiat 500 Topolino.

After the Second World War the quest for cheap motoring in a period of austerity continued. A whole new era of light cars appeared, including the Volkswagen Beetle, Renault 4CV and Citroën 2CV, as well as Britain's ubiquitous Morris Minor and Austin A30. The Topolino continued its success story in Italy with the newly-clothed 500C, before it gave way in 1955 to the revoltionary and time honoured Fiat 600. There evolved a whole range of minicars aimed at satisfying the demand for independence. From these machines – which obviously displayed their motorcycle heritage – came the bubble car, as well as a plethora of mainly German orientated vehicles representing both the bizarre and respectable. Born out of the search for a small but truly economical car was the tiny Fiat 500 Nuova, which, together with the 600, was the brainchild of Dante Giacosa. The 500 it was

which enjoyed the distinction of being a first car for hundreds of thousands of Italian families. Today, this diminutive car is still found in abundance in its native Italy, enjoying virtual cult status.

This, then, is the story of Fiat's baby cars. It traces their history back to the thirties and forties when a replacement for Italy's most popular small car, the Topolino, was first contemplated. In an effort to chronicle the exhaustive designs and prototypes – often originating from radical ideas – the search for the ultimate in economy cars is explained: a course of events which lead, eventually, to the overtly succesful 600 and its variants such as the eccentric, multi-purpose Multipla. The 500 Nuova, even smaller and more economical, followed but it was not without problems. It is surprising just how many of the world's greatest cars got off to a shaky start: early 500s were doomed to potential failure had not a rescue formula been found and a new car designed and built in weeks rather than months. A tribute to the success of the baby Fiats is the sheer numbers in which they were produced over a period spanning three decades, and the derivatives that remained in production around the world long after the last cars left Italian factories.

With a penchant for disguise, the demure little Fiats appeared in a number of roles, but none so formidable as that of the mighty Abarth. Sedate and sober family cars were transformed into valiant sporting machines capable of taking on the giants of motorsport and defeating then outright. From road-going cars to full-blown racing machines,

July, 1986. Dante Giacosa with the Topolino he helped create half a century before. After the Topolino came the 600 and then the Nuova 500 – Dante Giacosa is the key figure in the development of the baby Fiats; sadly, he died in 1996. (Courtesy Fiat [UK] & Fiat SPA Ltd)

Introduction to the new edition
After nearly four decades of building rear-engined models, the all-new Cinquecento, which was introduced in 1992, not only established new standards in small car design, but appealed to customers seeking fun motoring combined with economy. Six years later in 1998, the design of the little Fiat was again revised, and the new Seicento immediately amassed a loyal following. Other developments in March 2003 saw the unveiling of the Gingo, and, while it maintained all the traditions of the original Topolino and its successors, it evolved as the new generation Panda. The most notable event in the recent annals of the Fiat 500 occurred in 2007 with the arrival of the new baby, with its styling cues echoing the 1957 Nuova. Every bit the new baby Fiat in appearance, it nevertheless featured front-wheel drive. And for the diehard enthusiast there was the reward of opting for a twin-cylinder, rather than a four-cylinder, engine under the bonnet. Further model revisions were made in subsequent years, and for 2016 a number of design tweaks gave the car a sense of styling that even more evoked that of the original 500 Nuova to carry forwards those principles laid down by Dante Giacosa in the early 1930s.

the Abarth Fiats have won the esteem and admiration of some of motorsport's most respected personalities.

Amongst the most successful of all cars in an era spanning the 50s, 60s and 70s, the 600 and 500 Nuova – of which almost 6 million were built – have bequeathed to today's generation of baby Fiats the ideology of four decades past.

**Malcolm Bobbitt,
Cockermouth, Cumbria,**

I

AFTER ZERO

Geneva 1955

At every motor show there is always one car that steals the limelight. At Geneva, in March 1955, this accolade was Fiat's with their revolutionary small car, the 600. Innovation and wizardry provision of so much in such little space placed the newcomer from Turin apart from all others.

The 600 had the honour of being the only completely new car shown at Geneva; all the others were either a variation on a theme or a continuation of existing models. The 600 was so singular and representative of the new that no other car could have challenged Dante Giacosa's design, let alone spearheaded the trend of relatively minimal cars for mass markets.

Fiat had traditionally chosen Geneva as the launching ground for a new model: it was worlds away from Italy's often dire economy and the wealthy surroundings and Switzerland's strong currency provided a prestigious backdrop.

In their presentation of the 600, Fiat demonstrated a wholly intriguing and unusual view of the new car. The diminutive family four-seater, via an active display, was made to split apart, tilt and turn to show off its hidden talents. Whilst the car was going through its acrobatic routine its mechanical systems reacted to an on-road simulation to display a host of moving parts to great effect. A similar, if not identical, display promoted the car at Turin a month later and again in London at Earls Court in October.

The tiny 600 could not have enjoyed a greater impact. It seemed all of Europe's eyes were on Geneva and Fiat. On the eve of the Motor Show Fiat

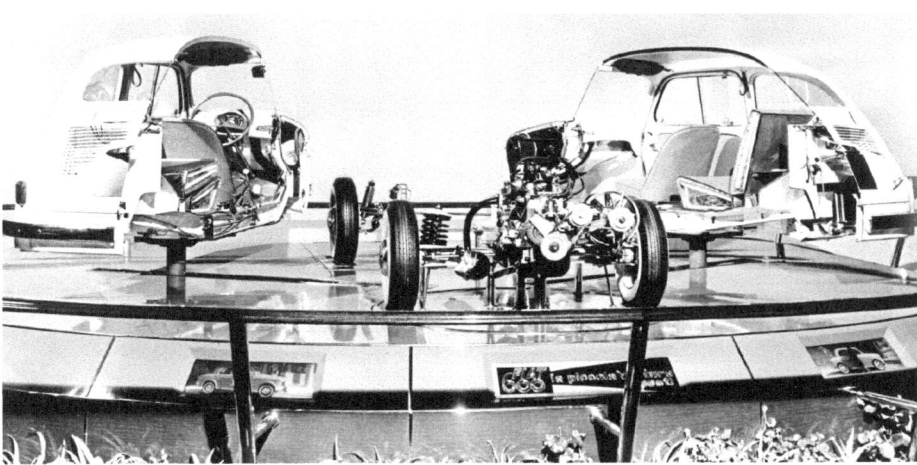

The 600 makes its debut at Geneva in March 1955. In an active display, the car split apart, twisted and turned. (Courtesy National Motor Museum)

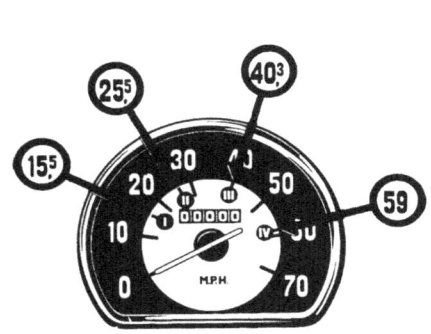

Ready for sale, one of the first batches of 600s destined for the Italian market. (Courtesy Fiat Auto (UK) & Fiat SPA Ltd)

achieved a coup; the city was besieged by what appeared to be an invasion of the little Fiats, sent to Geneva to promote the 600's launch. Thirty 600s could be seen continually driving through city streets – such a publicity stunt had not been witnessed since Citroën had invaded Paris with 5CVs in the early Twenties.

The 600 arrived at a time when European car manufacturers began heading out of years of depression; the Second World War had taken its toll and car building, after hostilities were over, had resumed with pre-war models and production methods originating from the 1930s and before. The demand for cars was enormous but little investment was available for new designs. Nevertheless, pre-war models were eagerly snapped up by customers fervent for independence. Such was the market for cars in Britain, where 75% of all production was taken for export, motorists clamoured for anything that was available.

As the years passed, one by one manufacturers brought out new designs, albeit often old technology wrapped up in modern clothing. There was, however, serious development: in 1948 Citroën showed its starkly utilitarian front-wheel-drive 2CV to an amazed audience who ridiculed the 'umbrella on four wheels,' the design of which could be traced back to 1936. Immediately after the war Renault unveiled the 4CV and, in turn, Volkswagen, under the direction of Ferdinand Porsche, helped restore Germany's motoring needs with the model so affectionately known as the Beetle. As for Italy, Fiat – the country's largest car builder – continued production of the Topolino.

With the introduction of the 600, Fiat was able to retire the legendary Topolino after a long and highly celebrated life. A new motoring market demanded more from a car than the Topolino could offer, illustrated by the success of the 4-seat Belvedere version, so the demure 'Little Mouse' was allowed to languish into history. The 600 rightly received huge attention purely because it was sensational. Lesser in size than the model it replaced, it was small by design but vast in capacity and potential. As if this were not enough, it signalled Fiat's commitment to the growing trend of relocating the engine and drive train to the rear of the car. It could be said that this was 'back to the future' for Fiat as the first Fiat car (1899) had been powered by a water-cooled 3.5hp two-cylinder rear engine of 697cc.

In Europe rear-engined designs had become fashionable for post-war cars: Renault, under the direction of Pierre Lefauchaux who had taken over the French giant from Louis Renault, introduced the 4CV at the 1946 Paris Salon. This small car, with its 760cc four-cylinder engine and unitary construction, had been under development throughout the war years: it was intended it should set new standards in re-establishing the French motor industry and getting Europe back on the road.

Meanwhile, in Germany, Volkswagen (people's car) owed the evolution of its rear-engined car to an unlikely relationship between Ferdinand Porsche and Adolf Hitler. Both men had a commitment to producing an inexpensive car designed primarily to provide transport for the masses. Registered in October 1938, the Volkswagen company began building cars in April 1939; after the war, manufacturing recommenced in 1945 with initial production reserved for military use. Three years later, a quarter of the cars leaving Wolfsburg were destined for export.

Aimed at winning sales in the market for cheap, minimal motoring, a number of minicars appeared during the late 1940s and early '50s. Amongst a myriad of models competing for a stake in what was considered an important and lucrative market, many were to adopt two-stroke engines and, in so doing, preserved much of their cyclecar and motorcycle heritage. Contenders amongst

One of the first brochures to advertise the 600, this English edition associates the new car with the successes of the Topolino. Smaller than the 500, the 600 is still a full 4-seater. (Author's collection)

these cars were Lloyd and Goliath (both part of the Borgward empire), Messerschmitt, Heinkel and Goggomobil. In Britain, Bond and Reliant added to an almost bizarre micro-car scene which was further coloured by smaller companies that fell into obscurity as quickly as they had appeared. An unlikely competitor in this market was BMW with its Isetta which, apart from being built under licence in Germany, was also manufactured in Britain at Brighton. Powered by what was essentially a BMW air-cooled single cylinder motorcycle engine, the BMW bubble car was later augmented by the slightly larger, but no less quaint, 600 and 700 series four-seat models.

Whilst the rear-engine format gained popularity in some areas, particularly Europe, the traditional layout of front-engine and rear-drive was still favoured in Britain and America, although acceptance of front-wheel-drive was gaining momentum.

The Fiat 600 arrived at a time when European sales of small or miniature cars with engines of less than 650cc were substantial and increasing. During 1955, 87,000 cars of less than 650cc had been sold in Italy: half of these sales attributed to the 500C alone. This is hardly surprising when considering that the Fiat concern was responsible for a large proportion of the Italian economy. In a paper delivered to the Society of Automotive Engineers at Detroit in 1957, Laurence Pomeroy, Technical Editor of *The Motor*, stated: "... whereas the largest automobile producer in Germany is owned by no one, and the largest car production unit in France is owned by the State, in Italy Fiat owns the State!" Of the three major Italian motor manufacturers, Fiat, Alfa Romeo and Lancia, Fiat was by far the largest with over 42,000 employees engaged in building a little over 218,000 vehicles in 1955. During the same year Lancia and Alfa Romeo built less than 13,000 cars between them.

Statistics show that for 1955, after the British Motor Corporation, Fiat was the largest European motor manufacturer followed by Volkswagen and Ford (GB). BMC built over 350,000 vehicles of which 42% were exported. Fiat, however, was a leader in supplying cars for home sales, exporting just 30% of its production. The Rootes

A convoy of early 600s somewhere in Britain. Note that each car has a number on the bonnet and an auxiliary interior mirror. (Courtesy Haymarket)

Group, where output of cars attained a figure of 96,000, was the most adept at exporting production with 44% of vehicles going abroad.

Fiat's huge contribution to the Italian economy was generated by a great deal more industrial activity than just its automobile concern. Apart from motor cars, the company not only manufactured commercial vehicles but extended its link with the nation's transport and defence industries, and indeed foreign trade, by producing both aircraft and military equipment. The Fiat empire was active in producing almost everything from raw materials, iron and steel, to household appliances and machine tools.

Fiat, the major shareholder of which at the time was the Agnelli family, amassed a massive turnover of $422m in 1955. Of this, vehicle production accounted for some 85%. Fiat was accepted as having a particularly successful policy of being self-sufficient and, unlike much of the British motor industry, did not have to rely upon external suppliers for body pressings and components. During 1955, the Fiat organisation produced 517,000 tons of iron and steel which included 75,000 tons of iron castings, light alloys and ferrous forgings for automotive manufacture.

The Fiat Story

The success and development of Italy's motor industry can be attributed almost entirely to Fiat whose major achievements lay in the period between the two world wars: in 1919 a mere 173 cars were produced by the company, yet, twenty years later, well over 52,000 cars were leaving its production lines. Nowadays known simply by the acronym FIAT, the company's ancestry reaches even further back, to 1899, when a group of three associates, keen on establishing an effective motor industry in Italy, formed Fabbrica Italiana Automobili Torino.

Giovanni Agnelli. (Author's collection)

Conscious that Italy had not met the automobile challenge with the same determination as had Germany and France, the new association was fearful of a mass importation of motor vehicles from France. The Fiat company was headed by Giovanni Agnelli, a former cavalry officer with a deep social conviction; with Agnelli was Count di Bricherasio, who had an aspiration of establishing a huge automobile factory centred around Turin, and Count Roberto Biscaretti di Ruffia who, even at that time, was fully committed to the love and development of the motor car. Later, di Ruffia would achieve further fame by founding Turin's motor museum.

Also involved with the original trio were Enrico Marchesi and Ludovico Scarfiotti. Marchesi, a qualified engineer, took on the role of managing director, a position to which he was well suited. Scarfiotti was elected chairman and Bricherasio vice-chairman. Giovanni Agnelli accepted the position of company secretary which was considered possibly the most arduous and important task. Di Ruffia, meanwhile, headed the board of directors.

Giovanni Agnelli was the prime motivator in establishing the automotive interests of the group, which included a certain Giovanni Battista Ceirano who had opened a cycle factory in the Autumn of 1898. There was some popularity for the English bicycle in Italy and Ceirano became an agent selling Rudge cycles. An enthusiast of motor cars and an ardent admirer of Aristide Faccioli's designs, Ceirano decided the future lay with building

The first Fiat car, the 3½HP designed by Aristide Faccioli. Four of the original eight cars are thought to have survived. (Courtesy Fiat Auto (UK) & Fiat SPA Ltd)

light cars. When Agnelli and his compatriots were looking for a suitable vehicle to put into production, it was Ceirano they approached as he was known to have already started building a prototype 3.5hp car to Faccioli's design. Known as the 'Welleyes,' the car's name no doubt derived from the influence of the British bicycle.

The Fiat Company was formed on 1st July 1899, although it was not registered until 11th July. Patents for Ceirano's 'Welleyes' car were soon acquired, along with Aristide Faccioli whose services were required in the position of chief engineer. A factory site of 12,000 square metres and costing 70,000 Lire (a little under £3000), was chosen in the Corsa Dante, home of the Turin Exhibition of 1898. By March 1900, when the factory was officially opened, Fiat had built its first car, the Tipo-A. Of the four examples thought to have survived, two are displayed in Turin at the Fiat Historical Centre and the Turin Motor Museum; the third is in America at the Ford Museum while the fourth is on display in Britain at the National Motor Museum, Beaulieu.

The Tipo-A gave way in 1900 to a 6hp car, built on the same principle as the 3.5hp but with a larger engine of 1082cc and, subsequently, a higher maximum speed of 28mph – 7mph faster than the model it replaced. Fuel consumption suffered as a result: at 18mpg (15lt/100km) it was less than half that of the Tipo-A.

Two further designs by Faccioli followed before his departure from Fiat as a result of a serious disagreement

Below: Giovanni Enrico with his 12HP, the first 4-cylinder Fiat. He succeeded Faccioli as chief engineer and with the 12HP achieved fame by winning the Fiat-Panhard event of 1902. The car was the first built in volume by Fiat and the first exported. (Courtesy Fiat Auto (UK) & Fiat SPA Ltd)

Ernest Eldridge took the land speed record in 1924 with the Fiat Mephistopheles. The 21-litre aero-engined car reached 146mph (235kph) at Arpajon, near Paris.

with Agnelli. The rear-engined 1082cc Corsa achieved Fiat's first competition successes: in April 1900 the Turin-Asti race was won with Castori at the wheel and in July 1900 the car took a double victory in the Vicenza-Bassano-Treviso-Radna event when Vincenzo Lancia placed the Fiat in the winning position with Felice Nazzaro in hot pursuit. This was the same Vincenzo Lancia who later went on to establish one of Italy's other famous marques, second only to Fiat during the 1920s and '30s.

Faccioli's last car for Fiat, an 8hp, featured a front-positioned engine, the first in the Fiat catalogue, although initial deliveries had retained the rear engine similar to the 6hp. Eight Fiat 8hp cars competed in the first Tour of Italy of 1902, an event which consisted of fifteen stages over 1000 miles. All the cars had the distinction of finishing every stage.

Giovanni Enrico replaced Faccioli following his departure from Fiat. Enrico, a civil engineer with experience of both steam and electricity, had been responsible for the installation of electric lighting for the 1884 Turin Exhibition. Staying with Fiat until 1906, Enrico's career was relatively shortlived; nevertheless he produced some impressive cars. The 12hp of 1901-2 was the first Fiat to have a four-cylinder engine; the 12hp Corsa, designed as a racing car, performed admirably, winning the Fiat-Panhard event at the end of 1902 and averaging the 187 miles (299km) at 21.33mph (34kph). Not only was the 12hp the first Fiat to be built in considerable numbers, it was also the first to be exported.

As Fiat grew in Italy so it turned its attention to markets abroad. A British subsidiary opened in 1903 and bodies built by Short of Rochester, Ward, Page, Mulliner and Young's of Bromley, were assembled on to chassis imported directly from Turin. Vehicles were built under licence in Austria and, in 1911, Fiat established a factory in New York. The American venture was not the success envisaged and lasted only until 1920.

Fiat taxis saw service in London, Paris and New York: the 'Type 1' taxi was the first Fiat designed expressly for commercial use and over 2100 2.2 litre vehicles were built. Each carried five passengers and 150kgs of luggage, returned a fuel consumption of 28mpg and maintained a maximum speed of 44mph.

After the Great War, Fiat reconsidered its strategy and looked towards mass-production. During hostilities the company had produced enormous numbers of commercial vehicles – 17,217 were built in 1917 alone, a figure not achieved again until the mid-1950s. Cavalli designed the first post-war Fiat, the 501, with mass-production methods allowing over 45,000 examples to be built in its life span of seven years. The 501 was a highly significant car, arriving at a time when mass-production techniques in Europe were first being established. In the same year, 1919, France witnessed the birth of André Citroën's first car, his Type A, which changed the direction of the French motor industry.

Immediately before the launch of the 501 Fiat took a daring look at absolute economy cars. The proposed baby would have been the first '500' but, as it happened, the project was abandoned as Agnelli considered the market unready.

Development at Turin continued throughout the 1920s at the cost of diminished racing activity, although 1924 saw the breaking of the land speed record with the Fiat Mephistopheles. Thundering along a prepared stretch of road at Arpajon, to the south of Paris, the car, fitted with a massive 21 litre aero-engine and driven by Englishman Ernest Eldridge, reached a fraction over 146mph (234.98kph).

Another success was the 509, mass-produced and aimed at an economy-conscious market. At just under a litre, the 509 appeared in a number of guises which included a saloon, coupé and tourer while a 'high-performance' version – the 509S – was also offered. The 509A was available in Britain and was the product of the British subsidiary factory at Wembley.

Fiat became the car maker for all: along with large luxury tourers within the 2 to 3 litre bracket, less ostentatious models afforded completely comfortable transport for the masses. The 514 emerged in 1929, but not before over 90,000 509s had been built; fitting conveniently within the 1.5 litre league, the 514 was extremely efficient even if the styling was less than inspiring. The same engine was fitted into the chassis of the six-cylinder version, the 522: the result was the 515 which combined spaciousness with economy but at the expense of performance.

Right: Exquisitely aerodynamic and enchantingly pretty, the 508 Balilla Mille Miglia is a legend in Fiat history. (Courtesy Fiat Auto (UK) & Fiat SPA Ltd)

Below: A wonderful example of Fiatmobilia, representative of the era. (Courtesy Fiat Auto (UK) & Fiat SPA Ltd)

Among the most famous Fiats was the Balilla 508 which had first been introduced at the 1932 Milan International Motor Show. Three-speed gearboxes coupled to 995cc engines drove initial models; later, four-speed models with an option of overhead valve engines were offered for 1934. Benefiting from slight re-styling, 1934 cars appeared less angular. Most appealing of the 508s was the Balilla Sports Aerodynamic Coupé, a delightfully proportioned design with true sporting qualities. Overall, 112,000 Balillas were produced which included vehicles for military use.

The 1500, first shown at the Milan Show in November 1935, clearly stated an emphasis on style. The 1.5 litre six-cylinder car was a superlative exercise in modern aerodynamics with sharply-raked air-intake and faired-in headlamps. Together with 1 litre models in a similar vein, the styling remained virtually unchanged for nearly two decades.

Giacosa and the Topolino

A most significant diversion into a market aimed at mass appeal occurred in 1936 with the announcement of the 500. The time was considered as being right for such a car and its status in automobile history has proved legendary. Virtually at once the tiny car won the affection of a nation who nicknamed it Topolino, Italian for Mickey Mouse, an endearment which has stayed with it ever since and by which it is better known.

The all-important link between the 500 Topolino and Fiat's later miniature cars is Dante Giacosa. He was 29 years of age when he attended a meeting at which the decision to put the car into production was made. Dr Antonio Fessia had been moved from Fiat's automobile and truck design office, where he was assistant director, to become director of the aero-engine section. Giacosa, as a departmental head noted for valuable work on water-cooled engines, was recognised by Fessia as having

Right: The 500 Topolino, apart from being charmingly demure was, for the era, quite streamlined. The corporate touch of Fiat design is clearly evident. (Courtesy Fiat Auto (UK) & Fiat SPA Ltd)

Below: A prototype 500 (the second prototype Zero A) showing its frontal styling incorporating faired-in headlights. (Courtesy Fiat)

particular abilities and he entrusted Giacosa with part of the 500's intricate design. It is not very clear as to how Antonio Fessia, in charge of aero-engines, became to be chosen by Giovanni Agnelli to oversee the Topolino project, especially when, as it appeared, there were other highly capable engineers within the automobile department.

Dante Giacosa originally joined SPA (Societa Piemontese Automobili) in 1928 with a degree in mechanical engineering. The following year, on 1st May after the company had been absorbed into the Fiat empire, he found himself as a draughtsman at the Lingotto works.

Being selected to design the engine and chassis for the Topolino was a tremendous fillip to Giacosa's confidence. The model designation 'Zero-A' managed to conjure up the image of Fiat's most spirited past model, the Tipo Zero whilst, at the same time, identifying it with the aero-engines division of the company. The body design was the work of Rodolfo Schaeffer, director of the coachwork technical department since 1929, who had conceived the idea that the minimal car should mirror much of the image of the streamlined 1500, although naturally completely scaled down in size. Designed as a 2-seater, it was envisaged the car should carry 110lb (50kg) of luggage or two children.

There was no question as to whether the layout of the engine and transmission would be anything other than conventional with a water-cooled 'four,' positioned at the front, driving the rear wheels. Front-wheel-drive, although developed on a mass-production scale and introduced on the Citroën Traction Avant '7' in the Spring of 1934, could not be considered due to Agnelli's antipathy towards this method of transmission. This had been brought about in 1931 by an experience with an experimental design known as the Tipo 500, an experimental car whose front wheels were driven by an air-cooled 2-cylinder engine. The designer, Oreste Lardone, was sacked when, on a trial run with Agnelli in the passenger seat, the car caught fire. Needless to say, the

As a van, there were several design differences other than body shape over the 500C Belvedere. A bench replaced individual front seats, a grille separated the cab from the load area and the spare wheel was concealed behind the front seat. Double doors were fitted at the rear. This depiction is from a 1949 sales brochure. (Author's collection)

project was abandoned, together with any further thought of front drive for many years to come.

Giacosa's brief was to produce a car that would be cheap to manufacture. By the same token it would have to be both functional and comfortable. Agnelli had decided upon a price guide of 5000 Lire which, to the design team, seemed unattainable, although it nevertheless continued to search for a formula for the ultimate minimal car. Schaeffer's eventual design for the Zero-A bodywork appealed to Giacosa, even if it did present a problem in positioning the engine within the limited space. Determining that the engine should have a capacity of 569cc, Giacosa sought to place the engine ahead of the front wheels – just as the practice with many front-wheel-drive cars today. Having decided upon the engine concept, the detail design was given to Virgilio Borsattino, who had been responsible for some excellent work on aero-engine carburettors. The forward position of the motor, squeezed literally in the raked front end of the car, did mean that not only had the radiator to be positioned behind the engine, but the gearbox had to be controlled by a ponderously long lever.

Final drawings were started on 1st June 1934 and were ready by that August – the fine timescale indicative of the simplicity of Giacosa's designs. The uncomplicated 2-bearing engine, without need for a water pump, relied upon thermo-siphoning for heat exchange; fuel was gravity fed and a simple pump distributed oil without pressure. The chassis followed the same simplistic approach: constructed for lightness it represented a straightforward A-frame. To cope with the Zero-A's diminutive proportions, prototypes were built without running boards, the first Fiat so designed, although they were fitted to production models. Wheels were non-standard and it was Pirelli who was summoned to Turin to design a special 4.25x15 tyre.

First outing for the Zero-A prototype took place on 7th October, 1934, and although it performed admirably it suffered from excessive engine noise. Taking a circular route north from Turin, the Zero-A topped 51mph (82kph) and demonstrated excellent road-holding made possible by its independent front suspension.

A second prototype resulted in relatively minor detail changes from the initial design: excessive engine noise was eventually overcome by re-working the crankshaft; the bodywork supported revised headlights, now projecting slightly from the front wings instead of being flush-mounted, whilst the air intake was made to resemble that of the 1500. An increased weight of 220lbs (100kg) was the result of design changes, although this was deemed acceptable and tooling commenced. In its definitive form the headlamp design was further altered, placing the lamps above the wings.

The Zero-A, officially designated the 500, was launched on 15th June 1936.

To celebrate 60 years of the City Car, the Topolino shared pride of place at the London Design Museum in 1993 with the Nuova 500 and Cinquecento. (Author's collection)

One of the few 4-seat Topolinos built specifically for the British market. 400 were built and only a handful survive. (Courtesy Haymarket)

It sold for 8,900 Lire, had a top speed of 53mph (85kph) and a fuel consumption of 48mpg (6ltr/100km). It received universal acclaim as the world's smallest mass-produced four-cylinder car and output soon reached 100 cars a day at Lingotto, a factory which had been built to accommodate such volume and production methods. According to Dante Giacosa, none were more enthusiastic about the 500 than the British who dubbed it the 'Little Mouse.' Well used to little cars, British motorists had been enjoying the ubiquitous Austin Seven since 1922.

Initially designed as a saloon, the Topolino also developed with a full-length folding sunroof, and it was this version that became the most popular. An extremely pretty little car, streamlined, with room enough for just two adults and luggage, it was also possible to accommodate two children on a makeshift seat. Every inch of space was saved: the two suicide doors (rear hinged) were fitted with sliding windows in order to gain interior width and the spare wheel was carried in a nacelle at the back of the car. There was no external boot lid and luggage had to go through the doors or, in the case of the coupé, through the open roof. A commercial variant was announced at the end of 1936 with a pay-load of 660lbs (300kg). Curiously, at prototype stage, the van was more aerodynamic than the car and was somewhat faster. Double rear doors and revised suspension arrived three years after its launch.

In France, the Topolino was built

Mechanical detail of the Topolino 500C as portrayed in a contemporary 1949 sales brochure. (Author's collection)

under licence by Simca as the Simca Cinq at the company's Nanterre factory in the Seine department. Simca had been established in 1934, primarily to build Fiats for the French market, the first 'French Fiat' being the 508 Balilla.

Major revision to the Topolino occurred during 1938 when the rear suspension was updated, utilising long leaf springs. By this time 46,000 cars had been built. Meanwhile, in 1937 a 500 took the world land speed record in its category with a speed of 90.6mph (145kph).

The Topolino became available in Britain, at a cost of £120, towards the end of 1936 and was shown at the London Motor Show to the curiosity of an interested, if not bemused, audience. Fiat (England) tried in vain to deny rumours that the car was known as Mickey Mouse, going as far as issuing a statement to this effect in *The Autocar* of April 3rd 1936.

The British market was treated to a special 4-seat version of the 500 in 1939, albeit only briefly. Only 400 cars were made which had been designed by Fiat (England) and were identified by their special bodywork incorporating rear side windows. A redesigned floor-pan had built-in rear footwells, and a proper back seat provided comfort for rear passengers. It was common for these cars to be fitted with bumpers and painted in a two-tone metallic finish.

500C with American plates pictured in Italy circa 1952. (Courtesy Maria Cairnie)

In 1948, after 112,000 500As had been built, the 500B debuted at the Geneva show. Cosmetically identical, apart from minor trim changes, the 500B used a more powerful engine, still of 569cc but with overhead valves replacing side valves to increase output by 3.5bhp. To go with 16.5bhp, brakes, suspension, clutch and gearbox all received major attention. A further variant was announced at the Turin Show in the Autumn of 1948: the 500B Giardiniera which fulfilled the role of a multi-purpose 4-seater. Whilst the maximum speed dropped 5kph and fuel consumption increased to 6.5 litres per 100km, 50kg of luggage could be carried in addition to four passengers. The 500B was relatively short-lived; 21,000 vehicles and a year later the Topolino was given a complete facelift that would last until its demise.

Geneva's 1949 Spring Show unveiled an almost totally new Topolino which bore an unmistakable resemblance to its predecessor and without loss of its original character. The 500C had a more contemporary appearance but happily retained the 500A's cheeky styling. The main body pressings remained the same as before but new front wings, shaped to incorporate the headlamps and a new front end, increased the bonnet length. Revised styling changed the shape of the tail and allowed not only increased luggage capacity but the spare wheel to be slid out of sight under the boot floor. Access to the spare wheel was obtained by pulling down a hatch cover, just above bumper level.

Still only a 2-seater, the 500C lost an inch from the overall length of the 500A. The Giardiniera, together with the Belvedere which was unveiled three years later in 1952 as an all-steel estate car, were further variants offering 4-passenger capacity. The 500C was by far the best-selling model out of the entire 500 series and accounted for 376,370 sales.

Simca's "Topolino" received a similar re-vamp, although the bonnet line

The difference in rear styling between the earlier and later 500s can be seen in this picture of a 500C. The rear hatch conceals the spare wheel. (Author's collection)

The styling of the 500C was also extended to the Belvedere. Body sides were built with polished ash and masonite panels. A roll-back roof and third door completed the package. (Author's collection)

was slightly different to the Fiat's, and was re-designated the Six. Whilst the 500C retained a popular following in its native Italy, the Simca fared less well in France, losing ground to the Renault 4CV and Citroën's 2CV.

As the first batches of Fiat 600s prepared to leave the factory for eager customers, they stood alongside the last Topolinos, of which over half a million had been produced since 1936 – 519,646, to be precise!

DESIGN AND DEVELOPMENT

Under the spotlights of the 1955 Geneva Show, the star attraction reflected all that was new. The petite Fiat 600 announced the coming of age of the small and economical family car, which had been born during the years of austerity following the Second World War.

The background

Willingness to change to less orthodox designs of small car was further advanced in Europe than Britain: Renault's 4CV was attacking the market with force; Citroën's 2CV had a job to keep up with demand and the Volkswagen ran true to plan: all attracting masses of eager buyers. In contrast, Austin were producing the A30 and A35 which resembled scaled-down versions of its A40 and A70 models, whilst Morris, now related to Austin under the BMC umbrella, continued churning out the celebrated Minor. Standard, recognising the need for a cheaper and utilitarian car, introduced the no-frills Eight in the early 1950s to compete directly with the cars from Longbridge and Cowley. Ford was still finding buyers for the de-trimmed Popular 103E, the last of the 'upright' models, even though the new shape 100E Anglia had been introduced at the end of 1953. The true contender to brave both unconventionality and mass-produced economy was the Mini, which was still some four years away.

To look at the origins of the Fiat 600 it is necessary to return to pre-Second World War Europe. Dante Giacosa had already earned considerable respect for his work with the Topolino and it was this that led to a more defined role in automobile engineering under the direction of Dr Antonio Fessia. When not preoccupied with later models such as the 508C Balilla and revisions to the 500, he spent some time returning to the design of aero-engines.

As the Topolino continued to enjoy an unqualified success, the question as to what should eventually follow it was never too far away. There is no doubt Giacosa possessed an affinity with the Topolino; he relished small cars, insisting their role was to provide cheap economical transport whilst generating as wide an appeal as possible. His respect for frugality serves as a reflection of his childhood and youthful days when it was important to save every Lire.

Concept

A little before the outbreak of war, Giacosa received promotion within Fiat's automobile division, taking over as assistant director from 1st January 1940. During the second half of the '30s he had been able to give some thought to future small models and went as far as preparing detailed drawings for eventual prototypes. Firstly, a car smaller than the Topolino was drafted, then, secondly, a model between the 500 and the medium-sized 1100. Code-named 400 and 700 respectively, neither car materialised as such, but it is for certain they exercised considerable significance on subsequent designs.

In considering plans for a small utility car every conceivable configuration was examined, even to the point of deciding whether it should have three wheels or four. Any further ideas of

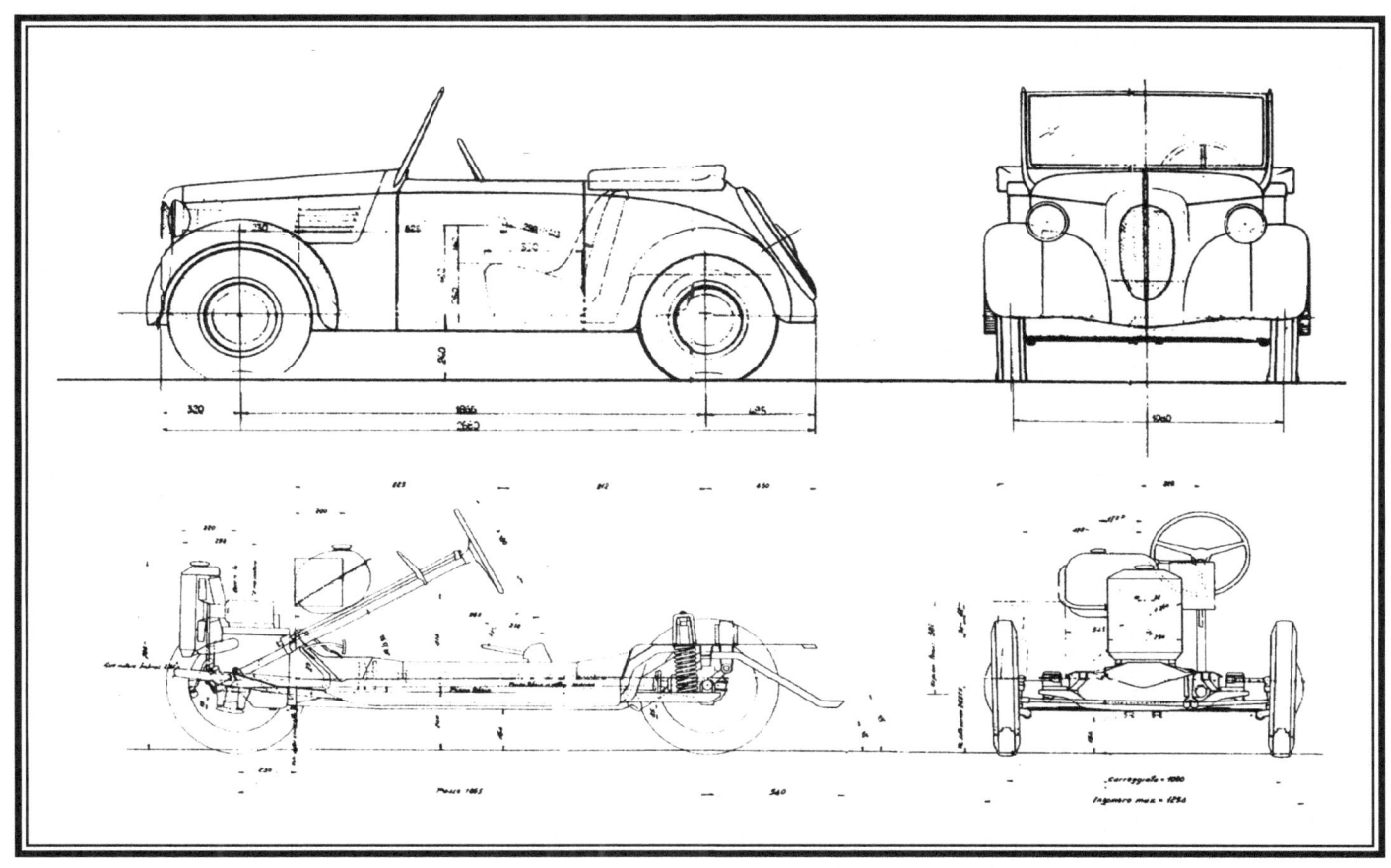

Two sets of drawings for the proposed 400 Minicar. Above are sketches for the bodyshell which date from 1941. Below, dating from 1943, are very faint drawings which show plans for the chassis. (Author's collection)

three-wheelers were immediately cast aside, rejected on grounds of design and stability limitations alone.(It should be explained that Giacosa later affirmed his belief that any motor car, however small or economical, must have four wheels).

The 400, a 2-seat design just as the 500 had been, was, in Giacosa's view, to have been the Topolino's eventual and direct successor. Together with the 700, which had been originally conceived as a 4-door, 4-seat saloon, the model range would have been evenly spaced to cater for the whole span of the economy market. Both cars were designed with conventional power and transmission arrangements; the 700 breaking with traditional Fiat policy at the time by adopting unitary construction. Such was the trepidation at this departure into the unknown, the senior directors of Fiat went as far as purchasing an Opel Olympia, which had been introduced in 1935 as one of the first volume-produced cars to employ chassiless construction.

A full assessment of the Opel and its build structure was made before allowing Giacosa to go ahead with his ideas. Citroën's monocoque Traction Avant, which had created such a furore on its introduction in 1934, was another early example of unitary build but it is likely this was rejected for evaluation on grounds of it having front-wheel-drive, to which Giovanni Agnelli had an aversion.

Development of the 700 presented particular difficulties: weight was the all-important factor and in keeping below 1433lb (650kg), which was considered to be the car's maximum, the engine's crankcase was made from aluminium and the gear casing from a light alloy. Under trials the engine leaked oil excessively and major redesign work was necessary before performance could be considered anywhere near acceptable.

Development of the 700 occurred at the time Fiat was building the Mirafiori works, where the car would have had the distinction of being the first new model to be built. A prototype car was submitted to Mussolini for his approval and it was only a matter of time before the subsequent directive was received to start production. Italy's entry into the Second World War stopped the project in its tracks and caused it to be abandoned. Today, only one prototype is thought to exist and this is displayed in Turin's Automobile Museum.

The 400 was conceived between 1939 and 1940 and shared similar principles to those of the Topolino, although it was somewhat reduced in size. If the Topolino was ever considered to lack refinement, the 400 would have been classed as totally utilitarian. Designed as an open 2-seater it was to be the ultimate in economy cars, giving the original Deux Chevaux a run for its money. Retaining side valves, the diminutive 400cc motor would have produced just 14bhp. Lessons learned with the Topolino's development were put to good use when it came to the 400: four-speed gearbox, independent front suspension, lightweight construction – just a fraction over 880lb (400kg) – were some of the features. The platform chassis was made to supply all necessary strength and rigidity and a light folding hood afforded weather protection. All this meant a car of the smallest proportions for which an attractive appearance had not been high amongst priorities. Lacking both the cheeky stance of the 500 and the sheer aerodynamics of the Balilla 508C, the 400 aspired to nothing other than an out and out economy utilitarian.

During the early days of the war, the design team, under the direction of Giacosa, worked upon a number of projects with the intention that certain models should be put into production as soon as hostilities ended. As often happens, fate played an intriguing trick, leading to decisions quite contrary to those originally intended. As the possibility increased of the Lingotto works being the target of enemy action, prototype vehicles were moved to Cigliano, situated between Turin and Milan, which was considered to be a reasonably safe haven. The design teams were sent off to Mirafiori, but only for a short period before intensified bombing made another move necessary, this time to an even safer location some little distance away.

Resuming work on the Topolino's replacement, further studies on the 400 project led the prototype car to be taken out of its hiding place at Cigliano. The design department was therefore devastated when the unthinkable happened and their premises were destroyed by a direct hit from an enemy bomb. Along with the buildings, which had been reduced to piles of rubble and twisted metal, was the one and only 400 car. All lost, Giacosa was spurred on to find an alternative design to replace the Topolino. The 400 and 700 together had served as a valuable experience, playing an important role in the eventual design of the 600 and, hence a little later, the 500 Nuova.

Tipo 100

The heart of the 600's development lay in designs sketched by Giacosa immediately following the 400 disaster. With obvious connotations of the 400 in mind, a chassis layout with a transverse two-cylinder rear-mounted engine and gearbox was devised. Of more importance and of direct relevance to the 600 were three diagrams, coded 'Tipo 100', which were seen as a key to future development. Resulting from current thinking, the drawings depicted a trio of ideas: conventional layout of front engine and rear drive, front-wheel-drive with transverse engine and, thirdly, a transverse rear-mounted engine. A common factor to each of the designs was the engine itself, which consisted of a 500cc four-cylinder in-line unit. Of the three, Giacosa favoured front-wheel-drive but dared not pursue his true feelings for fear of risking his future career and position within Fiat. A further incident which allows insight into Giacosa's inner thoughts is the existence of sketches, annotated '600 ESP AUTO', for a four-cylinder, side-valve engine with 58 x 60mm cylinders, which reflects designs for a small economy model – surprisingly with front-wheel-drive!.

Had it not been for the war the course of events and design of small Fiats might have been totally different; abandonment of the two existing proposals allowed Giacosa to reappraise the entire motoring needs of post-war Europeans, and Italians in particular. He considered it necessary to be able to produce cars in such quantities as to make them as cheap as possible by utilizing, where and when necessary, unconventional materials and technology. Aware that other manufacturers would be contemplating similar ideas, it was obvious that out of trial and error would arise wholly new conceptions.

The search for alternative engine and transmission arrangements had raised a whole new question as to the design of the gearbox. Giacosa believed that cars intended for a mass market should be built as simply and straightforwardly as possible, and in this respect the Topolino was seen as a landmark in automobile design. It followed, therefore, that the operating mechanism of the car should adopt

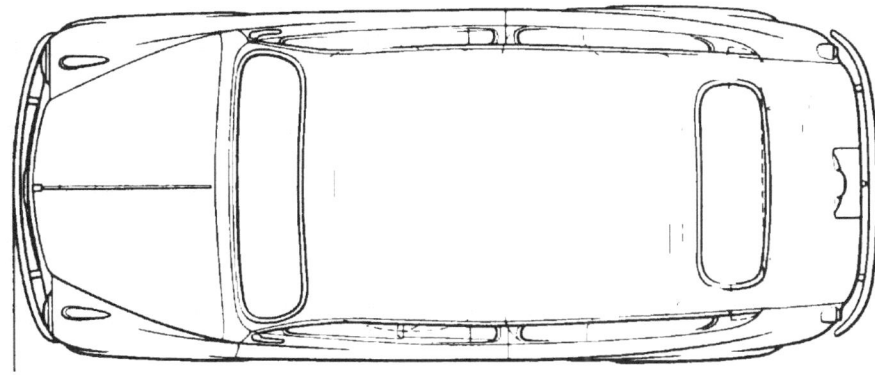

the same principle and what better than an automatic gearbox? As it happened, fully automatic transmission was rejected on the grounds of costs alone, but it was possible to salvage the concept of a semi-automatic system which employed the use of a centrifugal clutch. The technology of this system was well understood by Giacosa, who had already used a similar device on the Cisitalia racing car which had been based, albeit rather loosely, upon the 500's running gear. A further development of the centrifugal clutch was later used by Citroën to good effect on the 2CV and its derivatives.

Virtually no stone was left unturned in the pursuit of what promised to be the ideal minimal car; for a brief time the concept of an electric car received serious contemplation. The idea had come about almost by accident when shortages in fuel provoked alternative suggestions for powered transport; the engine of the departmental Topolino was replaced by an electric motor and power was fed through a bank of accumulators attached to the chassis. The batteries were rather cumbersome and unwieldy, weighing in the order of 924lbs (420kg), which meant that the Topolino had to be connected to the electricity supply for recharging almost constantly when not in use. The vehicle performed well enough with adequate acceleration, managing a maximum speed of 45kph, a little under 30mph, but obvious limitations were experienced, especially in distance capability.

A significant development in design arose out of J.A. Gregoire's plans for a minimal car. Gregoire, of Tracta fame, had used the Simca Cinq as a blueprint and comparison for his rigid but lightweight chassis, which was constructed from cast aluminium-alloy section. Aluminium with duralumin was used for the engine, a horizontally-opposed and air-cooled 600cc twin-cylinder affair. In making a thorough appraisal of the Gregoire, Giacosa was able to persuade Fiat's senior management to agree to the building of a number of prototypes to reflect both Gregoire's design and Fiat technology. Codenamed 102, permission for the project was given to build, by 1949, a series of test cars with a diversity of transmission arrangements which included both air and water-cooled engines with front-wheel-drive and a conventional water-cooled front engine with rear drive layout. It had been widely anticipated that Simca were to be nationalised by the French government after the war, in which case Gregoire's prototype would have been put into production as Simca's small car. In the event, Simca escaped nationalisation and continued building the Topolino under licence. As for the Gregoire, although production never materialised, it did achieve some fame as the basis for Panhard's Dyna series of cars.

The replacement for the 500 Topolino, coded 'project 100', received the blessing of Vittorio Valletta during mid-1946. Valletta, who was appointed president of Fiat following the death of Giovanni Agnelli, accepted the Topolino concept as being outdated and agreed the proposal to produce prototypes based on three designs enabling an evaluation between front and rear drive. Even the forward-thinking Valletta baulked at ideas thought to be too unconventional and issued an instruction that, while all possibilities be examined, there should be an effort to produce a 'conventional car'.

Getting closer ...

By 1951, after lengthy and detailed work on engine designs which included work on air and water-cooled units between 450 and 500cc, a particularly favoured concept was a four-cylinder horizontally-opposed 600cc unit with water-cooling. Its purpose was to drive a car built as a full four seater – the popularity of the 500 Giardiniera and Belvedere had been noted – with costs kept to a minimum but showing an overall improvement in performance and comfort. All this had to be in a form as small as, or even smaller than, the Topolino. Giacosa was convinced there were two choices only: front-wheel-drive or 'all at the rear'. Time was now of the essence: there had been protracted preoccupation with designing a replacement for the pre-war 1100 but the Nuova 1100 model had at last received its launch date of 1953. The 100 project was next.

Fiat experienced a difficult period throughout the first few months of 1951 and saw a continuing decline in sales. Management was forced to impose short-time working at production plants from the beginning of October, thereby reducing the working week from 48 hours to 40. In contrast to the gloom, reports which stimulated interest in Fiat's plans for its new economy cars began to appear about the same time. An account appeared in the

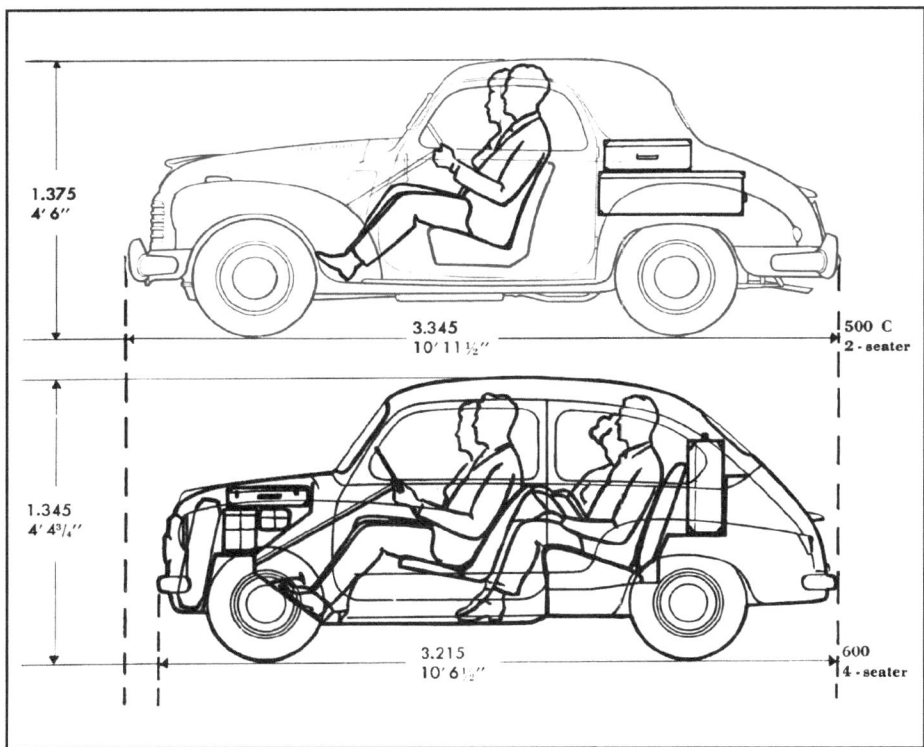

Interesting comparison between the Topolino and the new 600 as featured in an early sales brochure. (Author's collection)

The Motor of proposals by Fiat for a car smaller than the Topolino, nearer to the style associated with a motor-scooter, and powered by a 350cc engine. Commenting further on this strange hybrid, it was stressed there would be no lack of comfort which would be that expected from a conventional basic economy car. Another model, between this 'ultra-mini' and 900cc, was also mentioned but the article failed to go into further detail or supposition.

Relentless exercises in engine design, together with chassis and bodywork construction, proved to be a turning point in the 100 project. The decision on engine format and transmission layout was given over entirely to Giacosa, in return for which freedom he had to meet certain provisos: the weight of the car had to be kept to approximately 990lb (450kg), which allowed 550lb (250kg) for coachwork and 440lb (200kg) for the running gear; maximum speed had to be no less than 85kph (53mph) and, moreover, it was to be essentially capable of carrying four people with a reasonable degree of comfort.

As development intensified, the argument between front or rear drive became more acute, as did the question over the type of engine. Two cylinders or four, air or water cooling? these were the factors in question. There were two main considerations: front-wheel-drive with fewer limitations towards potential coachwork design, as against a rear-positioned engine which afforded reliability, lower build costs and a greater chance of keeping weight to a minimum.

In reality, Giacosa had little choice in his final decision as work had already begun on coachwork design with wooden framework erected to determine the minimum interior requirements to accommodate four passengers in comfort. Three prototype bodies were constructed, all using the same engine but utilising each of the three transmission layouts: front, rear and conventional. The outcome was quite clear: the rear-positioned engine accounted for less space, reducing the overall dimensions and therefore indicated lower build costs. Whilst there had been some erring towards front drive, the technology had caused some anxiety and was therefore discarded without fur-

Drawing showing early thoughts on body shape for the 600. Believed to be from 1951, the general outline of the definitive model is evident apart from the bulbous rear wings and semi-exposed headlamps. (Author's collection)

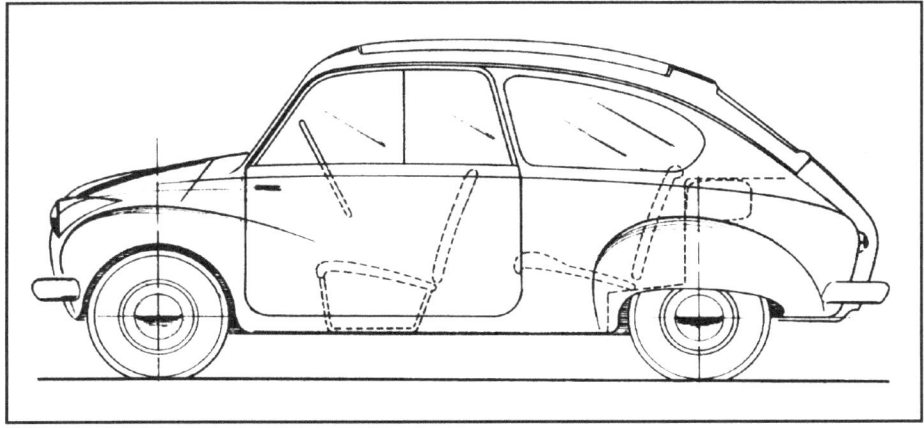

ther consideration. The possibility of a transversely mounted engine had been examined but the complicated drive arrangement was rejected as unreliable. As to the coachwork, Giacosa paid almost constant attention; regarded as a perfectionist he continually visited the workshops, checking progress and always acutely aware of the limitations that anything less than thorough design and lack of sensible space would create.

Gradually, the overall shape took effect with coachwork kept to an absolute minimum. Initial drawings represented a rounded but also streamlined design with semi-exposed headlamps faired into the body and doors. Half-enclosed rear wheels under bulbous wheel arches provided a slightly heavy appearance, which was amplified by a sharply raked tail. Not completely happy with the contours, Giacosa admits in his memoirs to often filing away the angular edges on plaster mock-ups and paying particular attention to the model's overall compactness. As to the interior layout, Giacosa was largely responsible for advice and direction on driver and passenger comfort in respect of leg room, seating position and steering wheel angle. His own generous frame was an ideal guide for comfort and access assessment and he spent many hours getting the interior layout to the correct specification.

Having reached a point when he was completely satisfied with the car's aesthetics, Giacosa turned to the engine which had provided one of the biggest headaches. Air-cooling suggested simplicity and two cylinders even more so; two-pedal operation took automation a stage further, therefore approaching Giacosa's dream of a car which would be largely effortless to drive. Eventually the answer was seen as an engine with its cylinders set at an angle of 150° instead of 180°, so leaving the valves at an almost horizontal position. A hydraulic torque converter was fitted between the clutch and the engine so as to dispense with the clutch pedal. Designs were completed by March 1952 with a road-going prototype ready by mid-summer.

Problems ...

Carlo Salamano, Fiat's most respected test driver, found the car awkward. This left Giacosa in the difficult predicament of admitting that further development was necessary before the design could be perfected. The problems were twofold: firstly the two-cylinder engine suffered chronic overheating which was likely to cause damage to the valves, a symptom that had prevailed all through the design stages; secondly, the semi-automatic gearbox had only three ratios when four were really needed to squeeze the

Installing the cooling system alongside the engine instead of in-line with it was an ingenious design which allowed the unit to be packed into a minimal space. (Author's collection)

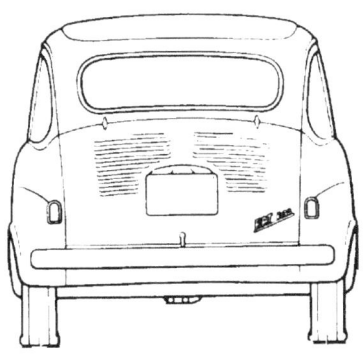

best results from the 600cc engine. Furthermore, changes between gears were dreadfully harsh and ensured progress was anything but smooth.

There was no time to perfect the engine and transmission design and Giacosa was forced to order an alternative concept with the minimum of delay. Gaudenzio Bono, General Manager of Fiat, whilst appreciating Giacosa's searches for a revolutionary car capable of attracting the mass market, allowed four months in which to find a solution. Literally taking his team of ten design engineers behind locked doors, work started at once on an in-line, water-cooled four-cylinder engine and conventional 4-speed gearbox, the format of which was quickly approved by company hierarchy.

By January 1953, after much feverish work, detailed designs for the new engine and gearbox were ready. The definitive outline of the 100 had by now advanced to the extent that a progress report to Valletta and Bono concluded that near-original specifications had been achieved. Unladen weight was calculated as being 1135lb (515kg), maximum speed 55mph (88kph) and engine capacity 570cc with an output of 16bhp. Although momentum was gathering at an ever increasing rate, difficulties still continued to arise. Installing the engine behind the rear axle in the conventional manner would have meant lengthening the vehicle, an unwise move and certainly one to avoid as it would involve increased weight and costs.

By taking what was considered the most unorthodox step of placing the radiator and cooling fan to the side of the engine, enough space could be saved to house the unit without further coachwork modification. There was an additional advantage in as much that with the cooling fan fitted onto the waterpump shaft, thereby pushing the airflow across the radiator, it was possible to avoid the necessity of installing a separate heater for the car's interior. Construction of the unitary body shell resulted in a full length strengthening 'spine' along the floorpan and in which the gear linkage, handbrake assembly and control gear for choke and starter were concealed. It was therefore a simple matter to use this tunnel to direct warm air into the cabin interior and defrost the windscreen. There was some question as to the efficiency of moving warm air against the direction of the car's motion, but the heating system worked well enough and so proved Giacosa's logical approach to the design.

Of fundamental importance, however, was the move away from a separate chassis to unitary construction. As far back as the early period of the Topolino this method of car design had been understood and favoured; the development towards a unitary design was, therefore, of some consequence. There is little doubt that the decision to build the 100 in unitary style was determined soon after the war when Giacosa visited Chrysler in America. During this trip he would have been inspired by some of the developments seen at the Budd company who, for years, had been leaders in automobile technology. A feature of Giacosa's researches in America was the front suspension he subsequently adopted for the 600: the transverse leaf spring arrangement performed so well, acting also as an anti-roll bar, that it was retained throughout the car's life span and beyond, remaining with the 500 Nuova and continuing with the 126 series.

Carlo Salamano encountered further problems when the revised prototypes were delivered to the test department. Serious defects in the car's stability became apparent due to oversteer, a tendency not uncommon with rear-engined cars. So acute was the instability, both Giacosa and Salamano were deeply worried the car might overturn whilst cornering sharply at speed. Not all was bad, though, the position of the drive-train had the effect of steadying the centre of gravity, irrespective of the car's laden weight, eliminating the need to redistribute braking power to each wheel. To establish a cure for the oversteer a whole series of tests was set up: the weight of the car was redistributed with little or no effect, even to the extent of placing weights upon a bracket protruding some 50cms (20ins) from the front of the vehicle; the battery was moved from the engine bay to the front luggage compartment where it remained in production cars. In the event, the problem was traced to the front off-side wheel which was over-inclining during cornering. The remedy was a reduction of the steering angle, made possible by modifying the steering rod joints whilst at the same time slightly lowering the rear suspension which consisted of coil springs and swinging arms. After that, the

On test in the mountainous region around Turin. In charge of testing the 600 was Carlo Salamano, Fiat's revered test driver. (Author's collection)

car behaved impeccably: Salamano and Giacosa were completely satisfied with test results and the 100 adopted a behavioural pattern of stability far better than the Renault 4CV or the Volkswagen.

By February 1953 the design of the Project 100 car had reached an advanced stage and Giacosa was able to complete the drawings for what he considered was the definitive car. At this particular time he was also engrossed with the idea of an estate version, the design of which was presenting its own difficulties but which, nevertheless, eventually saw production as the Multipla.

Acceptance

During mid-1953, amidst anxious prompting from Valletta who was concerned that production of the 100 should not be delayed any later than 1955 as he sensed the Topolino's sales could fall away to foreign competition, a meeting was called to discuss the final aspects of the project and to formulate a programme for production. The date was set for 15th July. In opening the meeting Valletta summarized the principles relating to producing a successor to the Topolino, together with options Dante Giacosa and his design team had been studying. In turn, Giacosa outlined the specifications of the 100 in great detail to the Presidential Committee who were responsible for approving every new model. He was careful to include plans for a rear-engined station wagon derivative, the only format that could comply with the weight limitation. Giacosa knew that a successful replacement for the Belvedere was essential and it was partly on these grounds he was able to secure his case for a rear-engined saloon.

The committee were virtually unanimous in its enthusiastic acceptance of Giacosa's design. Each member had been able to test-drive and evaluate the prototype cars but there were, quite expectedly, certain misgivings that called for some minor design amendments. Most significant were the demands for an increase in power which resulted in the engine being

During 1953, Dante Giacosa was absorbed in designing a replacement for the Giardiniera and Belvedere estate cars. The result was the Multipla, as seen here. (Courtesy Fiat Auto (UK) & Fiat SPA Ltd)

600 production underway at Mirafiori. (Courtesy Fiat Auto (UK) & Fiat SPA Ltd)

uprated to 633cc and 19bhp. Only Alessandro Genero called for caution: he asked for further durability trials as well as exhaustive tests on the car's transmission and drive arrangement. Genero favoured front-wheel-drive and was convinced this was the direction Fiat should be going in for development of the popular car.

Considering Fiat's historical policy on front-wheel-drive, Genero's statement was undoubtedly brave and forthright. It was a view he was not alone in sharing: later Dr. Antonio Fessia, in an uncharacteristic outburst and to Giacosa's surprise, confessed his allegiance to front drive.

The outcome of the meeting was the directive to put the 100 into production. Amando Fiorelli who, in 1946 had been appointed director of the Mirafiori works, undertook the tooling-up operation, a massive exercise costing 20 billion Lire – £6m.

In addition to tooling-up, ten cars were built purely for the use of the training and test workshop department to enable agents to become accustomed to the car, arrange after sales service schedules and note any defects. This period of evaluation, important for any new vehicle, led to a number of modifications on production models.

The motoring press was given their first look at the little wonder – christened the '600' by Fiat's marketing department – early in 1955. Journalists were taken to northern Italy where the high altitudes and severe winter conditions provided the test scenario with Fiat's dexterous Carlo Salamano in charge.

With 55% of the car's weight over the driving wheels, roadholding qualities proved to be exceptional, even allowing for the dire weather and road conditions. Fully laden with four passengers, a test car was taken up tortuously twisting mountain roads to a height of some 1097 metres (3600ft) before returning via a selection of lesser roads and tracks. Creating a huge impression, the 600 was hailed as nothing short of a miracle; smaller than the Topolino, yet able to carry four in comfort with luggage space behind the rear seat as well as under the bonnet. Fiat's

Putting the finishing touches to the 600. On the left can be seen the Nuova 1100 coming off the assembly line. (Author's collection)

tireless workhorse was set for a sparkling launch and a phenomenal career.

The Italian public was given its chance to see the 600 on home territory for the first time at the Turin Show, opened by the country's President on 20th April 1955. 'Fiat fever' reigned over the event with virtually all of the twenty specialist coachbuilders represented displaying their own version of the 600. Even the accessory manufacturers were geared-up for the occasion, one of the most elaborate special products being an entire luggage outfit especially designed for the 600 and manufactured from best quality pigskin. As for the car itself, it could be purchased for 590,000 Lire.

In Britain, the 600 appeared at the Earls Court Motor Show in October 1955 although it had gone on sale from 1st April at a price of £412.10.0 plus purchase tax. As expected, the 600's presence caused the same sensational reaction as at Geneva and Turin and attracted huge attention. The car was accompanied by sectionalised exhibits which cleverly demonstrated the wonders of micro engineering.

III

CHALLENGE FROM ITALY

The 600 was greeted with immense international interest, but nowhere more so than Italy, where it seemed every Italian was clamouring to get their first view of the car. The announcement of the 600 had come as little surprise, however, as it had been a very poorly kept secret: at least a year or so before its launch positive news and details were already emerging from Turin.

The spectacular arrival of the 600 at Geneva ensured both success and controversy; not only was the offering of a new model from the respected Fiat empire enough to arouse strong sentiments of emotive nationalism, but the seemingly illusory attempt to envelop four people, together with their baggage, into something so small was another matter entirely. Amidst this furore of attention, repeated a month later at Turin, everybody who was anybody insisted on being seen with the nation's new baby. As film stars caressed the 600's cuddly curvaceousness, so it became the star of films and the car for the stars. If it was good enough for Sophia Loren, it was good enough for anyone!

Small, but stamina, too

In true Italian style the 600 was both versatile and adept. To prove the point two production cars demonstrated its durability and stamina by completing 6240 gruelling miles (9984km) across

Early 600s had slender headlamp bezels, indicators on top of the wings and sliding windows. Sunroofs were not provided. The 600 was the centre of attraction at Geneva and, to get the car off to a flying start, two production cars completed a gruelling marathon from Calcutta to Rome in just eleven days. (Courtesy Fiat Auto (UK) & Fiat SPA Ltd)

The 600 was soon participating in motorsport. This early example is seen roaring out of a bend. Note the Abarth emblem on the front. (Courtesy Wally Pratt)

three continents from Calcutta to Rome in eleven days. The marathon, which was completed with an overall average speed of 30mph (48kph) is well documented, with reports telling of the cars encountering the poorest of roads that, more often than not, degenerated into rough tracks or worse. Appalling

Unitary construction was the key to the 600's success; smaller in size than the Topolino, it was possible to achieve seating for four in comfort. This illustration shows the bodyshell as a single unit with the rigid spine along the floor. (Author's collection)

weather conditions dogged the expedition and the two cars were hampered by the ravages of floods and desert sand storms. This feat of endurance – difficult enough in the best of conditions – was, therefore, all the more remarkable. Completed in legendary style, this performance of stamina was but just a curtain-raiser, adding to what has since been seen as yet another chapter in the history of the motor car.

A threat to Britain

As far as the British motor industry was concerned, *The Motor* saw the 600 as a challenge from Italy, predicting it would make further inroads into the European economy car market. This erosion of what had once been a market virtually dominated by Britain before the arrival of the Topolino could only lead to further loss of ground, with no apparent sign at that stage of Britain being able to survive this battle charge and order a counter-attack.

With an overall length of just 106.5in (3.2m) and a wheelbase of a mere 6 feet 6.5in (199mm), the shoehorning effect of packing so much into so little stemmed from the 600's unitary construction and ingenious engineering in the way the drive-train was stowed neatly behind the rear axle. Whilst by no means new, chassisless body design was relatively recent to Fiat, having first been adopted on the Nuova 1100 which had been successfully launched at the 1953 Geneva show. The effect and advantage of integral body design was plain to see: four passengers and luggage previously carried in the estate versions of the Topolino could now be quite comfortably accommodated within the confines of the markedly smaller 600 saloon. All this was achieved by welding the steel-pressing body sides and roof together as a single unit incorporating a punt-shaped floorpan, which itself had built-in rigidity in the form of a central rectangular box-section backbone. This spine proved to be particularly useful in providing a housing for the control linkages extending from the cabin to the drive-train In effect, the combined chassis and floorpan comprised three major box-sections: front integral scuttle and wheelarches, rear wheelarches

Family comfort as depicted in an early sales brochure. Note the luggage space behind the rear seat; this is in addition to the front luggage compartment. (Author's collection)

and power unit support and, consolidating the two units, the central floorpan and strengthening backbone.

More for less

It was certainly no accident the 600 had been designed as a small utility car, neither had it originated from a mere whim of impulsive engineering. It was created out of purpose and necessity. Although Italy enjoys a reputation for its flamboyant and expensively fast sports cars with exotic styling to match, there was another side to Italian life which reflected the restraints of the country's economy, terrain and climate. Whatever the design for day-to-day transport, the 600 had to combine the ingredients of in-built reliability with absolute minimal running costs, whilst being practically unaffected by the ravages of weather and altitude. A foremost requirement. was that the car should go anywhere, feeling at home negotiating tortuous roads or vying for a gap on congested narrow streets about town. The car's role dictated a design of uncompromising compactness and frugality.

In addition, the 600 had been designed to offer completely adequate comfort for the whole family, and at an affordable price, too. With a launch price of 590,000 lire, approximately £265, it was cheaper than the 500C Topolino saloon which had cost 625,000 lire upon its introduction. In Britain, however, import duties and exchange rates ensured a similar pricing policy did not follow suit: whereas the 500C coupé was listed at £403.10.0 (£572.15.0 including purchase tax), the 600 went on sale at £412.10.0 (£585.10.0 with purchase tax). The 600 found no shortage of home buyers and Italians queued anxiously to share its delights. Having caught the imagination and attention of the nation it was also accessible due to the low price tag and assisted purchase schemes available through S.A.V.A. This enabled many families to own a car – and a new one, at that – for the first time ever. S.A.V.A. had been in existence since 1928 and aimed at providing a simple hire purchase arrangement and reasonable vehicle insurance to encourage home sales of Fiats, thereby supporting Italy's motor industry.

The design of the passenger cabin not only eliminated intrusions such

Wide opening doors provided easy access to the rear seat, even though the doors are rear hinged. Note that the car in the photograph is of the second series with winding windows and a body moulding. (Courtesy Fiat Auto (UK) & Fiat SPA Ltd)

The 600 was also ideal for the business person. (Author's collection)

as the fuel tank and engine bulkhead, it also allowed the seats to fit snugly within the wheelbase without any compromise to leg room or rear passengers. Drivers and front passengers also enjoyed ample space; the convenient driving position was achieved by the clever positioning of the pedals which were fitted neatly between the wheelarches and under the front compartment which contained the petrol tank, battery, brake fluid reservoir and front seats.

When used as a four seater, additional carrying capacity other than the front compartment was provided by the convenient and amply-sized door pockets, while a deep recess behind the rear seat could accommodate at least a large suitcase. As for the seats themselves, although visually not over-inviting, they offered excellent comfort. Compared to the Topolino, Fiat 600 passengers enjoyed a degree of extra comfort with four inches added to the interior width, although the overall width had been increased by only 3.5 inches (88mm). Sliding windows, less bulky than the drop type, ensured effective space saving. Shorter and lower than the Topolino, the 600 managed to trim 5 inches (127mm) from the overall length and 1.5 inches (38mm) from the height respectively. The 'illusion,' therefore, was to be able to seat four passengers within the same wheelbase as the Topolino which, in saloon form, could only accommodate two, while the Giardiniera and Belvedere versions could just about manage four in cramped style. The car's weight was also something of a miracle: at 1250lb (567kg) it was just 14lb (6.35kg) heavier than the Topolino.

The two wide, doors allowed particularly easy access, even to the rear seat, as the front seats tilted forwards. Grab-handles were fitted for rear passengers' convenience in getting in and out of the rear and, as they were fitted immediately aft of the doors, undoubtedly provided some support over less even surfaces and hairpin bends.

In saloon form the 600 was never marketed as a four-door version: not only did the short wheelbase make it less than practical but, the rigidity of the body shell would have been adversely affected. Building-in the required extra strength would have involved considerable design changes, thereby increasing production costs by an appreciable amount, a measure that most certainly would have been deemed unacceptable, especially for a car in the economy market sector. Such variants were left to specialist coachbuilders but it is a matter of conjecture as to how many were actually made. Rear-hinged suicide doors, a feature of the Topolino,

Wide doors and a folding rear seat back-rest facilitated load-carrying. (Author's collection)

By mid-Fifties standards, the 600 boasted a relatively large window area. Curved windscreens were usually found on larger and more expensive cars. (Courtesy Fiat Auto (UK) & Fiat SPA Ltd)

Compact dimensions belie the amount of useable space in the 600. However, this contemporary brochure makes the car appear larger than it actually is. (Author's collection)

had been retained and was a practice favoured more by continental manufacturers than British: Austin, Morris and Ford had all adopted front-hinged doors whereas Renault and Citroën carried on with the front-opening type.

The sheer homuncular size of the 600 provoked speculative debate and almost disbelief: since the mid-Thirties the Topolino had continually been awarded the accolade for being the smallest production car – and now the record was being carried on by yet another Fiat, and one that appeared far smaller. There was a cheeky smugness surrounding the 600's rounded features, and for all its carrying capacity in relation to overall size, the design reflected an image of total proportion.

Compared with many cars of the era, the 600's window area appeared quite enormous, which gave it the illusion of a generously light and airy interior. The impression of space was further enhanced by the curved front and rear screens, a feature normally reserved for much larger and more expensive cars. Extensive use of brightwork helped contribute towards the 600's sparkling character: bumpers and hub caps were chromed, while other fittings were aluminium. Later cars had plated quarterlights and some models for the American market received chrome embellishments. To compensate for the lack of a frontal air-intake, a bright circular design incorporating the 600 emblem adorned the front panel. Surrounding the symbol, aluminium strips added to the overall effect, while on the front 'boot' lid the Fiat badge was the crowning glory.

Whitewall tyres, Pirelli 5.20 x 12 on 12 inch disc wheels gave the 600 that air of dash and smartness so associated with cars of the Fifties and early Sixties. Even for a smaller car the wheels appeared to be undersized: the Austin A30 had 13 inch wheels while the Renault 4CV sported the customary 15 inch variety; only the true minuscules such as the Goggomobil and Frisky had even smaller 10 inch wheels, apart, that is, from the NSU which also used 12 inch wheels.

The driving position was in no way compromised by the 600 being a 'baby car.' Compared to bigger cars, there was essentially some risk of shoulder-rubbing, especially with two large people. However, unlike some cheaper minicars, the pedals and controls were exactly to the same proportion as other conventional vehicles. As could be expected, accessories were kept to a minimum: the painted fascia supported a small binnacle directly in front of the driver and contained speedometer, oil pressure and fuel gauges, while warning lights indicated dynamo charge and water temperature. Housed in a separate panel in the middle of the fascia switches for ignition, lights, panel light and windscreen wipers were comfortably close to hand. Again in the centre of the dashboard, but mounted just under the windscreen, a simple direction-indicator control with built in warning lamp performed well enough. Highly unusual was the position of starter and choke levers which were mounted almost at floor level between handbrake and gearstick, using the central tunnel to conceal the control cables. Alongside the steering column a hand throttle further aided cold and winter starting.

Few luxuries above the necessities were provided for driver and passenger comfort, which was both understandable and even somewhat expected from a keenly priced economy car. The interior

For all its ingenious engineerring, the 600 was remarkably spartan. Note the central spine housing the control linkages. The key explains the controls and instruments.

1. Switch for lamp incorporated in rear view mirror.
2. Horn push-button.
3. Instrument cluster (five indications).
4. Ignition lock switch.
5. Direction indicator switch with incorporated pilot light.
6. Accelerator knob.
7. Screen-wiper switch.
8. Instrument cluster lighting lamp switch.
9. Front compartment lid catch control lever.
10. Gear shifting lever.
11. Parking brake control lever.
12. Carburettor starting device control lever.
13. Starter control lever.
14. Clutch pedal.
15. Brake pedal.
16. Accelerator pedal.
17. One of the two knobs controlling heating system shutters.

a. Insufficient engine oil pressure indicator.
b. Generator charge indicator.
c. Speedometer-mileage recorder.
d. Excessive water temperature indicator.
e. Fuel level gauge.
f. Fuel reserve indicator.

had a genuinely spartan appearance with rubber matting on the floor, the economy relieved only by an attractive seat covering in checked cloth material. In fact, the 600 was no more spartan

The instrument nacelle as installed on early 600s. (Courtesy Fiat Auto (UK) & Fiat SPA Ltd)

than its direct rivals, such as the Renault 4CV and Volkswagen Beetle or, for that matter, the Citroën 2CV. The latter model defied any hint of finesse with its canvas and rubber-sprung tubular-framed deckchair-type seats, together with complete lack of interior trim and refinement. Luxury in the grand touring style, however, was never an intention with the 600: it provided enough comfort, whether for a short run or long journey, and in executing its duties as a willing workhorse it gave all and asked precious little in return.

On the road

The charm of the 600 lay in its social acceptability and dexterity to go anywhere; its unpretentious nature allowed virtual anonymity and incognito travel. Overall design and easy driving were the 600's hallmarks: the short bonnet and curved windscreen maximised what was superb visibility and, even accounting for the rear-positioned engine, precious little bodywork overhung the rear wheels, making parking exceptionally easy, ideal in Italy where it is essential to compete for that convenient little space.

On the road, the 600's legendary stability was achieved by all-round independent suspension: upper wishbone and transverse leaf spring with telescopic shock absorbers at the front and coil springs with shock absorbers and swinging arms at the rear. Ingen-

The go-anywhere attitude of the 600 even included speed trials. Here, the Fiat seems to be holding its own against a Saab. (Courtesy Wally Pratt)

1. Kingpin 2. Upper swinging arm 3. Shock absorber 4. Steering knuckle 5. Transversal semi-elliptic spring 6. Resilient support for semi-elliptic spring 7. Rubber bumper

The design of the lower front suspension with its lower transverse leaf spring proved itself beyond all doubt and obviated any need for an anti-roll bar. This system continued for over thirty years and was used on the 126 models. (Author's collection)

1. Rubber bumper 2. Coil spring 3. Shutter, for air control 4. Swinging arm, complete 5. Shock absorber

The rear suspension was built as a unit to carry the drive train. Double-acting shock absorbers mounted within coil springs coped with the roughest terrain. (Author's collection)

iously simple, the design of the front suspension proved not only effective and space saving but also economical in production. The nature of the leaf spring, constructed from multi-sprung single leaves and clamped together with rubber-cushioned braces, allowed flexible wheel movement, while eliminating any need for an anti-roll bar. By fixing the leaf spring in two places directly to the body structure via rubber sandwich blocks attached to two brackets instead of a single central mounting, it was possible to attain a very consistent suspension geometry. In principle, the front suspension was not dissimilar to that of the Topolino, which had also relied upon a transverse leaf.

The rear suspension, with double-acting hydraulic telescopic shock absorbers mounted inside coil springs, together with swinging arms, was designed to support the engine and gearbox in a cradle. Triangular steel pressings supported the rear hubs and were attached, along with the suspension arms, to the bodywork by flexible bushes. The design not only allowed the wheels to travel in conical paths but eliminated the need for universal joints at the wheel end of the drive shafts.

As a general comparison with small French cars, whose suspension was notably soft, the 600's ride was firm but still comfortable even over bad road surfaces. The weight of the drive-train over the rear wheels and firm suspension resulted in extraordinarily good traction and surprisingly good handling, especially on tight-cornered Italian roads where an extremely positive tyre grip was essential. On snow-cov-

Possibly the 600's closest rival, the Renault 4CV. With the cooling system in-line in the traditional manner, more space was needed to house the engine compartment. (Author's collection, courtesy of the National Motor Museum)

ered roads the 600 gave an agile performance, made all the more reassuring by its weight distribution. In reviewing the ride quality, The Motor considered the car's suspension distinctly "vintage" in feel whilst The Autocar, looking from a different angle, found it "praiseworthy" but did find "a slight fore and aft pitching on certain surfaces."

The worm and sector steering arrangement adopted for the 600 was a direct descendant of that used on the 500C Topolino, only six greasing points were necessary which were restricted to the king pin brackets and split track rods, while the steering box required topping up at 3100 mile (5000km) intervals.

Getting the 600 started was one thing, stopping it was another: the braking system was effective enough, although early ears were fitted with a parking brake which operated on the transmission, a throwback to an era when there was a little less reliance on stopping power. Whilst transmission brakes were at one time commonplace, they had, by the end of the 1930s, generally been superseded by the now familiar mechanically operated wheel brakes. However, the practice of utilizing transmission brakes was retained by Fiat on some models until as late as 1960. Dual circuit braking offered complete safety and reliability, and brake drums were slotted in order to provide adequate ventilation and prevent any risk of overheating. Initially, brake shoes formed from a light alloy were fitted to the car, these were relatively difficult to adjust as they pivoted at the base of an eccentrically mounted fulcrum pin with further adjustment at the top of the shoe. Later brake shoes were self-centring, and manufactured from pressed steel, a far better arrangement allowing easier adjustment. The transmission brake, which was originally mounted on the front end of the gearbox, was later replaced by a conventional handbrake.

The engine

As has already been seen, one of the 600's particular attractions was the positioning and layout of the engine and transmission. For such a relatively small car, the effect of installing a four-cylinder water-cooled engine and drive-train into so confined an area was quite brilliant. Positioning the cooling system alongside the engine allowed a 'quart to fit into a pint pot,' making access to the engine compartment remarkably generous. The whole of the panel below the rear screen hinged upwards to reveal the works, with all the serviceable items, such as oil filler, dipstick, fan belt, air filter, distributor and radiator cap readily accessible. In terms of space efficiency the 600 has only to be compared with the Renault 4CV, also rear-engined and probably the Fiat's closest competitor. In adopting the conventional in-line arrangement for the radiator (which was squeezed against the cabin bulkhead and rear seat), the engine compartment was considerably larger. The additional space required to house the engine and gearbox unit is apparent from the overall length of the car: 1 foot 4 inches (401mm) longer than the 600. Taking into account the Renault's longer dimensions, four-door coachwork and bigger engine – 747cc as opposed to the 633cc of the Fiat 600 – performance difference was negligible. A mean top speed of 61mph (98.2kmh) was claimed for the 4CV with best at 64mph (103kmh), whilst 62mph (100kmh) was the stated capability of the 600. There is

Storming towards victory, this early 600 illustrates the soundness of the original engine design. The same block was used throughout the 600's lifespan and that of the 850 as well as for many a Fiat-Abarth. (Courtesy Wally Pratt)

no doubt that the Fiat benefited from a four-speed gearbox, a lively affair compared to the Renault's rather long-legged three-speed box.

The engine – considering the options and configurations originally evaluated by Giacosa – was relatively conventional: the four-cylinder 633cc motor, built in-unit with clutch, gearbox and differential, was suspended at three points by rubber mountings. The cylinder block, formed from cast iron, had an integral upper crankcase and an aluminium cylinder head with cast iron valve seat inserts and interior inlet passages.

Designed with economy in mind rather than performance, the 600 nevertheless was no slouch; with a compression ratio of 7:1, the engine reached maximum torque at 2800rpm, equivalent to about 35mph (56kph) in top gear. In order to save as much space as possible, water passages between the two outer cylinders were eliminated. This was an unusual practice, but to protect against overheating created by a situation of high engine speeds over long distances, an enlarged three-bearing crankshaft was provided, complete with lead-bronze bearings – an apparent luxury for an economy car. This precaution, which demonstrated a healthy regard to engine design and reliability, added to the costs but was considered worthy by Fiat.

The soundness of the original engine design is demonstrated by its longevity: the same block was used throughout the life span of not only the 600 and its variants, such as the Multipla and Abarth, but also the 850, eventual successor to the 600 series. Extensive use of aluminium, especially in the housing for the gearbox and final drive, allowed weight to he kept to a minimum. When installed in the car, the complete power unit comprising a full complement of components, i.e. gearbox, engine, differential carburation and cooling system, weighed just 238lbs (l08kg), a remarkable achievement at the time. The gearbox followed Fiat's design of the period in having synchromesh on 2nd, 3rd and top ratios only; in addition, second gear was attached to the main gearbox housing in a specially designed external casing, which also provided the bearing for the transmission parking brake. The cable-operated single dry plate clutch required no maintenance, the release bearing being packed with grease during assembly.

Carburation was provided by a Weber 22 DRA downdraught unit with manual choke and an air intake with a filter that could be adjusted for summer and winter conditions. The electrics, a 12-volt 28AH system, incorporated a conventional battery and coil ignition with a Marelli distributor.

Electrical equipment consisted of built-in headlamps and combined direction indicators with parking lights to the front and stop and tail lamps to the rear. Additional equipment included twin windscreen wipers, rear number plate and engine compartment

It was not always the case that Fiats were made by robots! (Courtesy Fiat Auto (UK) & Fiat SPA Ltd)

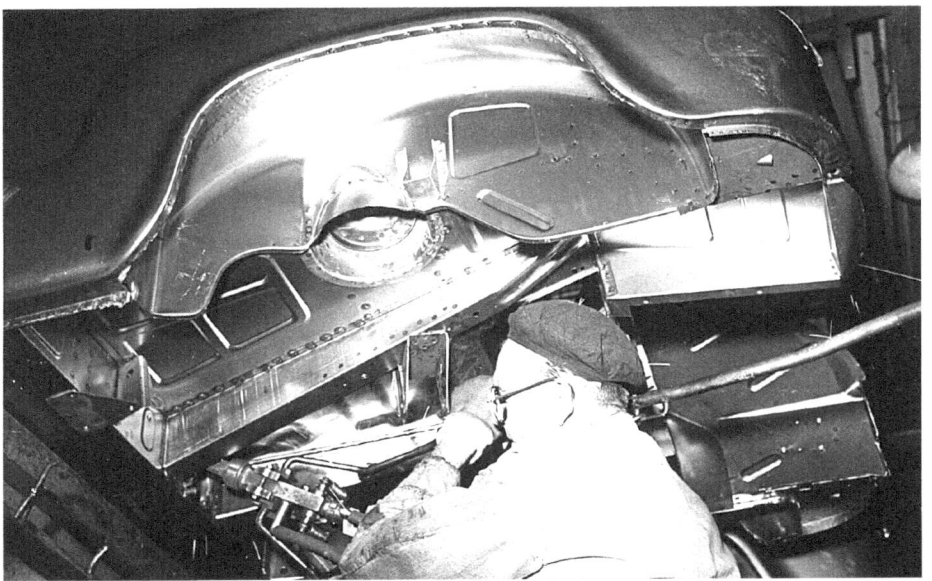

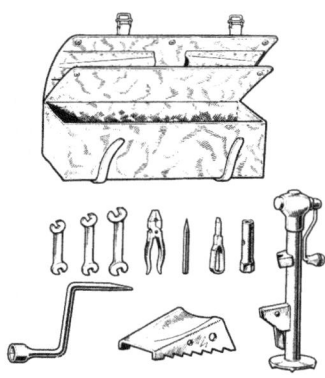

lamps, interior courtesy lamp combined with the rear view mirror and a single tone horn,

The cooling system, with its 0.95 imp gall (4.3 litre) capacity, included a water pump housed in a light alloy case and a wax element thermostat which had been designed robustly for the huge demands expected of it: long fast runs and mountain roads in high summer temperatures would take their toll. Designed to open up with water temperatures of 75-80 degrees C, an air outlet flap was controlled by the thermostat fitted to the lower part of the radiator. The flap became fully extended when water temperature reached 105 degrees C, controlling airflow through the radiator but not impeding water circulation.

The car's heating system was operated by opening a valve situated at floor level adjacent to the rear seat, warm air from the radiator was allowed into the passenger area by means of ducting incorporated within the central chassis backbone. Together with ducts at the base of the windscreen, two further controls in the front footwell directed heat at low level. The system was effective enough but required the occasional service and cleansing of the filter.

Performance figures seem hardly relevant in a car the size of the 600. The important factor was to keep going rather than top speeds and acceleration times against the stopwatch. Apart from Citroën's 2CV, the 600 relied upon the least number of cubic centimetres out of all the popular small cars at the time. But no matter, both Fiat and Giacosa were quite expert at squeezing every ounce of power from a motor, their experience in aero-engine design and manufacturing had seen to that. In view of its specification, the 600 was more or less written-off in terms of performance, the penalty in return for good economy and rugged reliability. In the event, there were to be some surprises and, in spite of its thrifty use of fuel, overall figures were by no means unimpressive.

Capable of extracting over 250 miles (402km) average cruising range from a tank of petrol (6 gallons, 27 litres), it was possible to achieve almost 60mph (96kph) from the 633cc engine. Through the gears, which *The Motor* found light, smooth and easy to use, with the gear change "a delightful experience," the 600 managed to keep up with the pack, showing on occasions a clean pair of heels to some of its rivals. The long-legged top gear, which was really in the style of an overdrive, was an asset in contributing towards particularly impressive economy and journey times over long distances.

In comparison with its contemporary British rivals, such as the Austin A30, Ford Anglia, Morris Minor and Standard 8, not to mention continental stablemates Renault 4CV, Beetle and 2CV, the Fiat's diminutive stature did not necessarily reflect a completely languid performance. The lightweight (only the 2CV was lighter), and dwarfish dimensions were a considerable advantage towards achieving results which, if not spectacular, were very respectable at least. In its native Italy, however, it is unlikely that many of its rivals, perhaps Renault and Volkswagen apart, could achieve the same performance under the notorious conditions for which the 600 was designed.

Under normal conditions it was possible to push the car to 15mph (24kph) in first gear which, by its nature, ensured a quick getaway, 25 (40) in second and a shade over 40 (64) in third. It is quite possible that Italian drivers with typical *brioso* manner could manage just a fractional extra squeeze of power. Austin's A30 was only marginally quicker: 27 (43) in second and 42 (67) in third, whilst the Volkswagen could do little better at 26 (42) and 45 (72) respectively. Only the Standard 8 showed any substantial improvement, managing 34 (54) in 2nd and 58 (93) in 3rd, although the 62mph (99kph) top speed was less than outstandingly superior.

The proving of the 600, which was carried out in the Italian Alps, showed the car to he virtually tailor-made for Latin drivers who were used to negotiating notoriously difficult roads. Hardly a temperamental car, it was characteristically an easy starter with use of choke and hand throttle when required. A light clutch and slick gearchange aided the car's overall performance, whether on mountain roads or as part of the customary debacle of town driving. The design of the braking system stood up to the harsh use demanded of it with no apparent sign of fade; the steering and suspension, too, performed very well. Even on hairpin bends the car's roadholding ability ensured sure-footedness with a light and easily controlled steering action.

Noise abatement was never the 600's strong point, as resonance

A Pininfarina-bodied special 600 similar to the vehicle shown at Geneva in March 1955. Note the reverse-rake rear window, a feature normally associated with the Ford Anglia and the Citroen Ami 6. (Courtesy National Motor Museum)

from lower gear ratios tended to be amplified within the car. As with all rear-engined cars, engine noise tends to be more prevalent than with conventional front engine layouts and the Fiat was no exception. At higher speeds and in third and top gears an ever present boom was present. But for all that the 600 was a delight to drive, far superior in roadholding and stability than its two closest competitors, the 4CV Renault and the Volkswagen Beetle. For all its small size, the 600 appealed to the Italians: used to the Topolino with just two seats and limited space for children or luggage, its successor offered all the advantages of a full four-seater with luggage space as well. Little wonder Italians were ecstatic about it and bought it in huge numbers!

From its introduction in March 1955 until the end of the year, almost 67,000 Fiat 600s were sold; by the end of 1956 the figure had increased to a staggering 230,000, accounting for almost 60% of Fiat's car sales for 1956. By the time of the London Motor Show of 1955, when the 600 had been on sale in Britain for only a relatively short period, it had already become a familiar sight.

Carrozzeria creations

The two prestigious European motor shows at which the 600 made its flamboyant debuts, Geneva in March and Turin at the end of April, were also springboards for the specialist coachwork designers to exhibit their latest creations. Naturally the 600 was featured quite extensively, which was remarkable in view of the short time the design houses had been given to apply their skills. The arrival of the 600, however, was too good an opportunity to miss and all the leading specialists displayed their own particular interpretation of the car. Whilst some coachbuilders offered elaborate interiors with special upholstery, built-in radios, extensive instrumentation and additional exterior trim embellishments, others applied their creativeness to exotic coachwork, often with sporting aspirations which included cabriolets. All the leading names could be found: Pininfarina, Viotti, Boano, Vignale, Siata, Ghia, Allemano, Monterosa and Zagato, to name but a few of the twenty or so coachbuilders represented. Much of the *elaborazione*, which went as far as sprucing up the interior trim, put as little as £65 to £90 on the price of a standard car which cost the equivalent of £330. For the full treatment, however, which possibly included special coachwork, a further £250 to £300 at contemporary rates could be added to the expected asking price.

Pininfarina devised its car with a reverse-rake rear window, a feature later adopted by Ford on the Anglia models, and by Citroën with its 2CV-based Ami 6. Monterosa produced an extremely sleek and pretty 2-seater coupé complete with front-hinged doors and wrap-around front and rear windscreens, the latter formed from plastic and moulded directly into the 'fastback' coachwork. Less successful was Canta who attempted a four-door version of the 600: not only was access severely

The exquisite lines of the Fiat-Abarth record Monza series car. Team Roosevelt was especially successful in racing; the chassis was virtually unchanged from the Zagato 750GT. Good for speeds of 95mph (150kph), the brakes were standard Fiat 600, making control of the car interesting, to say the least. (Courtesy Haymarket)

restricted but, in providing rear doors, the front seating position was moved forward and a front bench seat with a cut-out to facilitate gearchanging replaced the individual seats. With the handbrake, choke and starter controls repositioned ahead of the gear lever, the result was not at all becoming and made for a very uncomfortable and cramped driving position.

Viotti, like Monterosa, displayed an attractive little sporting coupé complete with air-intakes built into the rear wings and a two-tone colour scheme, Ghia, on the other hand, opted to retain the overall original styling of the standard 600 but added minor modifications to the wings and installed a dummy frontal radiator grille. Other embellishments included redesigned bumpers and a split rear seat backrest. Siata, again using the standard 600 shape, managed to enlarge the already wide-opening doors and elongate the car slightly by increasing the front and rear overhang. Boano, too, kept somewhat to the definitive design but, in offering internal refinements reduced the amount of passenger space, especially to the rear. Vipale, in displaying its *La Cherie*, managed to camouflage the 600's smallness by designing a two-door coupé with outstanding passenger accommodation. With coachwork design more attributable to that of the Fiat 1100 Nuova (even as far as a dummy front grille), it was considerably larger than the other offerings. The doors, front-hinged instead of the standard 'suicide' type, extended to almost the rear wheelarches. With special wheels, additional bodywork trim to include built-in driving lamps and a luxurious interior, the *La Cherie* was considered to be one of the most attractive exhibits.

By far the most outstanding variation on a 600 theme was the Zagato, oldest established of the specialist coachbuilders. This was a true sports coupé with sloping bonnet and aerodynamic rear styling. Thin windscreen pillars, made possible by a plastic roof, added to the impression of speed and, inside the car, instrumentation befitted a sporting machine of the highest calibre. To complement the styling, performance received some specialist attention: larger valves and carburettor, together with raising the compression ratio, pushed the top speed up to 82mph (132kph). To cope with the new-found power it was necessary to modify the suspension with larger dampers and springs. Two cars were entered for the 22nd Mille Miglia, staged between 30th April and 1st May, the thousand miles race over a section of Italy starting from Brescia, going south following

The Fiat-Abarth 750 with Bertone styling designed by Franco Scaglione. Build time was just 40 days before it was taking the records, cruising at over 90mph (144kph) and still managing over 40mpg (7l/100km). (Courtesy Haymarket)

the coast to Pescara, east to Rome and north back to Brescia via Bologna. The victor was Stirling Moss in a Mercedes 300SLR, the first British driver to win the event, and who, in so doing, smashed the existing record by some 10mph (16kph).

A year later at the 1956 show Bertone displayed a spectacular design for the 600 which incorporated Abarth engine modifications. The car's swept-down frontal treatment concealed headlamps behind pop-up flaps, but the main attraction was the engine, bored out to 750cc. By far the most outstanding design was surely the Fiat-Abarth-Bertone machine designed by Franco Scaglione: very aerodynamic, with fully enclosed wheels and a single closed cockpit, the car, with its modified engine and looking more at home on the race track or the Bonneville salt flats, had a top speed in excess of 130mph (208kmh) and could cruise at over 90mph (144kmh) returning a little over 40mpg (7 litres per 100km). These, and other Abarth conversions and variants, will be dealt with in greater detail in a later chapter.

To promote the 600, Fiat produced a range of sales brochures: early publications associated the new car with the company's historical 4-seater models from the horseless carriage through to the 501, 503 and 514. Bringing the story up to date via the Balilla and the 'new' 1100, Fiat was keen to link the 600 with the successes of the ubiquitous 500 Topolino. As well as promoting the maximum speed of the 600 – over 60mph (96kph) – economy was assured as consumption was stated as the same as the 500. Full use of colour was maintained with copious technical drawings displaying the workings of the car in ghosted view. Earlier brochures went into surprising detail concerning the merits of a rear-positioned engine and the space-saving design of the system, almost to the point of over sell. Fiat was less reliant than some other manufacturers upon vanity drawings – those showing the car, mostly overscale, in the comfortable environment of a familiar and happy smiling family of the 1950s. Instead,

Fiat quite naturally claimed the 600 to be a classic - just like the leaning tower of Pisa! (Author's collection)

42

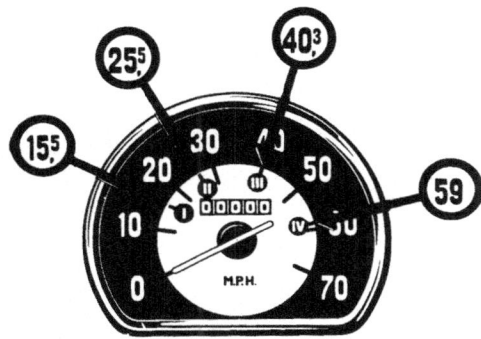

Fiat used location shots, still with the happy family, but with the aim of attracting the modern female driver. The usual exaggerated interiors were all there, as well as the inference that the 600 was easy to drive and easy to park, which, of course, it was. The advantages of the 600 compared to the 500 which it replaced are summed up in an initial brochure:

– *4 comfortable seats instead of 2*

– *Independent suspension on all four wheels*

– *Increased maximum speed: over 60mph*

– *Livelier acceleration*

– *Low fuel consumption (in relation to the increased performance and capacity)*

– *Maximum visibility*

If Fiat thought the motorist at large had to be educated to the 600's technology, auto journalists needed no convincing. *The Motor* hailed it as "outstanding" and "a remarkable small car"; Harry Mundy, reviewing the 600 in *The Autocar*, wrote of "the outstanding features of what may prove a classic design." By way of introduction to a road test, *The Autocar*, in a further review noted: "The Fiat 600 is one of those original designs which creates another milestone in the history of motoring."

A milestone the 600 has certainly turned out to be. In the first five years of production a shade under a million cars left the assembly lines.

IV

EVOLUTION AND BEYOND

New worlds

Fiat, in common with Renault and Volkswagen, looked west across the Atlantic to North America, in the hope of realising ambitions of opening up new markets in which to sell their cars. The American dream had failed before and ended in a rude awakening; now it was different with a market that was both receptive and willing to try any car from a European manufacturer. Renault had fared well selling 3500 4CVs and 1700 Dauphines to the Americans in 1956; a year later the figures had increased to 5000 and a staggering 28,000 respectively. By the early Sixties, half a million Renaults were being shipped across the Atlantic.

Volkswagen, too, did well in the New World with its Beetle. Volkswagen of America was launched in 1954 and in the first year over 32,000 cars were delivered with sales increasing eight-fold over the following ten years. In 1968 close to half a million Beetles had found customers in the United States.

Fiat, keen to join the export drive, leased two specially equipped ships to transport its cars across the Atlantic: firstly the Italterra, which was later joined by its sister ship, Italmare, carried their cargo of 600s and 1100s to Baltimore. Sadly, Fiat did not achieve the same level of success as rivals Renault and Volkswagen had enjoyed: after peaking at almost 38,500 units in 1959 American interest went into decline.

Looking to the southern hemisphere, Fiat drew up adventurous plans for a production plant in Australia, where the 600 would have been assembled in a purpose-built factory at Fisherman's Bend. Specialists and technicians from Turin were dispatched to supervise the establishment of the plant where it was anticipated at least 35% of the labour and material required in building the car would be Australian, rising eventually to some 75-80% local content. The plan was short-lived, as was the idea of penetrating the Canadian market. By an obscure route Fiat had hoped to sell its cars – the emphasis being on the 600 model – throughout Canada under an agreement with the Chrysler organisation. Some measure of success did materialise in Canada but not until 1968, by which time the nearest relative to the 600 to be marketed there was the 850 Spyder. There were successes, however, especially in New Zealand, but more of that later. In general, Fiat had to be content with the European operation which was its forte. In 1955, the year of the 600, some 250,000 vehicles were produced, 148,432 of which were registered in Italy.

A year after the glittering launch of the 600 and associated razzmatazz of a new model, the season of Europe's shows and salons got underway with the Brussels event in January 1956, where the 600 theme was still very much in evidence. This was further echoed at the Geneva Show in March and Turin in April, an indication of the extent of the 600's initial impact. The stylists and tuners also stayed with the 600, beautifying and powering it still further. Alongside Abarth, who displayed the full kit of parts to convert a demure 600 into a hot-blooded monster, were a host

Looking towards new horizons and new marklets. Fiat, together with other European car makers, turned to America. This brochure relates to export models for the USA; note the lack of body trim and combined sidelights and indicators below the headlamps. (Author's collection)

The agility of the 600 is well defined in this brochure illustration; the car is seen clinging to a less than solid road surface, perhaps ideal for the American market to which this catalogue referred. Note the American model's single combined sidelamps and direction indicators under the headlamps. (Author's collection)

For 1956 the folding roof once again became an option. At its launch, the 600 was sold only with a fixed roof. Note that the fabric roof unfolds almost as far back as the rear window. In Italy, this version was marketed as the Tetto Apribile and in Britain as the Convertible. (Courtesy Fiat (Auto (UK) & Fiat SPA Ltd)

Below: Sliding windows soon gave way to the more convenient winding type. The car illustrated may have been a pre-production model or a mock-up, given its dull and unreal finish. (Courtesy Fiat Auto (UK) & Fiat SPA Ltd)

The Multipla

The Spring shows of 1956 were of considerable significance, especially Turin which gave Italy its first glimpse of the Multipla, Fiat's all-purpose, all-service vehicle which had been launched in time for the Brussels Show. Neither estate car or saloon, the highly distinctive and efficient.Multipla can safely be tagged one of motoring history's anomalies. Replacing the beloved 500 Belvedere and Giardiniera, the Multipla was one of the first cars to demonstrate the serious art of people-carrying, luggage-carrying or, more often than not, both! The full story, however, of this very unusual vehicle, its development and evolution, is told in greater detail in a later chapter.

Fiat v. Dauphine

Although the focus of attention was still upon the 600, it had to share some of the limelight with a new contender in the popularity stakes: the Renault Dauphine. Renault had no intention of eventually replacing the 4CV with the Dauphine – the 4L and front-wheel-drive was planned for that – it was, instead, intended to complement it and use many common components. The Dauphine appeared as Renault's saviour and with it the company hopefully envisaged an upsurge of sales in what was seen as an important and lucrative market both at home, in France, and throughout Europe and the USA.

of extravagant styling exercises by some of Italy's most famous creators. Not to be forgotten, of course, was Fiat's standard bread-winning 600 models, updated with modifications for the new year.

At its launch, Fiat's baby car had lost one of its main attractions over the Topolino, the folding sunshine roof. In answer to an almost audible lament at its demise, the Tetto Apribile became available again for 1956 – not just an opening fabric panel for the benefit of the driver and front passenger, this was a full-length opening roof, folding back almost as far as the rear screen and so transforming the entire character of the car. In Italy, the 600 with sunroof was known as the Trasformabile, in Germany as the Cabrio-Limousine and in Britain the Convertible. There was, however, a price penalty for such luxury with 45,000 Lire – a little over £20 – added to the price. With the sunroof came further modifications: an interior courtesy light was fitted and the engine compartment lamp made to operate via an automatic switch; an additional 1.18in (30mm) was added to the length of the radiator, the interior heating was improved and, while more on the mechanical side, the front suspension was reviewed and strengthened.

Winding windows gave the 600 a cleaner and less cluttered appearance. This Fiat publicity photograph suggests the latest in Italian architecture as well as motor cars. (Courtesy Fiat Auto (UK) & Fiat SPA Ltd)

An early publicity photograph of the Multipla to coincide with its launch at the Brussels Show in January 1956. The Multipla was Giacosa's 600-based answer to the popular Giardiniera and Belvedere versions of the Topolino. (Courtesy National Motor Museum)

Further modifications to the 600 resulted in the appearance of bright body side mouldings and hooded headlamp bezels. (Courtesy Fiat Auto (UK) & Fiat SPA Ltd)

Windscreen washers were fitted as standard from 1957, the year of the Suez crisis and petrol rationing. In a publicity venture to demonstrate their economy, Fiat sent a 600 and Multipla on a mammoth tour through 33 countries. (Courtesy Fiat Auto (UK) & Fiat SPA Ltd)

Still retaining the rear-engined layout, the Dauphine boasted a modern design combined with economy and comfort, even if it did initially have a three-speed gearbox when other manufacturers were going for four. Its 850cc engine propelled the car to 70mph (112kph) with a meagre fuel consumption, usually not less than 40mpg (7lt/100km), but as it

This quite dreadful contemporary brochure shows the 600 on an airfield runway, almost under the rear fuselage of an aircraft. (Author's collection)

happened its handling fell far short of the 600's. The appearance of the Dauphine just a year after the launch of the 600 must have caused Giacosa a little concern and no doubt had some influence upon both the future and design of the 600's eventual successor, the 850.

1957

Apart from the 'D' version which will be discussed later in this chapter, some of the most significant changes and modifications to the 600 range occurred two years following its initial appearance in 1955. Mechanically, the car changed surprisingly little: the electrical system received a boost with a 32AH battery replacing the original 28AH type; steering and suspension received further minor modifications and easier starting was made possible by alterations to the carburettor. Other changes included the redesigning of the windscreen wiper assembly, a new wiper switch and attention to the ignition system.

The most obvious change was the provision of wind-down front windows which replaced the sliding type, a relic of the Topolino since 1936. A new instrument panel, neatly padded, added grace to the fascia which appeared less cluttered by relocation of the headlight and direction indicator switches to the steering column. Re-designed front seats provided increased driver and passenger comfort, a windscreen washer added to safety and the car's aesthetics were given a filip with the addition of door and body mouldings as well as headlamp cowls.

The gloom of world crisis surrounding the Suez affair of 1957 affected the motor industry very substantially. Petrol rationing and a total drop-off in sales of new cars had a recessionary effect on what had been post-war boom years. Lucky was the manufacturer who was able to offer an economy car and even luckier if its performance outweighed its frugality. There was frantic interest, therefore, when rumours began to circulate about a new Fiat, smaller even than the 600 with economy to match. This was not the first occasion such rumours had surfaced and Fiat was somewhat reluctant to provide any statement. Due probably to the renewed interest in small economy cars and pressure from an increasing number of enquiries, Fiat eventually succumbed and released an ambiguous but curt message in early March to the effect that the company would "at the right moment make an announcement from Turin." A few days later Fiat, in common with other Italian car builders, announced extensive price increases which on average ranged from 3.5-5%. The 600 suffered the most stringent price rise with 7.5% slapped upon it.

Of the three traditional Spring shows, Geneva was the only event to take place in 1957. The Brussels Show had been cancelled and Turin decided to defer until the Autumn. Fiat had relied upon the glamorous Swiss occasions to promote its cars, taking advantage of this renownedly auspicious venue which was free of the gloom of the Italian economy. It was with some disappointment, therefore, that the 600's future baby relative, the 500 Nuova, was conspicuous by its absence and it was left to the 600 to fly the Fiat flag. Naturally the styling specialists were again in attendance, offering their gems to customers looking for something a little different. Lombardi decided to return to the four-door concept for its version of the 600 and showed a particularly interesting pillarless saloon. *The Motor* claimed it to be "entirely practical" although there is little evidence to show the car was supplied in anything but minimal numbers.

In the early part of the Suez crisis, and a few days before petrol rationing came into force during January 1957, Fiat was quick to arrange a spectacular event to publicize the performance and economy of the 600. Two vehicles, a saloon and a Multipla, were hurriedly prepared for a mammoth tour and demonstration throughout 33 countries. Driven hard in what can only be described as appalling weather and conditions, the Multipla, it is claimed, completed the tour returning a remarkable 41.6mpg.

1958 & 1959

Less extensive but no less important were the changes for 1958 and 1959. A facelift to the 600's interior for '58 was quite evidential, a light grey colour replaced the original beige for the steering wheel, instrument panel, sunvisor and rear-view mirror. The light and direction indicator switches were also changed to light grey, although the other control knobs were finished in black. A choice of colours for the interior trim became available: carpets, panel coverings and seat material could

Interior of the 600 for 1957. The seat trim has been revised and fabric door pockets have replaced the original box type. (Courtesy Fiat Auto (UK) & Fiat SPA Ltd)

Revisions to the 600 interior included a light grey finish instead of the original beige, a redesigned instrument cowl and additional indicator lamps fitted to the fascia. These modifications applied to 1959 model cars. (Courtesy Fiat Auto (UK) & Fiat SPA Ltd)

be specified in either blue, beige, red or green. On the mechanical side, a new clutch featured rubber dampers and the generator received modification to its drive gear. 1959 saw the arrival of a new rear-view mirror, front direction indicators and rear tail lights; electrical and mechanical improvements included a combined ignition and starter switch as well as slight adjustment to the carburettor. By far the most important change was the disappearance of the transmission parking brake in favour of a conventional handbrake actuating the rear wheel brake shoes. Only on the 1200 Granluce did the transmission brake continue to feature on Fiat's production cars, and then only for a short while before it was superseded a year later in 1960.

Further changes for 1959 affected the external styling: wing-top light units disappeared and, instead, sidelights were fitted below the headlamps while direction indicators were repositioned to the side of the wing. Bright trim on the body sides was also slightly modified. (Author's collection)

Between 1955 and 1960, Dante Giacosa and his department had been busy with a number of projects which included developing the 500 Nuova and formulating ideas for the 600's eventual replacement. Combined with this were plans for a new Simca, the 1000, which would project the car into the next decade and on into the Seventies. Simca had, following the demise of the Topolino and therefore the Simca Six, concentrated upon the Aronde which had been introduced in the Summer of

Sharing the limelight, a Nuova 500 poses with the larger 600. In the background, parked in the garage is another 600, possibly a saloon. Whereas the 600 in the foreground has winding windows, the Nuova is the Economy version with fixed windows, opening quarterlights and a full-length sunroof. (Author's collection)

repositioned beneath the headlamps. Repeater signals were placed on the side of the wings ahead of the bright trim. Swivelling quarter-lights fitted into the front doors allowed improved ventilation and a redesigned engine cover, with a greater number of louvres, ensured more effective cooling.

The 600D signalled the arrival of a larger engine, increased from the original 633cc to 767cc. 600Ds can be recognised by front window quarterlights, slightly revised rear direction indicators and modified engine covers with a greater number of cooling louvres. The increased power of the 600D allowed a top speed of 68mph (110kph), as against 62mph (100kph), with only a minimal increase in fuel consumption. (Author's collection)

1951. Although the 600 had become Italy's best selling car and had seen several design changes which, in general, were of a relatively minor nature, Giacosa was in the process of updating it in the form of the 600D with an appearance planned for the late Summer of 1960.

600D

The 600D arrived after the traditional summer shutdown of the Fiat factories. Revised body detail immediately distinguished the "D" model from earlier production: front indicators were removed from the top of the wings and

Essentially, however, the "D" designation referred to the new engine: type "100D 000" when fitted to the saloon and "100D 008" for the Multipla.

The new engine gave the 600D a significant boost in power. From the original 633cc, its displacement

Profile of the 600D showing its modified windows. (Courtesy Fiat Auto (UK) & Fiat SPA Ltd)

Centre: Although little had changed in interior design, more comfort was afforded by the 600D's modified seats. (Courtesy Fiat Auto (UK) & Fiat SPA Ltd)

Bottom: Folding the back seat rest forward allowed a huge increase in the 600D's luggage capacity. (Author's collection)

increased to 767cc, providing a maximum horsepower rating of 32bhp. Through the gears the 600D displayed much greater energy, culminating in a top speed of 68mph (110kph) against 62mph (100kph): 19mph (30kph) was possible in 1st, 28 (45) in 2nd and 44 (70) in 3rd. Modifications were not limited to the engine: the original bypass cartridge oil filter was replaced by a centrifugal type and the cooling system radiator received a larger diameter inlet and outlet. Either a Weber 28 ICP 1 or the Solex C28 PIB-2 carburettor was specified; revised brake cylinders improved stopping power whilst a larger battery and redesigned starter motor helped put the car into motion. Other modifications included a revised air cleaner, external crankcase oil vent, rear wheel toe-in and a higher final drive ratio.

As revisions and modifications improved the performance of the 600, so the gross vehicle weight increased by just 22lb (10kg) which, in turn, allowed a far greater useful load, increased from four passengers and 66lb (30kg) to four passengers and 110lb (50kg). The interior trim of the 600D remained similar to the original model, although versions intended for the British market had seats trimmed in leathercloth instead of fabric. With the fitting of a combined ignition and starter switch on the fascia, only the choke control remained mounted at floor level, this being situated between the gearlever and handbrake.

Testing the 600D, *The Autocar* re-affirmed its affection for the car; *The Motor*, too, was generally complimen-

Front and rear profiles of the 600D. Note the increased number of air vents in the engine cover. By 1960, output of the 600 series was running at a little over half a million cars a year (Courtesy Fiat (UK) & Fiat SPA Ltd)

tary but had rather severe reservations over the suspension and ride which it found to be "less pleasing by modern standards." The power increase had a marked effect on the car's performance, providing an extra degree of flexibility. Higher maximum speeds in each gear helped the general progression enormously: 0 to 50mph (80kph) took 23.8 seconds, 8 seconds quicker than with the 633cc engine in 1955, although *The Motor* in its test knocked a clear 3 seconds from this figure.

From the quarter-million vehicles produced by Fiat in 1955, output had doubled by 1960 to some 531,000 units. Of the half-million plus vehicles, a little over 291,000 had been registered in Italy. The 600 was still Italy's most popular car with 891,000 having been built until introduction of the 600D. This was matched only by the 1100-103: during its production years spanning 1953 to 1962, 1,019,378 units were sold.

Production of the 600 in 1959 reached the dizzy heights of 1000 cars a day as export markets were explored. Czechoslovakia began taking the 600 from 1959 and eastern Europe was seen as an important future market, not only for the 600, but other models in the Fiat catalogue which could eventually form the basis of local assembly. Poland, of course, under the direction of FSM would be a major source for small Fiats in the years ahead. By the end of the 1960s Fiat had as many as twenty five production and local assembly plants throughout the world, all delivering models of one sort or another.

The turn of the decade saw a revolution in European car design. The rear-engined Renault 4CV gave way to the R4 in 1961 whilst the Dauphine, now with a four-speed gearbox and 38bhp, continued its success story and was the first French car to exceed production of over two million vehicles. Renault also achieved success outside France with the Dauphine; in Italy it was built under licence by Alfa Romeo and in Brazil by Willys-Overland. The R4 steered a new direction for Renault, it adopted front-wheel-drive and a five-door hatchback-style bodywork to become known as a "hold-all on wheels." Early examples were fitted with a tiny 603cc water-cooled four-cylinder engine which was completely lethargic in operation. A larger, and much more successful, 747cc unit took its place. The 4 had been designed to steal custom away from Citroën's 2CV and in so doing employed soft loping suspension with exaggerated body roll, basic utility, and a similar fascia-mounted, push-pull quirky gear change. The 2CV theme, however, was extended and the "Tin Snail" was joined by an up-market version, the Ami 6, complete with reverse-rake rear window similar to Pininfarina's version of the Fiat 600. Renault's 4 outlived the 2CV, the last examples left production lines in Morocco in 1993 though the 2CV was in production from 1948 till 1990.

In Britain, the side-valve Fords had given way to the new and stylish Anglia, complete with overhead valve engine and reverse-rake rear window. Standard-Triumph launched the Herald using the Triumph marque and so announced the demise of the Standard Eight and Ten; the Herald was unusual in that it retained a separate chassis when modern convention dictated unitary construction. As early as 1958 BMC had introduced the Farina-styled Austin A40 as an additional model to the A35 which continued in production until late 1961. The ubiquitous Morris Minor marched on to the magic million figure late in 1960 and then settled down for an easy run until the turn of the following decade. The real challenge, however, appeared in August 1959 in the shape of the Mini which was initially marketed under two badges as the Austin Seven and Morris Mini-Minor.

Alex Issigonis had managed to swing BMC's faithful A-series engine and gearbox sideways, packaging them into a single unit to adopt front-wheel-drive, just as Giacosa had imagined when considering alternative engine and transmission arrangements for the Fiat 600. The Mini's 848cc engine and front-wheel-drive gave a new meaning to performance for the small British car, 70mph (112kph) was attainable, as was a claim by the manufacturer of 50mpg. Arguably one of the most successful cars in British motoring history, the Mini, a full four-seater with a small luggage compartment behind the rear seat, was 9 inches (229mm) shorter than the Fiat 600, 1 inch (25mm) wider, and a fraction over 2 inches (50mm) lower.

Surprisingly, the concept of the rear-engined layout was not dead in Britain. Hillman, under Rootes Group management and in response to an increasing demand for small family cars, produced the Imp at its new and purpose-built factory at Linwood in Scotland. Rootes' engineers had decided upon a design keeping power away from the steered wheels and, in order to save as much space as possible whilst retaining simplicity, mounted a light-alloy 875cc engine behind the rear wheels driving them via an all-synchromesh 4-speed gearbox. At the time Rootes considered the Imp revolutionary, but it failed to achieve the success expected.

Germany's Volkswagen plodded on with the Beetle which retained its original overall appearance apart from relatively minor detail changes. Engine capacity remained the same – 1192cc – although for 1961 the power unit and gearbox received a substantial modification which produced 10% more power, quicker acceleration and a higher top speed coupled with synchromesh on all gears.

Also in Germany there had been a return to the small car and minimal motoring: the NSU Prinz, Goggomobil TS400 and Auto Union DKW Junior had made an appearance. In Holland, the Daf 600, with its idiosyncratic belt-driven automatic transmission, became popular while, a little later in France, the rear-engined Simca 1000 appeared alongside the Panhard PL17 and Citroën's weirdly characteristic Ami 6.

On home ground in Italy there had also been a move towards a smaller and more economical car with a return to ideas first realised during the dark days of the Second World War. In the

One of the most significant changes to the 600 occurred in 1964 with the adoption of front-hinged doors, the result of new Italian safety regulations. (Courtesy Fiat Auto (UK) & Fiat SPA Ltd)

Rear styling changed little with the move to front-hinged doors; later models received modified bumpers and overriders with rubber protectors. (Courtesy Fiat Auto (UK) & Fiat SPA Ltd)

summer of 1957 Fiat finally announced a new 500 – the 500 Nuova – again masterminded by Dante Giacosa. The Cinquecento Nuova, heralded as a new Topolino, suffered a shaky start but development since its introduction resulted in the launch of the 'D' version at the same time as its big brother, the 600D.

Price reductions for the British market were announced for the 600 range at the end of April 1961, which no doubt reflected the growing and ever-hostile competition from a new generation of smaller family cars. Nearly £60 (including tax) was slashed from the price of the basic model and £56 from the de luxe version – an advantage of the de luxe car was its sunroof, sadly, a feature not on offer by most British manufacturers. Vehicle production in Italy was on the up and up: almost 171,000 more vehicles were produced in 1962 than 1961, pushing the total number of Fiats leaving the factories up to 930,000. Taking the

increased popularity to heart, Fiat initiated a sales drive for the United Kingdom market and commissioned a new reception and preparation department at Dover.

Safer doors

The next major change to the 600 occurred in 1964 when its suicide doors were replaced with the front-hinged type. The 600 was amongst the last to retain front-opening doors, a relic of the golden days of motoring. Pivoting the doors at the front gave the 600 a more modern appearance and external door hinges disappeared. The changes, however, were not modern enough to see the car through the remainder of the '60s without further modification

Interior of a 1964 car with leathercloth seats. (Courtesy Fiat Auto (UK) & Fiat SPA Ltd)

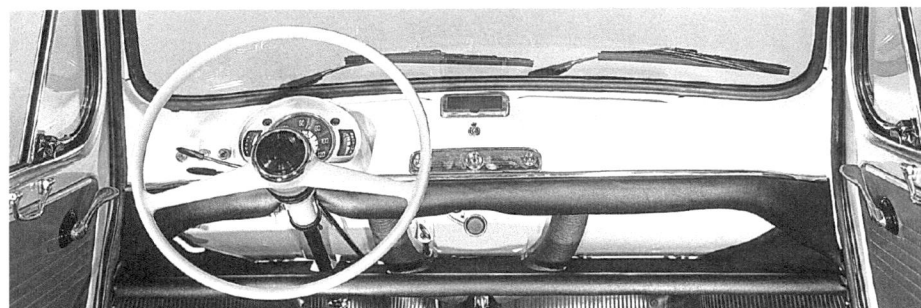

The dashboard of 1964 cars retained clean and uncluttered lines. (Courtesy Fiat Auto (UK) & Fiat SPA Ltd)

From the Turin Show of 1965, the 600's appearance was changed again to reflect styling trends. The front compartment lost much of its brightwork and body trim mouldings disappeared. Larger headlamps were fitted while mechanical changes included a larger fuel tank and the adoption of a centrifugal-type oil filter. (Author's collection)

and a year later at the 1965 Turin show yet another – the final – design change took effect. In general, the lines of the 600 were subject to some tidying-up: new rear light clusters were fitted in the tail, side trim mouldings were removed and the front of the car underwent minor, but still significant, restyling. Gone was the circular 600 emblem and the associated brightwork that had adorned the car since its launch. In its place was a simple Fiat badge with a narrow trim either side of it. New and larger headlamps were fitted, and in the front compartment a bigger fuel tank held 6.8 gallons (31 litres) of petrol which reduced the number of visits to the filling station. Overriders on the bumpers, which had been fitted on introduction of the 600D, now received rubber mounts to provide added protection, especially when parking. In Italy, the 600 was listed until 1969 although production continued into 1970 before being transferred to other factories throughout Europe and South America.

Coinciding with the design changes of 1964 a further development of the 600 theme was realised with the introduction of the Fiat 850. Winner of the 1964 Car Of The Year Award, thankfully the 850 arrived at a time when both Fiat and Italy needed a new small and economical family car most desperately. The 600 was still selling well but Italy's economic situation had taken a serious tumble in 1964; amongst the most noticeable victims was the motor industry. Home registrations of new cars fell drastically, resulting in a reported downturn of business by some £43.5 million. Fiat's export market was less affected and remained reasonably buoyant, managing to offset losses to some degree. The 850 was seen to stimulate sales throughout its particular market sector which, naturally, had an encouraging affect upon sales of the

The 600L was a product of Barcelona and received SEAT badging although marketed as a Fiat. Known as the 'Especial,' the L had de-Luxe trim with cloth seats and a padded fascia. (Author's collection)

600. By 1965 a turn-round in Italy's economy had been achieved: production of Fiat vehicles recovered to about 3500 units a day and exports also regained ground to represent approximately 30% of the country's total vehicle output. It is interesting to note that during the period of recession, BMC managed to make inroads into Italy's automobile market, doubling its share of sales during the first three months of 1965.

There was no concealing the 850's parentage. The overall shape and character of the 600 was quite in evidence although the body styling was altered and updated. The basics of the 600 were all there, even to the layout of the power unit and drive train. Marketed in two models, Standard and Super, both were identical in appearance; the Standard produced 40bhp whilst the Super boasted 42bhp and a maximum speed of 78mph (125kph), which was 4mph(6.4kph) faster than the basic model. Coachwork of the 850, whilst retaining a healthy resemblance to that of the 600, consisted of the familiar two-door design but with an elongated 'boot' area at the rear housing the engine compartment. Although virtually a foot longer (305mm) than the 600, the 850's wheelbase increased by just an inch (25mm), therefore providing a negligible amount of increased length to the cabin space. Where the difference was most apparent was the width, where almost 2 inches (50mm) were added which enabled Fiat to claim the 850 to be a four- to five-seater car.

600: the Universal car

In essence, the 600 changed little during its production from 1955; on the last cars, 600Ds with front-hinged doors, the interior was virtually the same as earlier models, even the fascia had hardly changed. Production of the 600 was not limited to Italy: in Germany it was marketed as the NSU, in Austria as the Steyr-Fiat, in Yugoslavia as the Zastava. in Spain as the Seat and in Argentina as the Fiat-Concord. 600E and 600L versions also made an appearance, these were the product of the Seat works in Barcelona, from which all export markets were supplied from 1970. Although Fiat assembly plants had been opened up worldwide, Barcelona remained the only point of production for both the 600D and 850 saloons destined for the European market.

The 600L, designated Especial, was the de luxe version of the "E" and sported a superior interior finish which incorporated cloth trim and a padded fascia. The 600E adopted the traditional Fiat 600 logo and came with vinyl upholstery and a plain, painted dashboard. Externally, the "E" and "L" models were all but identical apart from ventilation grilles positioned immediately behind the rear side windows of the "L." A further version was the Fiat 600R, a product of the Argentinian factory designed for the important South American market. Devoid of wheel hubcaps and bright body mouldings, a dummy air-intake adorned the front panel and a fender attached to

57

Following the cessation of 600 production in Italy, European manufacture was centred at Barcelona at the SEAT works. The 600E appeared with basic trim, leathercloth seats and a plain painted dashboard. (Author's collection)

the bumpers provided protection to the lights and lower bodywork. The "R" version received a power advantage over previous 600s, the 767cc engine was extended to 797cc with an output of 36bhp to match. The Argentinian 600 emerged as the country's most popular car and in the years between 1959 and 1971 nearly 167,000 units were delivered. The contract to assemble cars in the Argentine came into effect during 1960 and lasted well into the '70s.

On the sporting side, Fiat, through such masters as Abarth, Zagato and Pininfarina, brought about a return to the racing successes of pre-war days. The Sestriere rally of 1958 in a Zagato-designed Fiat-Abarth was taken in style; in Turin, Abarth was busy modifying 600s to 750cc and at the same time found a market for the product in the United States. Abarth was responsible for promoting the sporting aspect of the 600, having made a fleet of cars available at the 1956 Turin show for the general public to test drive. From 1956 to 1964 the Fiat-Abarth Berlina, which was based on the standard 600 saloon, remained Abarth's most successful selling car.

Motorsport
The 600 began to show its worth on the international sporting scene. Under the guise of the Fiat-Abarth 750 Berlina it was class winner in the 1956 Mille Miglia, even beating a Zagato-bodied car. It was also a popular contender in the Monte Carlo rallies, its performance over snow and ice making it eminently suitable for such events. The Fiat-Abarth 850TC, a development of the 600, was the overall winner in the 1961 FIA European Championship for touring cars and at the 1965 Monza four-hour race Fiats dominated the scene. Abarth, too, was responsible in part for the development work on the original 600's power unit, uprating it to 767cc for the 600D.

Abarth was not the only specialist to pay attention to the 600, although there is little doubt it was the most successful. Siata produced relatively small numbers of 735cc engined cars in Spain whilst in Britain MPG and H, a London based company, converted and tuned standard 600s so that they became capable of speeds of well over 80mph (129kph). The latter specialist retained the original bodyshell but bored the engine to 850cc. With new pistons, the compression ratio was increased to 8.9:1 and the standard Weber single-choke carburetter was discarded in favour of a Fish unit, all of which allowed the engine to be taken up to 7000rpm. Such conversions allowed the 600 to compete outright with 850 Minis which were starting to take home the trophies.

In Britain, the 600 was showing a clean pair of heels to many cars more powerful at Silverstone and Brands Hatch. There have been few more suc-

A 600D comes out of a corner with the front offside wheel clear of the ground. This particular car was a well-known visitor to trials and rallies and had an engine conversion similar to that on Abarth cars. (Courtesy Wally Pratt)

Built for the Argentinian and South American market and considered by Fiat to be very important, the 600R was a derivative of the definitive model. A small dummy air-intake is fitted to the front compartment while the engine is a 797cc unit. Note the special wheels and bumpers. (Author's collection)

cessful behind the wheel of 600s than Wally Pratt, whose first car dated from 1955/6 and his second car, a 600D, from 1965. The sporting fraternity followed the 600's progress with interest and Wally was soon to become a celebrity on the circuit. It is a tribute to both the 600's sound design and Fiat's engineering that almost forty years after the 600's introduction it is still performing and winning on the racetrack.

Trials with the earliest cars during 1955 showed that it was feasible to achieve a maximum speed of virtually 60mph (96kph); it proved possible, however, for the Abarth version of the 600, with its tuning and conversions, to push that speed up to over 84mph (134kph) and 91mph (146kph) at best. The story of the Abarth, together with other variants, is a fascinating one which is dealt with in a later chapter.

Production of the 600 continued in one form or another well into the Eighties with some 2.5 million cars accounted for. The 600 is truly a world-class car and one of the most successful ever. As a car for the Italians it was perfetto, providing four wheels and independence with dignity, all at a time when the nation's economy began to prosper. Italy took the 600 to its heart and it has become a living legend. The 600 can be found in virtually every country and far-flung corner of the Earth, carrying out totally reliable and faithful service just as Dante Giacosa and his design team intended it should.

V

A NEW TOPOLINO

Although the ill-fated 400 project was abandoned after the prototype car had been destroyed in a bombing raid during the Second War, the significance of the proposal was such that its concept dominated Fiat's designs for small cars over the following four decades. There is still evidence of its original identity, half a century later, in the form of the smaller Fiats emerging from eastern European countries where manufacturing continues under licence.

Whilst the 600 was undergoing final stages of development, Dante Giacosa chose to return to the original principles that led to the Topolino in 1936. Not that he was unhappy with the 600 as the 500's direct successor; on the contrary, it fulfilled the role admirably. His aim was to realize the design of a very small car other than something so utilitarian as to be totally disregarded. A return to the 400 concept was the project that Giacosa contemplated.

Giacosa's reasons for re-kindling the 400 theme were twofold. Firstly, he was, perhaps, concerned that the absolute minimal car concept was about to be lost and, after all, the Topolino in this respect had been outstandingly successful. Secondly, Germany, which was still struggling to rebuild the fabric of its society, was showing a strong tendency to return to the principle of the cyclecar in a quest for an independent and cheap form of transport. The result in Germany, as elsewhere, was the appearance of a whole plethora of micro-cars, based somewhere between the motorcycle and a genuine light car.

The new Topolino, the Nuova 500, represented minimal motoring for the small family, as this rather poor, but original, press photo shows. Although capable of accommodating two children, the car was, in essence, a 2-seater. (Courtesy Fiat Auto (UK) & Fiat SPA Ltd)

The Nuova 500 came about to provide a real alternative to micro-cars and bubble cars such as the Isetta illustrated here. The popularity of such minicars stemmed from Germany where independent transport was sought at minimum price. (Author's collection)

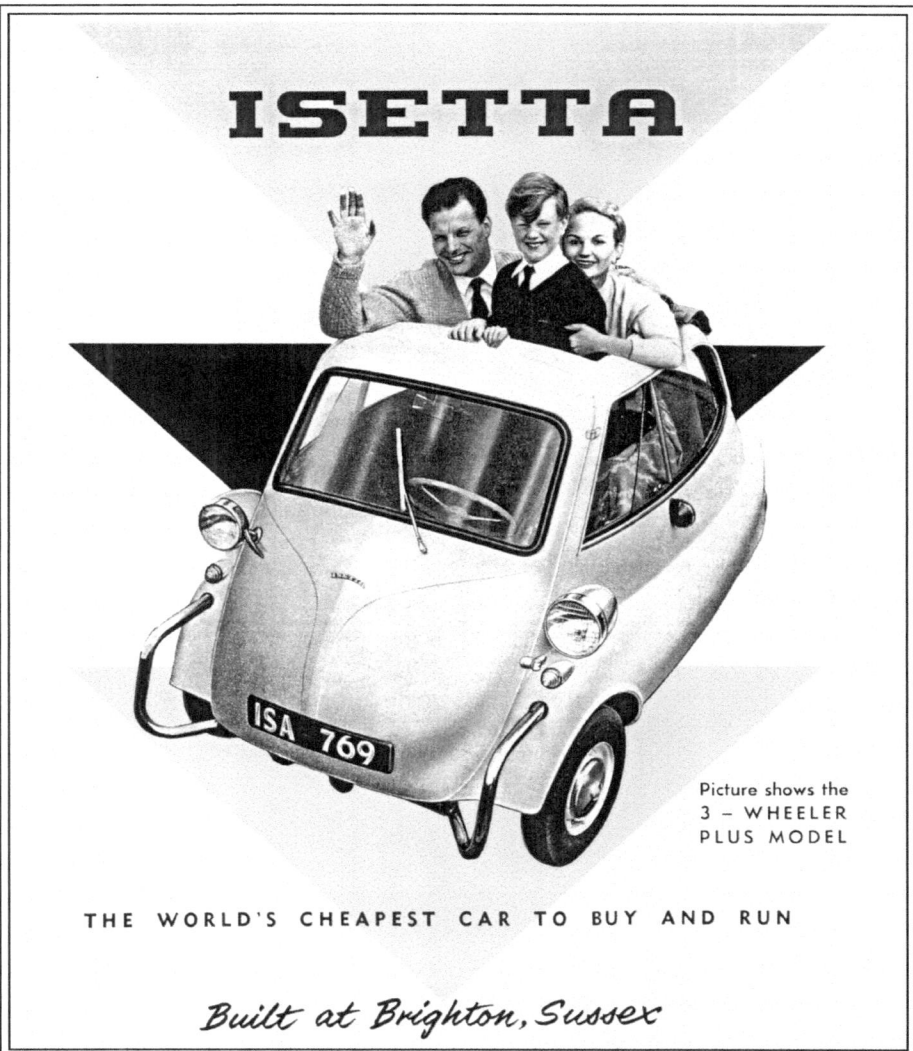

This included the curiously novel bubble car which started a love-affair that lasted into the early Sixties when the bubble burst and a new generation of minis appeared.

The micro-car era

The Paris Salon was often the launching pad for an assortment of odd machines, usually described as interesting or unique but by nature more eccentric. Their popularity was phenomenal with strong followings for such vehicles as the Fuldamobil, H einkel, Isetta, Trojan, Zundapp and Messerschmitt. One micro-car in a league apart from the others was the 1958 Vespa 400 which was built in France to an Italian design against a background more famous for scooters of the same name. This was more significant than perhaps all the other micro-cars, but more of this later.

Britain was another source of eccentric micro-cars which, although often built in relatively small numbers were nevertheless partly responsible for the demise of the motorcycle and sidecar. The like of the Bond, Reliant and BMW Isetta provided a degree of comfort far greater than the motorcycle combination and at little extra expense.

The appearance of the 500 Nuova was not only due in part to Germany's intense desire for rock-bottom motoring, but to a greater extent to the months and years of development associated with the 400 project. Such a high significance had been placed on its design that even almost to the date of the launch the Nuova 500 was still recognised and referred to as the 400. To get to the hub of the Nuova's development it is therefore necessary to return to immediate post-war Germany and Fiat's manufacturing plant at Heilbronn where the Topolino was built under licence as the NSU-Fiat.

Genesis

For sure, a Topolino-style car, smaller than the 600, was being considered at Turin before the German micro-car explosion occurred; Italians had taken to the Topolino with great affection but there was still a market for an even cheaper and more basic car, even if it afforded only minimal comfort and protection. During the months immediately before the 600's launch, an unbelievably hectic period in the Fiat calender, Giacosa somehow found time for relaxation by way of studying drawings of what he considered to be the ultimate in minimal motor cars with one particular exercise intriguing him above all others. Based upon Corradino D'Ascanio's design of the Vespa motor scooter, which was built by Piaggio to world acclaim, the diminutive four-wheeler, totally spartan and unorthodox, provided a wholly-effective answer to the city-car. Perhaps fifty years later the same design with little touches of restyling here and there might have received the accolade of yet another award-winning 'concept car'.

The 'city-car' notion was not quite abandoned by Fiat in the shorter term,

Everybody loved the Nuova as this original advertisement emphasises. (Author's collection)

Some of the original ideas for the 500 originated from drawings inspired by the Vespa motor scooter, created by Corradino D'Ascanio and built by Piaggio. (Author's collection)

however; ten years after the design inspired by the Vespa, a return to a similar principle was made in the form of an experimental electric micro-car, completely utilitarian and capable of seating three abreast in deckchair-type seats. Whilst never developed any further than scale models, the Vespa-inspired exercise did serve as an indication that Giacosa had taken notice of, and was concerned about, events leading to the popularity of the micro-car. Even as long ago as December 1951 Fiat was seen to be looking at the micro-car concept with a design intended to invade the motor-scooter market. With an engine of approximately 350cc the proposed vehicle was to have had a price tag double that of a scooter but with conventional controls and comfort of sorts. The car's criteria was that it had to be very cheap to buy and maintain.

Equally concerned at the increasing popularity of the micro-car was Piero Bonelli, director of NSU-Fiat Heilbronn. The Topolino 500C had been in production in Germany since 1949-50 and, knowing development was underway on a replacement, Bonelli was dismayed that Fiat could lose out to a growing market. Bonelli urged the directors at Turin to instigate designs for a locally-produced micro-car without delay: the outcome was that Bonelli provided drawings and ideas from within his own plant as well as from the coachwork division at nearby Weinsberg.

In the meantime, and by way of digression, Dr. Antonio Fessia, Giacosa's former departmental head, had returned to Fiat and was sent to Heilbronn to head-up a design department under Piero Bonelli with the intention of producing a small economical car. In the event Fessia's stay at NSU-Fiat was not a happy one: the relationship between Bonelli and Fessia soured almost to breaking point and the eventual prototype was a virtual disaster. Fessia's design for an air-cooled twin-cylinder machine should have been ideal as the recipe included front-wheel drive and unitary construction. The styling, although compact in appearance, was perhaps not readily admired for its attractiveness. Carlo Salamano made no attempt to hide his personal opinion – he hated the car, as he did a further prototype which had been designed with a water-cooled twin-cylinder engine. After a period of abortive trials the projects were abandoned and the prototypes returned to Fessia in no uncertain manner.

The Vespa 400, one of the more successful minicars with its roots in motor scooter history. Dante Giacosa's Vespa motor scooter-inspired ideas never came to fruition although, ironically, it was the Nuova 500 which led to the Vespa 400's eventual demise. (Author's collection)

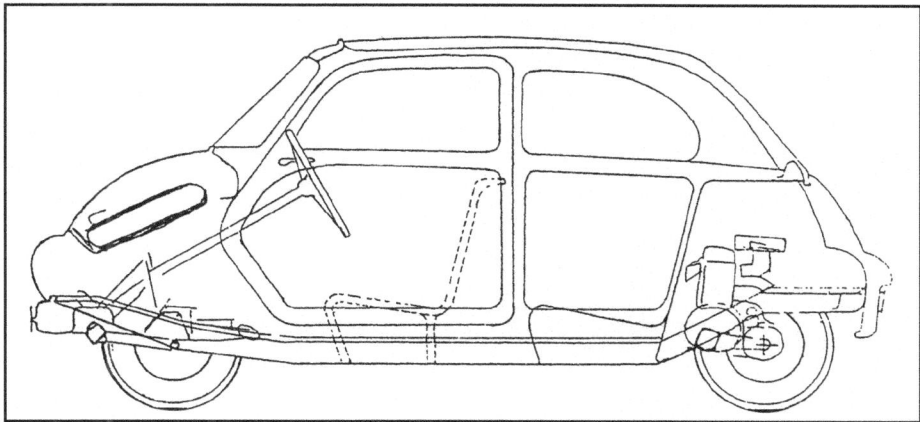

Bauhof's outline sketch for a minicar smaller than the Fiat 600 was designed to compete with the many utility miniatures finding their way onto the market. The overall shape bears some resemblance to the definitive 500. (Author's collection)

The key figure in NSU-Fiat's quest for a minimal car was a young engineer by the name of Bauhof to whom Bonelli had entrusted the project. Bauhof had opted for a choice of two engines; firstly a single cylinder unit based on the Ilo design and, secondly, a two-stroke unit incorporating a double piston. Neither proved entirely satisfactory. Giacosa was not a lover of two-strokes but agreed to put the Ilo engine under test in the Turin workshops where it was found not to meet the objectives and design Fiat considered necessary. What was of interest, though, was Bauhof's coachwork design, a simple two-door, four-seat convertible with the engine mounted directly above the rear wheels. Almost to the point of being stark, the utilitarian interior was simplicity itself. In essence, this prototype, which had been constructed at Weinsberg and dispatched to Giacosa in Turin, bore more than a passing resemblance to the eventual definitive model. The design from Heilbronn had made such an impact on Giacosa that he admits to taking Bauhof's ideas into account in later designs.

If any of the aforementioned ideas had any connotation at all with the design of motor-cycles or scooters, they were entirely abandoned when Giacosa drafted his proposals for project 110, a car smaller than had been outlined in the 100 project which managed to recapture the spirit of the immortal Topolino. The 110 project was quickly given the model designation "400," again recapturing an earlier era, but it had far more in common with the 600 than the original 500. It shared unitary

Prototype model of the Nuova 500. At this stage the project models were still referred to as the '400'. Evident is Bauhof's styling influence as well as similarity to the eventual 500. (Courtesy Fiat Auto (UK) & Fiat SPA Ltd)

construction, a rear-mounted engine and transmission system and similar styling, although it was considerably smaller and amazingly compact. If there was a problem in designing the Nuova then it was in ensuring it should not compete with but complement the 600. To do this, Giacosa followed Fiat's tradition of devising its small cars essentially as two-seaters, just as the Topolino had been, and before that even the 500 of 1918.

Serious development commenced soon after evaluation of Bauhof's prototype in 1953; engine choice was relatively simple as Giacosa had already

One of a series of mock-ups for the 500. Here the car has excessive rear drag and a sloping back, making it scarcely possible to seat two children at the rear. Note the exposed headlamps. (Courtesy Fiat Auto (UK) & Fiat SPA Ltd)

Below: This rather faint drawing for a further 500 prototype shows the car to have a longer roof line, making it possible to seat 4 adults. This design was abandoned in case the car competed directly with the 600. (Author's collection)

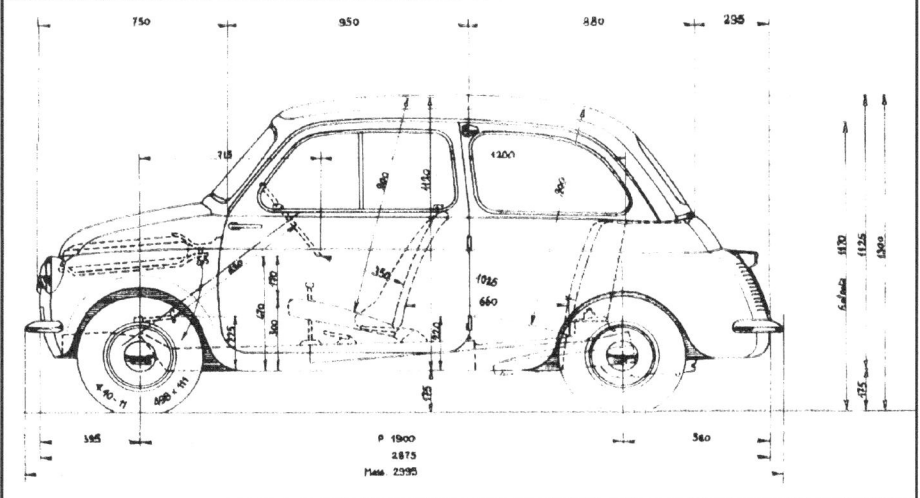

established that he wanted an air-cooled vertical twin with a displacement of approximately 500cc and output of 14bhp. The question of engine design had, of course, been thoroughly examined in the development of the Tipo 100 prototypes which led to the production of the 600. Water cooling was rejected on grounds of weight and an effort to retain as much simplicity as possible. To this end, a rear-positioned layout was chosen, not only to avoid complexity but to keep costings to a minimum. This drive-train arrangement was eminently suitable for a car of moderate performance, which, perhaps, is a slight exaggeration in Fiat 500 terms. There were certain disadvantages with air-cooling: fuel consumption was at the mercy of the larger and more powerful cooling fan than that normally required for a water-cooled engine, and noise was generally greater. These factors, however, were disregarded on the grounds of the car's improved overall weight and minimal performance.

During the earlier stages of development it was anticipated that many – or at least some – of the components from the 600 could be shared with the 500 Nuova; this did present certain difficulties for there was more than a risk that the overall weight of the car could be adversely affected. The decision was simple: to engineer the car to the running gear of the 600 gave rise to too many complications and it was therefore decided to let the Nuova's design run its own course.

Defining the details

Surprisingly, it was not until mid-October 1954 that the 110 project received its first official discussion by the Presidential Committee when it met to review future and prototype models. By the time this meeting occurred, Giacosa had already put much of the car's development into place. Giovanni Torazza, a young engineer with a brilliant perception for knowing what was required, who had been poached from Lancia where he had worked under the direction of Gianni Lancia since leaving university, was given the task of designing the engine. The gearbox, meanwhile, was entrusted to another engineer, Mosso, whose job it was to devise a completely new unit that could be installed transversely, along with the engine, over the rear axle. Just as he had done with the 100 project, Dante

Front profile of the 4-seat prototype. It was not until a replacement for the Nuova 500 was eventually sought that Fiat designers returned to these drawings for inspiration. (Author's collection)

COLOUR GALLERY

A nicely restored 1938 rhd Topolino. (Courtesy Malcolm C. Elder)

This picture of a Topolino 500B Belvedere Station Wagon dates from a c1948 press release.

COLOUR GALLERY

The front cover of Fiat's 1949 sales brochure for the then new Topolino 500C, a model which Fiat claimed to be "a new stage in the progress of the 'big car' in miniature." (Author's collection)

This superb colour cutaway of the 500C Topolino is taken from Fiat's 1949 sales brochure. Note how the four cylinder engine is ahead of the front axle line. (Author's collection)

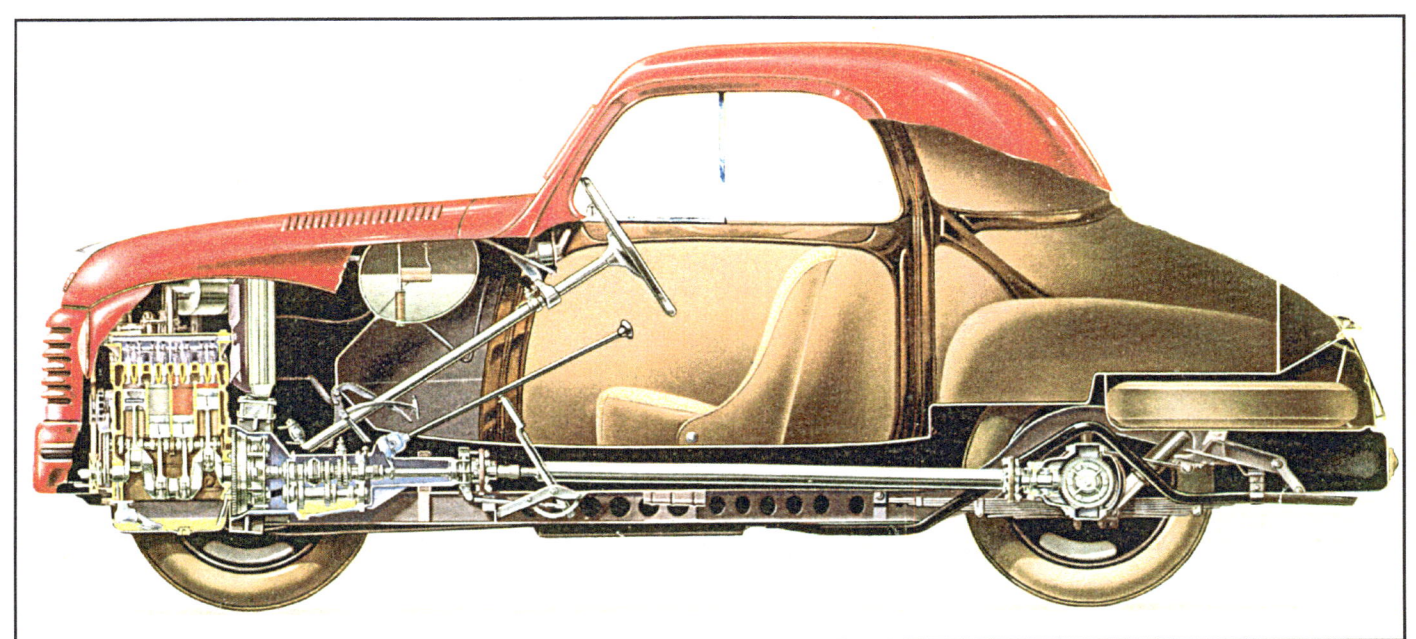

COLOUR GALLERY

The front cover of a typical 1950s sales brochure for the Fiat 600D. Sliding windows were a relic of the Topolino and a sunroof was not available on early models. (Author's collection)

Page from a sales brochure of 1960/61 illustrates features of the Fiat 600 – including a particularly garish colour scheme of pink and red!

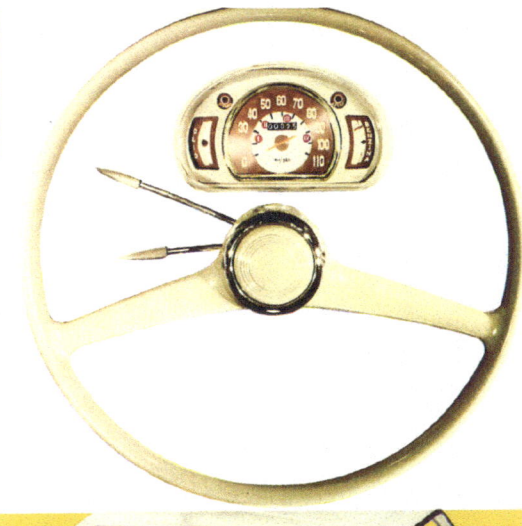

COLOUR GALLERY

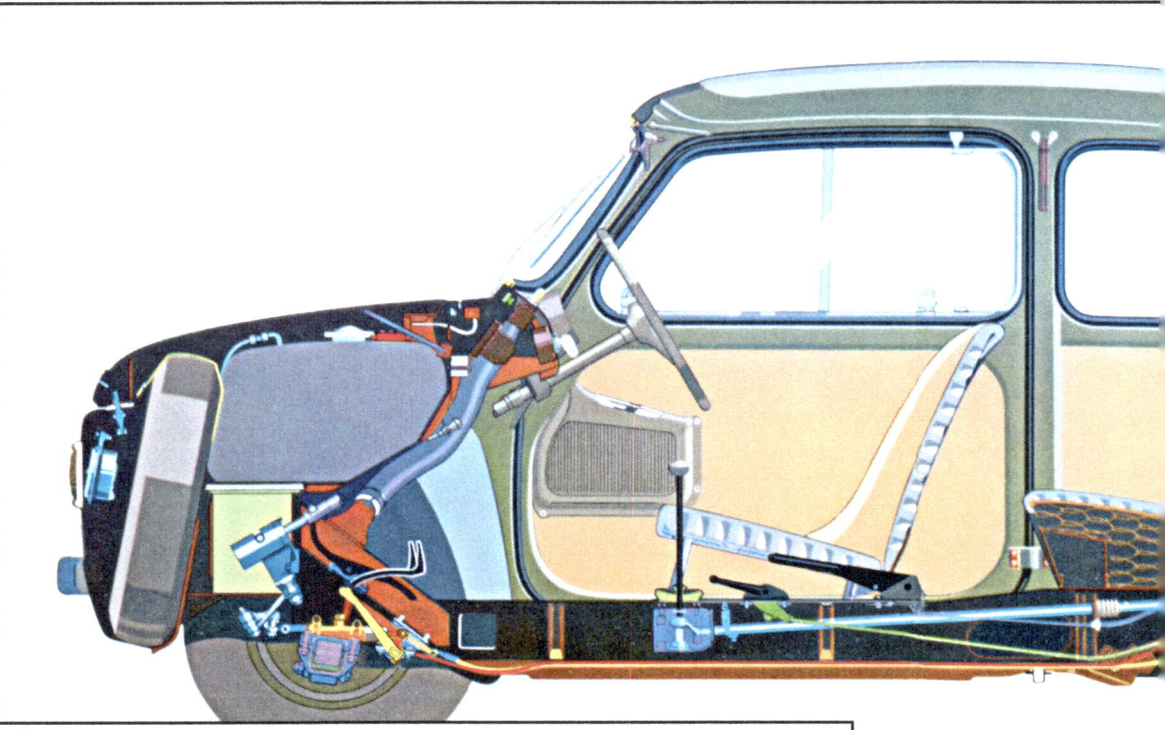

speed about 60 m.p.h. (95 km)
load 770 lbs (350 kg)

While the **600** with its four seats has given a great impulse to the popularity of the very small car, the **600 Multipla** (all service) increases this success, with its two versions: 6 seater and 4/5 seater. Both these versions offer facilities for dual use; also transport of goods when desired. Further, in the 4/5 seater version the back rests of both seats can be folded down, thus providing a uniform and cushioned platform.
The **600 Multipla** increases the usefulness of the **600** for family motoring and business purposes.

COLOUR GALLERY

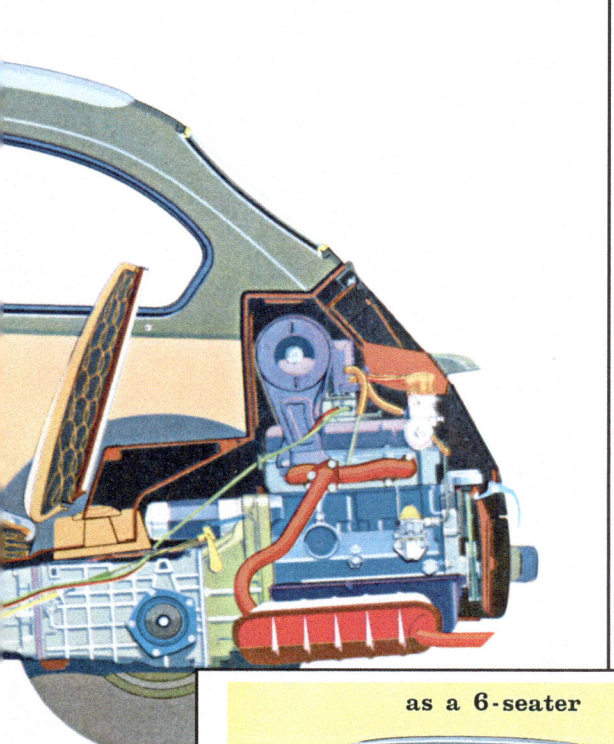

Left: Brochure cutaway drawing graphically illustrating the construction of the 600. (Author's collection)

Far left: This contemporary sales brochure page shows just what an effective people carrier the ingenious Fiat Multipla was. (Author's collection)

Below: This page from a contemporary sales brochure illustrated the Fiat Multipla's truly amazing versatility. (Author's collection)

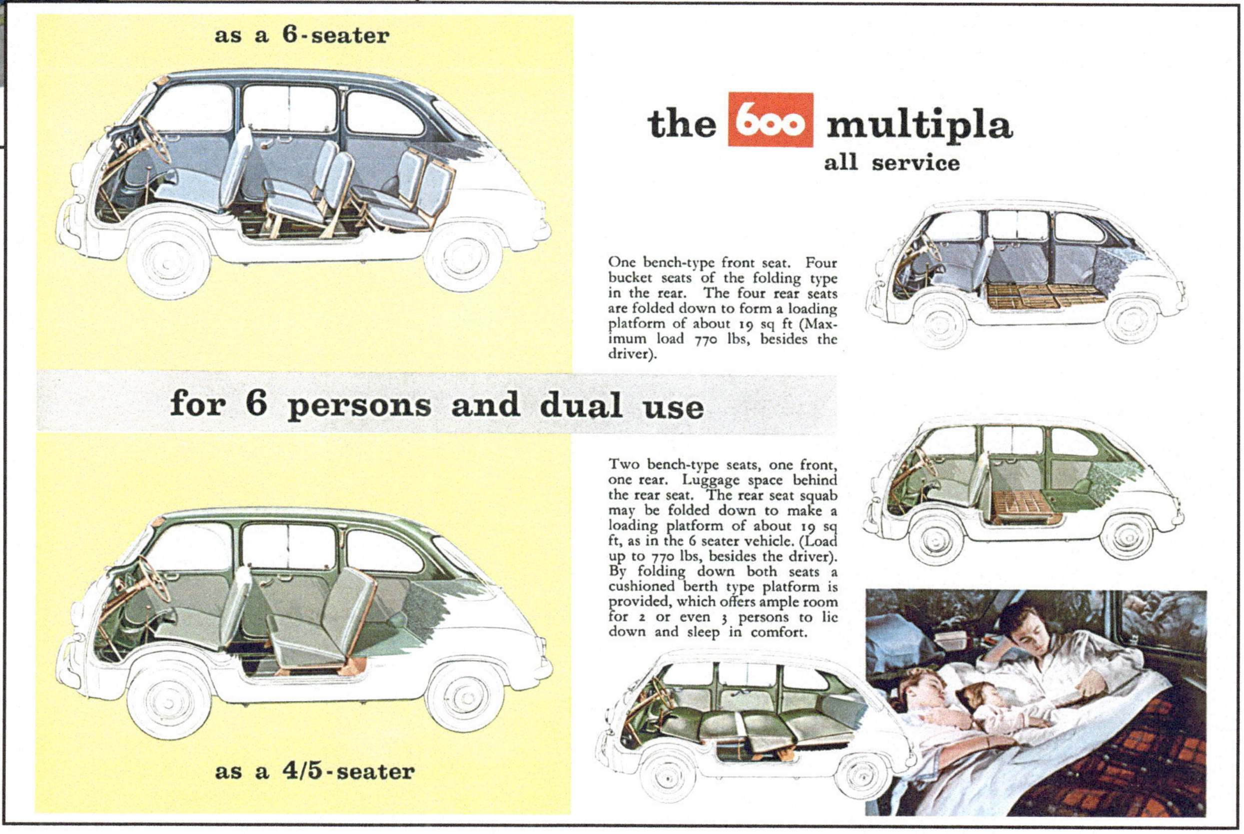

COLOUR GALLERY

an engineering success, economic progress

FIAT
the new
500

With the **new 500** Fiat has made further progress in the field of the small, ultra-utilitarian, economical car: technical progress in the design and construction will provide an economic and social advancement of this car to a greater number of people than ever before.

The **new 500** is a two-seater, but with ample room in the rear. The features and performance of the new car are very modern. This model brings still greater success to a model famous among Fiat cars: the "**500**," which in 1936 started the development of the small utility-car.

From the "**500**" to the "**new 500**."

speed about 55 miles (over 85 km) per hour

This brochure illustration shows two 500 Nuovas, the leading car with sunroof open and the second car with sunroof closed. The original Nuova 500 was far too slow and economies too drastic, the result of which was that the model was total disaster. (Author's collection)

s peculiar to the new 500 expo

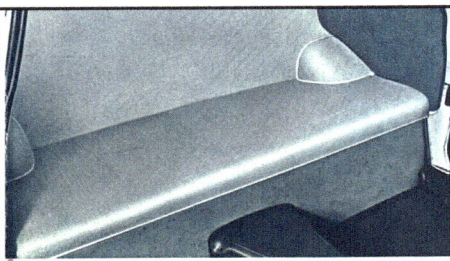

Rear bench seat with sponge rubber cushion.

Wind-up windows and draught deflectors with stop.

Levers on steering wheel controlling headlamps and self-cancelling direction indicators.

Headlamps with rims, wheel emb mium trimmings

the body
Very roomy car. Adjustable tilting front seats. Sunshine roof.

the new 500 standard version

70

COLOUR GALLERY

Above: Cutaway taken from an early sales brochure illustrates the cleverness of the Fiat Nuovo 500's mechanical packaging, which allows maximum people space.

Double-page spread from an early Nuovo 500 sales brochure illustrates the new car's export market features and the 500's all-round versatility.

COLOUR GALLERY

Above: "Your dream ... the new Coupé." NSU-Fiat's Weinsberg 500 Coupé made an enchanting variation on a theme. Trim level was superior to the Fiat 500 and note the sliding fabric sunroof. (Courtesy National Motor Museum)

The 500 lives on; the 1990's Cinquecento's purpose the same as the Nuova 500 and the Topolino before that. (Courtesy Fiat (UK) & Fiat SPA Ltd)

Drawings and proposals for a new 500 led to some interesting designs, including this pretty version which is similar to the eventual Autobianchi and NSU-Fiat derivatives. (Courtesy Fiat Auto (UK) & Fiat SPA Ltd)

Giacosa assumed direct control of the bodywork design, working closely with a chosen colleague, Alberti. A thorough and practical engineer, Alberti displayed many of the same attributes and qualities as Giacosa when perfecting the final shape of the 600.

By the end of August 1954, two principle designs were ready, complete with full-scale plaster mock-ups. The first example bore a somewhat uncanny resemblance to the 600, although naturally much smaller and sporting a stubby, but rounded, frontal area. Against the definitive model, the rear styling appeared rather awkward, having excessive drag and looking less than tidy. This was due, in part, to its long sloping roof line, designed to prevent the car from being a four-seater, which would have only just accommodated two tiny children in the back. This design was, therefore, very much different from the second mock-up which had been built as a full four-seater with a longer roof line and less raked rear styling. Coded as project 110-540, this version was abandoned as it clearly competed with the 600 and would have compromised sales of both models. It is interesting to note, however, that this design was re-appraised years later when consideration was given to the Nuova's eventual replacement in the form of the 126.

At the meeting in October 1954, specific parameters were established for the specifications of the Nuova: weight had to be kept below 814lb (370kg), fuel consumption was to be no more than a little over 60mpg (4.5 litres per 100km) and a top speed of 53 mph (85kph) should be possible. At that stage, side-valve engines had not been entirely ruled out but would have meant an engine of 500cc – in the case of opting for an overhead valve engine the 14bhp maximum could be achieved from 480cc. In retrospect it would have been most unlikely that a side-valve engine would have been chosen, especially as the Topolino had already received an overhead valve engine as early as 1948 in its 500B form. A timescale was also devised which gave little leeway for protracted experiments: the first prototype was required by June 1955 with production scheduled to commence a year later. As if all this were not sufficient, the Presidential Committee, which consisted of, amongst others, Valletta, Montebone, Bono, Fiorelli and, of course, Giacosa, determined that a four-seater version should be prepared for the German market under the direction of NSU-Fiat, and that an Autobianchi variant incorporating greater luxury also be produced.

Fiat was facing the challenge of a new decade and the Sixties era when the Nuova was officially included into an already full and chaotic schedule. Not only was the company actively searching for the right answers in respect of their smaller and more economical cars, it was also preparing front-line models which were to extend across its entire catalogue. Apart from continued research on larger and more powerful vehicles, work was well advanced on the 600 programme with the Geneva launch only a few months away. By the same token, the Multipla and its commercial variants were proving something of a headache with their announcement looming ominously nearer. The design team was therefore stretched to the limit but, nevertheless, the 500 Nuova was treated with exactly the same level of enthusiasm and attention to detail as ever. Time had run out for the faithful Topolino which, by now, had begun to show its age and

Today, motor car design is computer-aided. Before this technology a proposed car would be built to scale in wood. (Courtesy Fiat Auto (UK) & Fiat SPA Ltd)

This rear profile of a wooden scale model illustrates the exacting standards employed in the design department. (Courtesy Fiat Auto (UK) & Fiat SPA Ltd)

appeared distinctly vintage with its origins dragging back two decades to the Thirties.

Although the deadlines imposed upon the 110 project had, perhaps, seemed almost impossible to achieve, the situation was not as desperate as first feared. Much of the groundwork, which always resulted in months of detailed research and development, had been completed during the earlier stages of the 600 programme and provided a clear direction in which to proceed. By the end of 1955, five engines had been built for exhaustive testing: experiments had been conducted using the 600's gearbox whilst a detailed examination of Volkswagen's Beetle engine had helped achieve a desired cylinder barrel design. The first engine prototype was ready by May 1953, an air-cooled vertical twin of 479cc; then came a series of modified units which consisted of a horizontally-opposed twin and two further vertical twins, one with overhead valves, the other with side valves. The fifth version was deemed the definitive model and followed in principle much the same concept as the original engine. The specification included a displacement of 479cc and vertical cylinders with overhead valves. In essence, the engine was practically identical to its forerunner apart from slight modifications to facilitate easier tooling and build.

Throughout its development period, the Nuova was plagued by problems resulting from vibration of the engine and transmission system. Several modifications and remedies were sought, even to the extent of

Ideal for a couple and a child, but could the Nuova 500 really accommodate all that luggage? (Courtesy National Motor Museum)

The same couple and child: the limited space is clearly illustrated, but it looks as though they managed to squeeze in the luggage! (Courtesy National Motor Museum)

designing a flexible or "elastic" system of suspending the engine within the bodyshell. While this proved relatively satisfactory, further complications were highlighted which signalled the need to return to the drawing board for a close look at the basic design of the engine. The problems had first shown themselves in the initial prototype which had been completed only a couple of weeks following the October 1954 Presidential Committee meeting. The excessive vibration was so marked that a decision was taken to abandon any further idea of a transverse engine and to return to a more conventional in-line arrangement.

These early problems caused some dissension between Giacosa and Oscar Montebone, head of Fiat's research and development department. This was not the first occasion the two had not seen eye to eye – the rift extended back to 1952 when Montebone was side-stepped, unfairly in his opinion, in a move to rationalise the technical departments. Montebone was made assistant director of automobile production while Giacosa was awarded the directorship of the automobile department. In the event of the current difficulties it was Giacosa who gave way to Montebone's claims of faulty initial design, not because he accepted the claim – on the contrary, he considered Montebone's findings hasty and ill-conceived – but in the interests of progress and in order get the project underway.

However, difficulties with the 500 Nuova development refused to go away. Gaudenzio Bono, General Manager of Fiat since 1946, had always supported Giacosa: he had backed him entirely during the gestation period of the 600 but now it seemed that Giacosa's stand for an air-cooled vertical twin engine worried him. Perhaps Bono considered that for such a minimal car the engine did not have to be engineered to such exacting standards and that a flat-twin, or even a single cylinder motor, would have been more suitable. The tension was not eased by complications with the carburation, which could have been resolved quite simply, and by the question of excessive noise, which was less easy to remedy. Detailed tests showed that an effective solution to engine noise was twofold: firstly, the camshaft drive gears would have to be redesigned using nylon-reinforced plastic; secondly, to eliminate the noise problem completely it would be necessary to increase the weight over the front wheels by some 88lb (40kg) – a matter which was rejected without further ado. Giacosa was therefore faced with the unhappy task of requesting Bono to agree a delay in the development programme.

The problems between Giacosa and Bono were not restricted purely to the Nuova 500 project; their relationship affected the viability of other models under consideration throughout the Fiat catalogue. It was most likely for this reason that Vittorrio Valletta packed the two off to the USA to join a party of Fiat senior management in a further study of America's motor industry.

While he was away, Giacosa left Oscar Montebone in day-to-day charge of the Nuova. On his return, he found progress not exactly to his liking: development of the flat-twin engine had been pursued to the point where it was virtually ready for approval, having undergone stringent testing. Montebone had fully expected the engine would receive its final approval at the end of October 1955, only days after the American party returned.

At the October meeting, discussions were held on the general progress of all models in the planning stage and, as expected, the question of the proposed 400 arose. Unexpectedly, however, the go-ahead for the flat-twin was not granted but instead Bono instructed that its development be carried on until perfected. A further meeting was arranged for the early part of January 1956 when it was anticipated the committee would make final decisions and approve production dates.

As the January meeting opened, it was, ironically, Bono who scored an own-goal. After detailed reports on the Nuova's progress, amongst other models, Bono still worried whether the proposed car might result in damaging some of the potential sales of the larger 600. He suggested looking at a proposal for an uprated version, to be known as the 600A, which would be equipped with a larger and more powerful engine, preferably an air-cooled flat-four. Giacosa, obviously irritated at the General Manger's continual meddling in engine design and specification, not to mention his obsession with horizontally-opposed engines, seized his chance. He reminded Bono that such studies had already been carried out in the greatest of detail and rejected on cost grounds. No more was said by Bono upon the subject which was rapidly closed. Giacosa had won the day, regained his credibility, and was allowed to continue development of the project in his own experienced manner.

Any further idea of a flat-twin or flat-four engine was dropped and final tests were started on the air-cooled vertical twin that was to power the definitive model. The final experimental example of the engine proved to be a refined version of the original design and, therefore, a tribute to its original concept. In producing the definitive engine all the development problems were taken into account and ironed out: noise levels were reduced to the point of acceptability and the inbalance that dogged earlier development was practically cured, although some vibration was still evident.

The protracted controversy over the design of the engine and transmission did not prevent continued progress on the overall styling of the Nuova which had developed from the original 1954 drawings and scale model. Incorporated with the 400 project was a design for an Autobianchi version which, at the time, was considered too up-market to be sold under the Fiat banner. In order to avoid any loss of sales from Fiat to Autobianchi it was intended that a monetary premium be levied on the latter, so putting the car more within the Fiat 600 price range. Accepting that sales would therefore be limited, it was planned that even-

An early 500 Nuova in mountainous surroundings. A car of the first series, it is identifiable by an absence of any trim. (Courtesy Fiat Auto (UK) & Fiat SPA Ltd)

tual production should not exceed 50 cars a day – as opposed to the proposal to build 500 Nuovas a day. The Autobianchi, coded as project 110B, will be described in greater detail in a later chapter.

The general construction of the 500 Nuova followed, quite naturally, that of the 600 although few, if any, components were interchangeable. Unitary construction with integral floor-pan complete with its rigid central spine was again apparent, but in miniature. If the 600 had caused so much controversy with its midget-like proportions, the Nuova was diminutive to the extreme. The difference in size could be most appreciated when the two body shells were placed side by side when the 600 overshadowed the 500 to the point of making it appear quite dwarfish. Whilst originally the 600 had been claimed as the natural successor to the Topolino, it really was the Nuova which became its logical descendant as its size and market position clearly defined it as a minimal two-seater.

The endeavour for the ultimate economy car was further evident from Giacosa's work on the body pressings and his approach to the car's construction. Economies in build cost had certainly led to the 600's success, but for the Nuova these economies were pushed a stage further to reduce the overall weight and cost to an absolute minimum. An area in which Giacosa had been extremely anxious to make reductions was the cost of door pressings, traditionally expensive due in part to the amount of wasted material involved. By effectively reorganising the method of cutting out sheet steel, waste material which had previously been sent for scrap was eliminated to the extent that distinct savings were made.

Less obvious economies were often considered and then abandoned in the interest of efficiency. One such example

The definitive version of the Nuova 500. This was preceded by months of feverish work getting the design right and ironing out difficulties. (Courtesy Fiat Auto (UK) & Fiat SPA Ltd)

Manufacture of the 500 in progress. These early cars, identified by the louvres under the headlamps, are ready to be fitted with their running gear. (Courtesy Fiat Auto (UK) & Fiat SPA Ltd)

was the front luggage compartment: initially this had been designed with a fixed hood instead of an opening type similar to that found on the 600 model. The spare wheel was made to stow behind the dashboard and the fuel tank incorporated within the scuttle above the driver and passenger's feet as similarly found on the Topolino. Such economies were later thought to be too extreme and final prototype models had a self-contained front compartment with opening lid which contained the spare wheel in the nose, fuel tank and battery.

The green light

The meeting of the Presidential Committee in January 1956 provisionally set the Nuova 500's production date for Spring 1957, allowing a little over a year in which to prepare the definitive design. Along with the 2-cylinder engine which had caused so much aggravation, a relatively simple 4-speed gearbox provided the transmission in similar fashion to that of the 600. Whereas, however, the 600 benefited from a synchromesh gearbox, the Nuova received a "crash" box which bore evidence of further economy. There was some relief for the design team – which had been working at a crazy pace, trying to perfect the Nuova – when approval was at last given, signalling the start of tooling-up operations.

Even in the final stages of the car's design feverish work was necessary to get the production lines ready. Along with the elation of seeing a car through from initial drawings to the plaster mock-up, and on eventually to the road-going prototype, there were still weeks if not months of frustration and, sadly, tragedy. Working closely with Giacosa and his team, but under the direction of Carlo Salamano, Luigi Vestidello, Fiat's second-in-command test driver, was killed at the wheel of a Nuova 500 prototype. The accident happened whilst on a test run when a head-on collision caused the total destruction of the car. Vestidello's death was a serious setback to the Nuova's final development: apart from the loss of a highly respected test driver and an integral member of the design team, there was naturally some concern as to whether the car had been in any way to blame or whether the tragedy could have been prevented. Vestidello had been involved at all stages of the prototype's testing and his enthusiasm and careful dedication to the Nuova's development was sadly missed.

As Fiat's marketing department prepared to launch the car, the project number 110 and model designation 400 were considered meaningless. Fiat had always reserved the 500 notation for its popular minimal cars and thus it seemed appropriate that it should continue. Seen as the new Topolino, the car quite obviously sought to be associated with the company's earlier triumph and was therefore christened the 500 Nuova.

During the tooling-up period, prototype 500s were exhaustively tested throughout the region surrounding Turin. For something like a year, sightings of the cars were almost commonplace and even in Turin itself they were constant visitors to the city's streets. Due to its prominence, albeit in test guise, there was some speculation that it might make its first public appearance at the 1957 Geneva show and, by the same token, disappointment at its absence. It is interesting to note that *The Motor* suggested the car might not be ready until the Turin Show in November, further indication that the car was not as far advanced as had been presumed. Of further interest still was the report that some prototypes were still fitted with horizontally-opposed engines.

The aftermath of Suez was much in evidence at the 1957 Geneva Show which saw more than a sprinkling of economy cars on display. Amongst some of the strangest miniatures was the Meadows Frisky with styling by Michelotti and built especially for the show by Vignale of Turin. This micro-car had gullwing doors which gave access to a cramped interior with seating for two adults. At a squeeze, two children could be accommodated on a rear seat that straddled a tiny two-stroke engine mounted above the rear wheels. Goliath displayed their latest model with its flat-four engine whilst the Isetta 300 appeared with a BMW badge. The Heinkel bubble car was seen in two versions: a 175cc three-wheeler and its stablemate, the 204cc four-wheeler with its rear wheels set very close together.

Great launch but cool reaction

Having missed the opportunity of Geneva at which to introduce the 500 Nuova, Fiat were rightly keen to launch it as quickly as possible. The dilemma was whether to wait until Turin in November or go for a Summer

launch, therefore breaking with tradition of using the hype of an international event to get the car off to a good start. In the event, Fiat chose a Summer launch. Tooling-up, although nearing completion was, by the Spring, not quite ready. Mirafiori was in the throes of being extended to enable a possible production of 600 cars a day in addition to those assembled at Lingotto. Fiat's marketing department swung into action to heighten the excitement of the announcement of the new car: "Great Little Auto" was the catchphrase that heralded the arrival of the 500. Television viewers were able to see live reports direct from the assembly lines at Lingotto and even Giacosa was invited to be interviewed alongside his creation.

Motoring journalists descended upon Turin at the end of June 1957 to try the 500 Nuova for themselves. Perhaps they were inspired by the car's diminutive size, substantially smaller than the 600; perhaps it was its performance and road-holding, considered to be more stable than the 600, even if its performance was only just adequate for Italy's traffic conditions. 55mph (88kph) was the claim by Fiat although on test runs only 50mph (80kph) was possible. If it lacked outright performance then

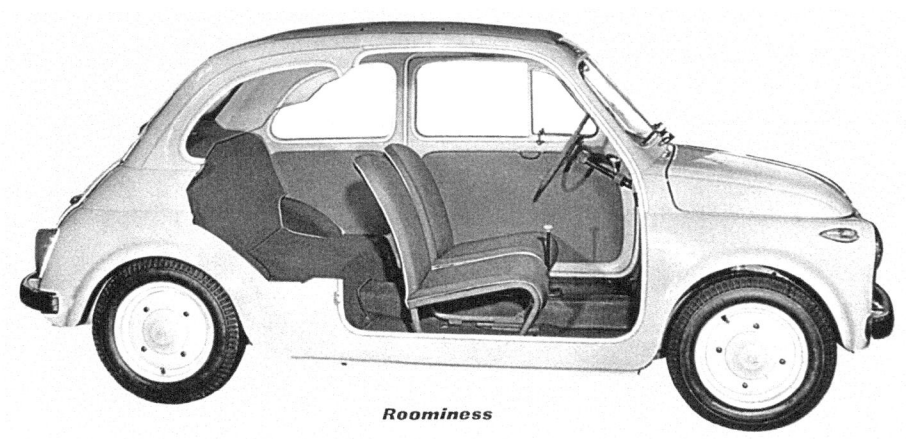

This cutaway illustration clearly shows the 500's spartan interior. The rear platform, intended for luggage, could be an uncomfortable seat for children. All windows were fixed except for the front quarterlights, ventilation was provided by air vents below the headlamps and, of course, the roof opened. (Author's collection)

economy was certainly its forte, with over 60mpg (almost 5 ltr/100km) well within reach. As for comfort, there was sufficient room for two adults – so recreating the Topolino idiom. If there was a drawback it was the lack of headroom – however, in Italy the norm was to drive with the hood open, thereby providing tall drivers with enough room!

In true Latin style the 500 Nuova took to the streets of Italy with all the pomp and occasion that could be mustered. Hundreds of cars, or so it seemed, left the factory assembly lines, each with an attractive Signorina standing through the open roof. The cavalcade went on to tour the streets of Turin before departing for the grandeur of Rome. The Nuova had many admirers keen to be seen with the miniature marvel, amongst which were Jane Mansfield, Juan Manual Fangio and Giovanni Montini, the future Pope Paul V1.

After its launch in Italy, the Nuova made its debut in Britain at the end of July with a consignment of fifty cars shipped over from Turin. Fiat arranged a press day at Brands Hatch with four cars continually circumnavigating the racing circuit to the delight of invited guests.

In spite of the Nuova initially being well received by the media, all, however, was not well. The predictions for a rush of sales just did not happen: it was something of a damp squid. Criticism was levelled at the car's lethargic performance and the hardly significant 479cc and 13bhp; moreover, it failed to be any threat to the out-and-out microcar market. There was worse news, too: the engine and transmission vibration had refused to go away. On its launch, Fiat dealers throughout Italy were instructed to line up their cars on garage forecourts, ready for instant trial and with engines running. Reports suggest it was a common sight to see cars vibrating so badly that, in extreme cases, their rear wheels were bouncing off the ground!

The blame for the early failure of the 500 was quickly laid upon Giacosa and his design team. In turn it was pushed back just as speedily to the Presidential Committee who had been insistent that the Nuova should not be allowed to compromise the 600 in any way. Economies had been taken too far

The Nuova 500 put hundreds of thousands of Italian families on the road. It was an ideal first car. Early 500s, in common with the Topolino, did not have a rear seat; children made do with a cushion on the luggage platform. (Courtesy National Motor Museum)

The Nuova 500 in delightfully period pose. Early cars, with their fixed windows and absence of trim, were dreadfully underpowered. This contemporary advertisement clearly illustrates that Fiat were hoping to make the car attractive to women and families wanting a second car. (Courtesy National Motor Museum)

at a time when the motor industry was recovering from the Suez crisis and, before it, the years of austerity.

In truth, the Nuova was dreadfully underpowered and too utilitarian by far. This was emphasized by it not having opening windows apart from the front quarterlights; even the penny-pinching sliding windows had been sacrificed in the quest for cheapness. There was no question, however, that the underlying principle of the Nuova was anything but brilliant: the car should have been met with the accolade it deserved. For its launch price of 465,000 Lire – equivalent to approximately £300 in Italy – the Italian market demanded more than an out-and-out micro-car.

All, however, was not lost. The Turin show, which was seen by Fiat as the most important event of 1957, was still some three months away which allowed barely enough time for the Nuova to be given a second chance and a re-birth.

Scuttling back behind closed doors, Fiat's design teams, now with the full backing of the Presidential Committee, worked feverishly on a modified Nuova in time for November and Turin.

VI

SMALL IS BEAUTIFUL

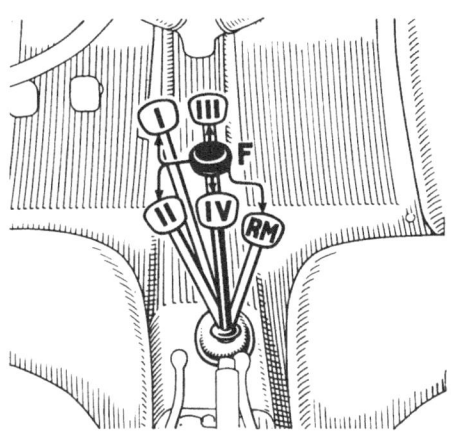

Although a new Topolino in character, the 500 Nuova shared only three common features with that of its ancestor: a transverse leaf spring for the front independent suspension; a full length folding sunroof and identical door hinges. In its appeal, of course, the 500 Nuova shared a lot more, providing economical and carefree motoring for the masses (it could carry two adults and luggage and, at a push, two small children also) who could not have previously afforded a motor car.

A real baby car

The 500 Nuova was considerably smaller than the Topolino and, for that matter, the 600. Compared to the original 500 of 1936, the Nuova was a good 12 inches (305mm) shorter and 2 inches (50mm) narrower. As for the engine and transmission, a 479cc upright twin replaced the 569cc four-cylinder motor, air-cooling superseded water and, following in the wake of the 600, the engine was mounted in the tail. For the first time in Fiat history, the 500 Nuova pioneered an air-cooled engine. Whereas the Topolino had a traditional chassis, the Nuova 500 was of unitary construction, sharing practically all the same principles of the larger 600.If simplicity was the goal of the 1936 500A, so it was with the 500 Nuova: *The Motor* found it to be a "modern version of an old favourite" and *The Autocar* summed it up quite simply as "a new Topolino."

Although the new 500 was substantially smaller than the 600 there was no mistaking the family resemblance. At some 9 inches (230mm) shorter in length, 2 inches (50mm) less in width and 3 inches (75mm) lower in height than its bigger sister, the 500 Nuova was a miracle of design and engineering. The difference in size was most noticeable in the length of the wheelbase – 6.56ft (2m) on both the 600 and Topolino but only 6.03ft (1.840m) for the 500. The doors of the 500 Nuova, which, on first inspection, appeared overly large, were a further indication of the car's overall diminutive proportions. Fiat, somewhat surprisingly, reverted to the use of rear-hinged doors for the 500 even though the safety lobby by this time had all but put a end to the practice of using suicide doors. As it was primarily a two-seater, there was less inconvenience with front-opening doors than if the car had been a full four-seater.

Right from its introduction the 500 Nuova appeared with a folding head in true Trasformabile fashion. The roof fully extended to incorporate the rear window which, instead of glass, was made of transparent plastic. Looking as if it had been turned out of a jelly mould, the Nuova was more rounded and curvaceous in design than its 600 stablemate. Where the 600 had distinct front wings, the front compartment lid of the 500 extended fully across the entire frontal area, so smoothing out the line of the car. As a result, the combined front indicators and sidelights, which, on the 600, had been mounted on top of the wings, were repositioned on the 500 to be incorporated on the leading edge of the front side-panels above the wheelarch flanges and adjacent to the headlamps. The rear of the car was neater in detail than that of the 600,

Designed for the young, the new generation 500 gave the promise of effortless motoring and independent holidays. (Courtesy National Motor Museum)

there was no rear seat as such, leg room for driver and passenger was especially generous and in the case of getting luggage or children in or out of the back, the seats tilted forward for easy access. The only real complaint was the position of the brake pedal on the left hand side of the steering column, which required some getting used to.

The controls, too, followed on from the principle of the 600. The unitary construction provided a rigid backbone onto which the gearlever, handbrake, starter and choke levers were all positioned, the spine running the length of the car's interior and concealing the linkages. The gearchange, for all its remoteness of control and lack of synchromesh was, once having come to terms with it, remarkably light and efficient. Even for 1957 a crash gearbox was controversial: gearchanging needed patience with double de-clutching to avoid noisy clonks and grating of gear teeth.

As for instrumentation, the 500 Nuova was, by design, basic in the extreme. A tiny speedometer mounted into a single pod-shaped nacelle on an almost otherwise bare fascia peered at the driver through the two-spoke steering wheel. Incorporated within the speedometer were warning lights for parking lights, dynamo charge, oil pressure and low fuel. The lack of a fuel gauge was considered acceptable in view of the car's economy, a red warning lamp indicating when approximately a gallon of fuel remained in the 4.6 gallon (21.5 litre) tank. This arrangement was better than that of the Citroën 2CV which had a dip-stick in the tank.

purely due to its smaller dimensions. Naturally, the engine compartment differed in layout as air-cooling demanded less space than a water-cooled system. The petite features were further enhanced by the smaller engine compartment cover which bore less ventilation louvres.

The interior of the 500 followed in similar vein to that of its bigger sister although the Nuova was generally more spartan. Compared to most conventional cars the seats appeared narrow, cramped and uninviting.However, appearances were deceptive: once in the car ample comfort was afforded, especially to those more used to the seating arrangement of the Topolino. Because

With the **new 500** Fiat has made further progress in the field of the small, ultra-utilitarian, economical car: technical progress in the design and construction will provide an economic and social advancement of this car to a greater number of people than ever before.

The **new 500** is available in 2 versions: the **standard version** and the **export version.** This latter has, besides two bucket seats in front, a full-width bench seat at the back special accessories and trimmings.

Symbolic advertisement for the 500 Nuova. The car shown at the top is an export or Normale model and is equipped with hub caps and winding windows. There is little doubting the model is aimed towards the young mother. Shown at bottom left is the economy version stripped of trim and with fixed side windows. (Author's collection)

In the centre of the fascia switches controlled windscreen wipers, direction indicators and parking lights while, below the dashboard, a hand throttle assisted starting and provided relief for the driver's right foot on long journeys. Each side of the car, under the fascia, simple controls provided interior ventilation from louvres positioned beneath the integral headlamps.

This early publicity photograph illustrates the plain interior and spartan dashboard. (Courtesy Fiat Auto (UK) & Fiat SPA Ltd)

In terms of living with the Nuova 500 the economies in build were clearly evident: only the front quarter-lights opened, all the other windows were fixed which, apart from being somewhat inconvenient, was also claustrophobic. Body trim was virtually non-existent and, apart from the bumpers, there was very little bright-work – even the hub caps were dispensed with!

On the road
Performance from the minuscule 479cc twin was negligible; the 13bhp engine

The 500 production line. The connecting linkages can be seen hanging from the centre tunnel. On the left of the picture is a 600 assembly line. (Courtesy Fiat Auto (UK) & Fiat SPA Ltd)

Below: There was only one way to drive the 500 – with accelerator at perpetual full throttle! (Courtesy Fiat Auto (UK) & Fiat SPA Ltd)

(4 ltr/100km) for the Heinkel and 60mpg (4.75 ltr/100km) for the more powerful Isetta.

These figures, whilst somewhat academic, do serve to illustrate the competition the 500 faced. By comparison, however, the Fiat was in a totally different league in build and design, being a truly conventional car built on large car principles. It therefore enjoyed a degree of comfort and durability over some of its rivals which clearly had evolved from motorcycle aspirations and origins.

struggled and puffed to propel the 500 at anything over 50mph (80kph) although Fiat claimed a top speed approaching 55mph (88kph). This was in total contrast to the Goggomobil, of which over 250,000 were built, with its puny 293cc rear-mounted engine which could attain 60mph (96kph) at a push and still return over 60mpg (4.75 ltr/100km). Even the considerably larger Citroën 2CV with its 425cc air-cooled flat-twin could reach somewhere near 50mph (80kph) and still return an unbelievable fuel consumption of well in excess of 50mpg (5.5ltr/km). In comparison, the slightly larger BMW 600 with its 585cc air-cooled flat-twin managed almost 62mph (99.1kph) and still gave 55mpg (5 ltr/100km) at a steady 50mph (80kph). Bubble cars such as the BMW Isetta with its 298cc engine and the 174cc Heinkel, on the other hand, both had top speeds of 50mph (80kph) with fuel consumptions of well over 70mpg

For the Turin Show Fiat introduced an uprated and less spartan 500, the Normale. Here, the external differences can be seen: winding windows, hub caps and body side mouldings. The sunroof, instead of continuing as far as the rear window, opens only as far as the door pillar. (Courtesy Fiat Auto (UK) & Fiat SPA Ltd)

Below: From Autumn 1957 uprated 500s received a new engine, still of 479cc but with 15bhp instead of 13bhp. (Courtesy Fiat Auto (UK) & Fiat SPA Ltd)

The Motor in its first full road test described the 500 as scarcely being lively. The only way to drive the car, it noted, was virtually at perpetual full throttle. Under most conditions the 500 was found to understeer; push the Fiat to its limits though and oversteer would occur resulting in a slide of the rear wheels. Although quite gutless in output, the tiny engine had the capacity to be thrashed almost to the extreme; it was possible to wind the miniature twin up to almost 4000rpm and keep it there over vast distances which in some way made up for its lack of acceleration.

Where others found little to commend the 500 Nuova, Bill Boddy, writing in Motor Sport, appreciated the car's finer points such as excellent road holding and brakes. Michael Sedgwick, too, found the 500 a car apart: he equated its performance with that of a sporting 1.5-litre of the 1920s, complete with the delights of heavy brakes, high noise level, uncomfortable pedals and the need to double de-clutch for every change up or down.

The 600's influence is clearly evident in the 500's suspension and unitary construction. The front suspension followed the design of the larger car with its lower transverse leaf spring and upper wishbones. A telescopic damper above each wishbone controlled the suspension while the rubber mounted leaf spring allowed effective road holding without the need for an anti-roll bar. Five spring leaves made up the transverse spring assembly which was held together with polyethylene anti-friction pads and two rubber-cushioned clamps.

The rear suspension formed a cradle incorporating double-acting hydraulic shock absorbers within coil springs. A swinging-unit was formed by joining the longitudinal suspension arms with the body structure and a steel pressing on the wheel assembly thereby supported the complete engine, gearbox and transmission system on three rubber mountings. This arrangement of suspension eliminated any need for a universal joint on the drive shaft at its wheel end, a de Dion type joint being used at the inboard position.

Worm and sector type steering gear was utilised for the 500 Nuova; for such a small car a more simple method might have been considered, however, to ensure absolute stability and road-holding no expense was spared. With the steering gear housing attached to the scuttle, a symmetrical three-track rod system with an idler arm formed the steering linkage.

Similar sized tyres to those on the 600 – 5.20 x 12 (125 x 12) – were used for the 500 with the result that due to the

The overall diminutive dimensions of the 500 can be gauged by the size of the doors in relation to the rest of the car. (Courtesy Fiat Auto (UK) & Fiat SPA Ltd)

Below: Further modifications between the Economica and the Normale were larger headlamp trims and an upholstered rear seat. (Courtesy Fiat Auto (UK) & Fiat SPA Ltd)

500's smaller dimensions it appeared extremely well-shod. For true microcars, 10 inch tyres were often used, as demonstrated by BMW's four-seat 600. As for braking, the hydraulic system was conventional enough: the footbrake acted on all four wheels while the mechanical parking brake acted on the rear wheels only. This is in contrast to the transmission brake used on the Topolino which was retained on early 600s. For simplicity, the master cylinder was mounted directly to the brake pedal, and the cast-iron brake drums incorporated spring-loaded adjusters which acted automatically on each shoe. Although now considered perhaps a little feeble, the drum brakes operated efficiently enough, bearing in mind the car's performance.

Engine

At the time of its introduction, the 500's engine was the cause of some controversy, not because it was a twin-cylinder unit, nor that it was air-cooled, but due to the method by which the cooling air was delivered to the unit. As for the engine itself, this was quite conventional with its two-bearing crankshaft mounted within a pressure diecast crankcase. Cast iron cylinder barrels, deeply finned to aid cooling, bolted directly on to the face of the crankcase; the pistons were formed from light alloy and the connecting rods had lead/bronze big ends.

The chief aid to cooling was the 8.8inch (223mm) centrifugal fan, belt-driven from a light alloy pully and running at 1.75 times engine speed, delivering air at ambiant temperature collected from the louvres immediately below the rear window and forcing it over the cylinder head, barrels, and crankcase, as well as around the sump. The crankshaft to which the fan pully was attached also served as an integral oil filter which, being so efficient, only required cleaning at 30,000 mile intervals.

The warm air drawn off the engine could either be externally extracted or, by opening the heating valve on the central tunnel, used to heat the car's interior. The warm air, drawn along a duct in the floor, entered the car through vents adjacent to the front seats and often managed to render the handbrake lever what seemed like red-hot! Air from the cooling system was also directed to the air filter and carburettor, thereby eliminating any risk of freezing in winter conditions.

The initial coolness that greeted the 500 Nuova on its introduction had been enough to send shivers throughout the echelons of Fiat management. In Italy, the car was a great disappointment, not from design or styling points of view but because of its overall lack of performance and utility. The most prominent mechanical shortcoming was the weakness of the driveshafts

an engineering success, economic progress

Left: Most popular in Britain was the Normale model; the car shown has a full-length hood. (Author's collection)

Right: This superb brochure illustration shows the 500 Sport, the first Nuova 500 to receive the 499.5cc engine. Together with special trim, early series Sports had steel roofs with built-in strengthening ridges. (Courtesy National Motor Museum)

which had a tendency to break with alarming regularity. Potential failure so quickly on the heels of success with the 600 resulted in a grim atmosphere at Turin: strain and tension, virtually to the point of rancour, brought about a series of high level managerial changes.

Getting it right
Summer and Autumn of 1957 were not particularly happy periods for the design team employed in revamping the Nuova. Relief and consolation were, however, provided by Dante Giacosa who guided his team with his usual careful and quiet efficiency throughout a feverishly busy programme aimed at resurrecting the project and re-establishing Fiat's esteem. During the three months that preceded the Turin Show Giacosa proved miracles were possible. With a certain degree of free-handedness, granted in some respect in recognition of the Presidential Committee's failure to fully comprehend the market requirements of the 500, the design team prepared to meet, for the second time, the challenge of a new Topolino ...

As the Turin Show opened in November 1957 to the usual fanfares and delightfully exotic cars created by some of Italy's most revered designers, Fiat triumphantly unveiled a more powerful and substantially modified 500 Nuova. Known as the "Standard" – or Normale – it went on sale at 490,000 Lire, an increase of 25,000 Lire over the launch price. The original 500 Nuova, complete with its ultra-utilitarian specification and lower price of 465,000 Lire, was retained and redesignated the Economy 500, although it was given the same power increase as the Standard model. By re-vamping the Nuova in this way, Fiat was seen to offer a choice of models, a marketing ploy which saved loss of face and averted what could well have been a catastrophe.

Discarding the lethargic 13bhp engine in favour of a 15bhp unit, it was possible to tack an extra 3mph (5kph) onto the maximum speed, pushing it up to 56mph (90kph). Still from a displacement of 479cc, the extra power had been achieved by modifying the camshaft, redesigning the carburettor and using a higher compression ratio.

There were considerable differences in specification between the Standard and Economy versions of the Nuova. The Standard had winding windows fitted to the doors in place of fixed glass; waist-level side mouldings, hub caps and headlamp bezels to enhance appearance, while an upholstered rear seat added comfort. Direction indicator and light switches on the fascia were replaced by more convenient stalks on the steering column. Completing the package, a "Nuova 500" badge was fitted to the engine cover and, as an optional extra, a fan for the interior heater was available.

The arrival of the Standard 500 was enough to kickstart some real interest in the car which, in Italy, offered remarkable value for money at the equivalent of approximately £300. The export market was slower to respond: for example, it was not until early 1958 that the modified version was available in Britain where it went on sale at £556, compared to the Economy model at £526. In the first year of production 28,482 500s left the factory gates, although only 12,505 of those found customers in Italy.

The 500 Sport
After the advent of the 15bhp engine, a further significant development was the appearance of the 500 Sport – "a car for the enthusiast." With its engine uprated still further to 21.5bhp and a displacement of 499.5cc, this was not a car for the faint-hearted: maximum speed shot up to 68mph (109kph), thus necessitating the extra rigidity provided by the adoption of a steel roof with three strengthening ridges built into it. Apart from the all-steel body, Sport versions could be identified by their light grey paintwork with red flash along the body sides: the only colour scheme to be offered. The 500 Sport was available from August 1958 and had already achieved fame by winning its class in the Hockenheim 12-hour race a short time previously. The Liege-Brescia-Liege micro-car rally, also in 1958, added to the Nuova 500's achievements while Abarth had produced a Zagato-bodied machine, sleek and fast, which accounted for first, second, fourth and fifth places. Out of the thirteen cars that finished, seven were Fiat 500s.

In producing the 500 Sport, the engine was re-worked to engineer the camshaft in case-hardened steel rather than cast iron; modify inlet and exhaust valves, revise combustion chambers, enlarge carburettor choke and reduce cooling fan speed. This specification made for the fastest 500 at the time. A year later in 1959 the Sport was offered with a sunroof. Instead of the folding roof extending fully to include the rear screen as on early 500 Nuovas, the Sport was given a roof that opened only as far as the door pillars, therefore retaining the extra rigidity required.

Fiat introduced the Sport as the "Car for the enthusiast." Only one colour scheme was offered; light grey paintwork with a red flash along the side. (Courtesy Fiat Auto (UK) & Fiat SPA Ltd)

Second series 500 Nuovas showing the Teto Apribile. Sidelights have been moved to below the headlamps in place of the air vents and direction indicators moved to the leading edge of the front wings. The smaller picture shows the Trasformabile with basic trim level. (Courtesy National Motor Museum)

An interesting feature of the Sport version is that the first series of cars had body details similar to the Nuova Economy, apart, that is, from the provision of hub caps. By the time the sunroof version had made its appearance, the front ventilation louvres had disappeared and in their place were fitted small circular side lights, so complying with safety regulations. Taking the place of the original combined indicator and side lamps on the front wings, small amber-lensed indicators were fitted.

Changes to the Sport model coincided with the announcement from Turin at the end of April 1959 of modifications to the 500 Nuova in general. The Economy version became known as the Convertible – or Trasformabile – while the Standard version changed to the 500 Sunroof. In Italy this was the Teto Aprible which could be identified by its shorter opening roof. British customers were given a price advantage on new 500s: the Convertible sold for £497 while the more luxuriously equipped Sunroof model was available at £525. Performance remained generally as before, only the Sport versions having the larger 499.5cc engines.

After initial deliveries of 500s in 1957, sales took a dive in 1958 with somewhere around 6000 less cars finding customers. Out of the 22,844 cars produced, less than 10,000 were registered in Italy. In 1959 there was a massive upturn in demand with 66,273 cars built, representing an increase of 300%.

Giardiniera

In May 1960 Fiat, recalling earlier successes, announced a Giardiniera version of the 500 Nuova. The inherent problem of designing a rear-engined estate car was the amount of space required for the power unit. Two major hurdles had been overcome, firstly in providing a flat loading platform and, secondly, by opting for a suitable power to weight ratio bearing in mind the

Frontal trim of the second series cars is tidier with repositioned sidelamps and indicators. (Courtesy Fiat (UK) & Fiat SPA Ltd)

Right hand drive second series 500. This car is shown on display at the London Design Museum to celebrate 60 years of the city car. (Author's collection)

increased dimensions over the saloon. In the event, and unlike the Multipla for which forward control had been adopted, the solution was to use the 499.5cc engine instead of the 479cc unit, turning it on its side and laying it under the rear floor.

The Giardiniera at first appeared oddly out of proportion, increased body length accentuating the narrow track and overall width. In fact, of course, the Giardiniera was a very practical car in as much that it offered space enough for four adults plus a degree of luggage or, alternatively, two adults and a massive 440lb (200kg) of luggage. Based upon the Standard version of the 500, the Giardiniera benefited from opening front quarter-lights, winding windows in the doors and sliding windows at the rear. In addition the sunroof folded back three-quarters of the roof length, in line with the centre of the rear wheels. Even if the rear-hinged doors were restrictive for loading, the full height rear door, hinged on the left, provided particularly easy access. Surprisingly, a five-door version of the Giardiniera was never contemplated. A point of interest with the estate car is that it retained suicide doors throughout its production, even when later saloon cars were built with front-hinged doors. By lifting a panel on the load platform, just as in the later 126 Bis hatchback, the engine compartment could be completely revealed and was readily accessible.

Overall, the Giardiniera was 8.5 inches (215mm) longer than the saloon; the wheelbase gained an extra 4 inches

Right: The interior of the Giardiniera has a flat loading platform made possible by turning the engine on its side. The 499.5cc engine was used instead of the 479cc unit. (Courtesy Fiat Auto (UK) & Fiat SPA Ltd)

Below: Profile of the Giardiniera. Surprisingly, a 4-door version was never contemplated; however, access to the rear was not difficult in spite of the front-opening doors. (Courtesy Fiat Auto (UK) & Fiat SPA Ltd)

FIAT 500 station-wagon

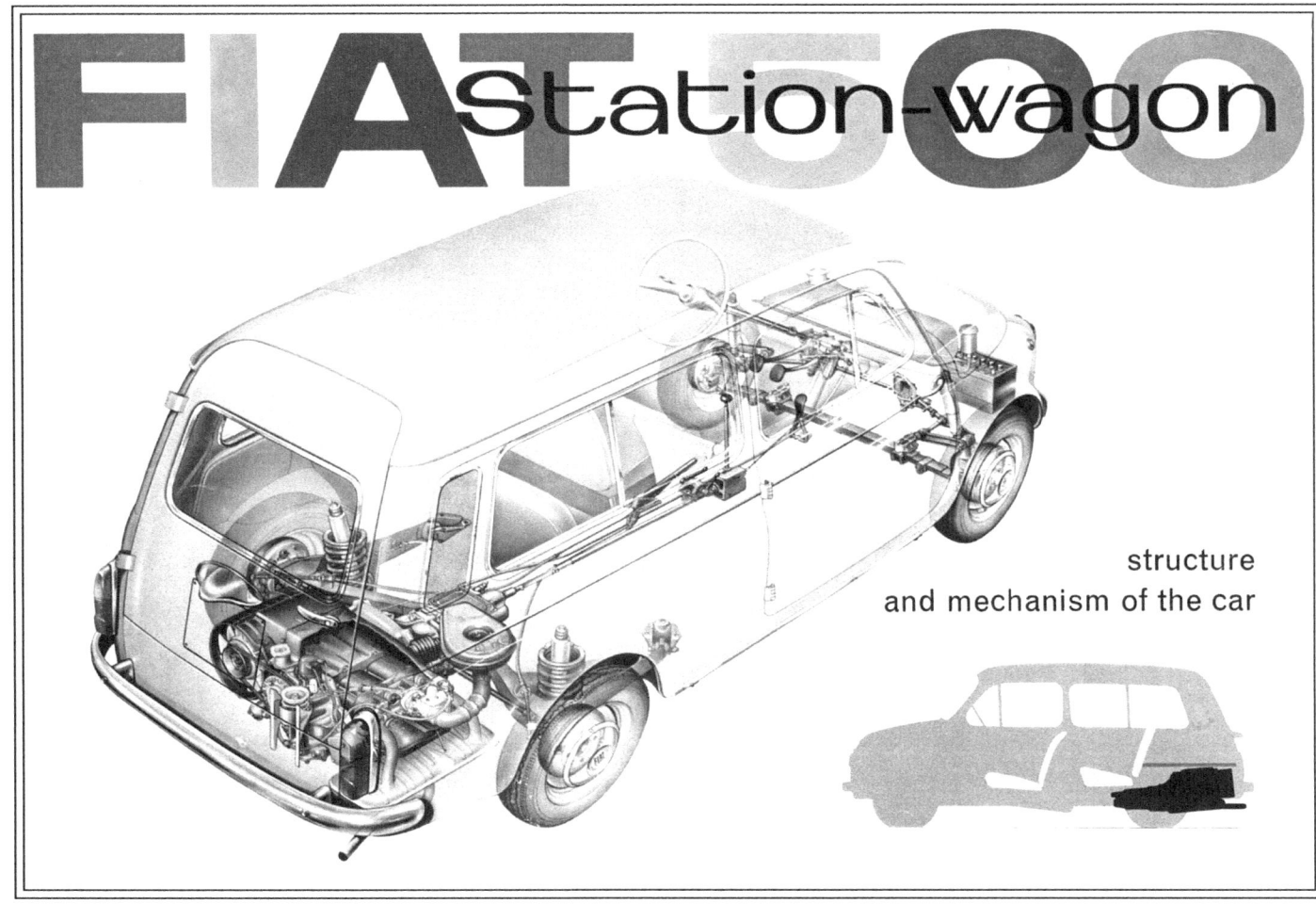

structure and mechanism of the car

Apart from turning the engine on its side so that it lay flat under the rear floor, the Giardiniera was mechanically similar to the 500 saloon. Air was drawn in through the ports adjacent to the rear windows and over and around the engine. Placing the cooling louvres at high level saved road dust from being drawn into the car. (Author's collection)

(100mm) and 1.25 inches (29mm) was added to the height. The extra weight, somewhere around a hundredweight (50kg), presented an added burden even for the extra power of the larger engine and, as a result, performance was affected. Up to 40mph (64kph) acceleration was quite brisk – in 500 terms at any rate – thereafter lethargy set in. Usually, 50mph (80kph) was the expected top speed although on test and in ideal conditions 60mph (96kph) was achieved at the expense of some fuss and bother. Through the gears, however, the Giardiniera outpaced the saloon, showing a clean pair of heels on 0-30mph (0-48kph) figures by a good 2 seconds.

To cope with the extra power and weight, the Giardiniera was given additional braking capacity with 8.3 inch (210mm) diameter drums, front and rear, in place of the normal 6.7 inch (168mm) drums. Fuel consumption, surprisingly, did not suffer as might have been expected: at a steady 30mph (48kph) in top gear the Giardiniera had a clear 7mpg (10 ltr/100km) advantage, although this was whittled down to just 3mpg (5 ltr/100km) at 40mph (64kph). At 50mph (80kph) the saloon nudged slightly ahead.

Although mechanically similar to the saloon, the Giardiniera relied on cooling air collected from grilles positioned on the body sides alongside the side windows and between the rear pillars. Air was thus drawn in through the ports and over the engine. The decision to mount the louvres at high level, rather than at engine height, was taken after trials showed there was less chance of road dust being sucked into the engine cowling and that engine noise would be reduced. Laying the engine on its side to fit horizontally under the floor meant that some re-designing of the engine itself was necessary. A new timing cover enabled easier access and servicing while the carburettor was fed air through an oil-bath type cleaner. To enable quick access to the dipstick and oil filler, a separate small hatch saved lifting the entire engine cover.

The 500D appeared in the summer of 1960, soon after the launch of the 600D. A short sunroof and larger tail lights immediately identified the 500D. The 499.5cc engine was universally adopted. (Author's collection)

Below left: Modified tail lights identified the 500D from earlier cars. Note the Nuova logo is still used. (Courtesy Fiat Auto (UK) & Fiat SPA Ltd)

A commercial variant in the form of a 5cwt (250kg) van was also marketed, but under the Autobianchi badge. This, and other variants, are described in the next chapter.

500D

Apart from the introduction of the Giardiniera in May 1960, and the appearance of the Nuova Sport two years earlier, the first significant change in model designation occurred in 1960 with the launch of the 500D. The new model appeared quickly on the heels of the 600D immediately after the annual summer shutdown. Coded as project 110D, the 500D retained all the general features of the Nuova and, more importantly, kept the same cheeky go-anywhere character.

As the 500D entered the Fiat catalogue, so other versions took their leave. The Sport models were withdrawn, as was the Convertible. The 15bhp engine was also discarded

A small rectangular-shaped fuel tank made it possible to fit a suitcase in the front compartment of the 500D. (Author's collection)

With its 35 cubic feet of luggage space, the Giardiniera offered a tempting package for those seeking an economy car with a lot of plus features. At a mere £29 above the cost of the 500 Nuova, it represented good value. Although the new Giardiniera appeared four years after its forerunner's namesake, Fiat was not slow to latch on to the connection between the 500 Station Wagon and the Topolino 500C Belvedere, and even the original 500A saloon of 1936. For all its appeal and useful payload, the Giardiniera never enjoyed the success of the saloon. In its first year of production, 27,367 Giardineras were built: compared to a total of over 84,000 saloons.

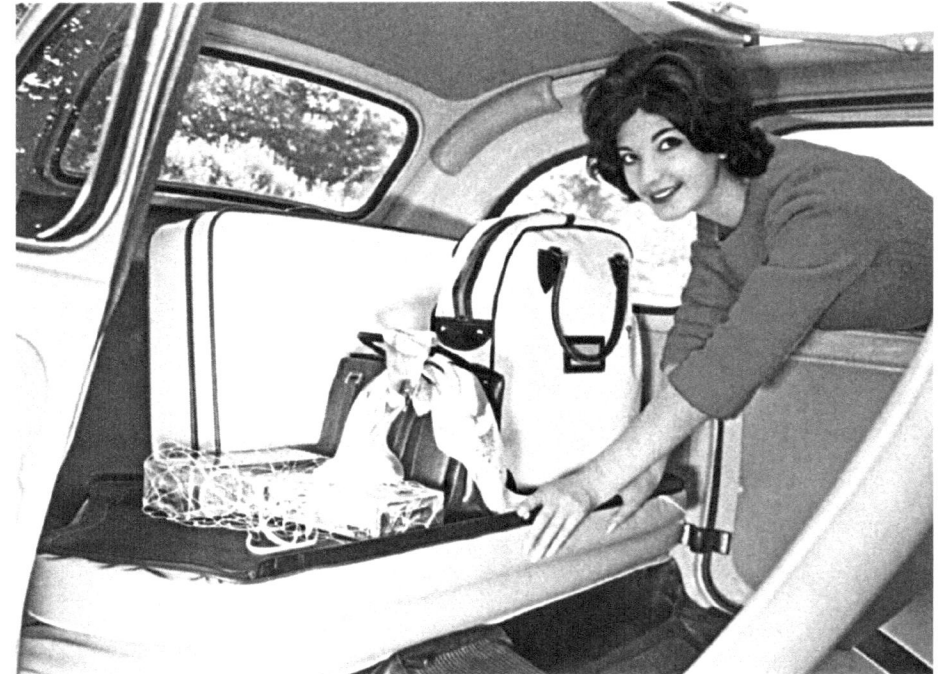

Inside the cabin of the 500D, the rear seat back folded forward to increase luggage capacity. (Author's collection)

as the 499.5cc unit was universally adopted. Externally, the 500D could be identified by its short sunroof and larger tail lights, but it was internally that the main differences applied. By re-shaping the fuel tank it was possible to provide more luggage space in the front compartment, although it is too much to infer there was anything other than room for occasional items. The

500 D sun roof saloon

rear seat received a folding back-rest which improved luggage capacity enormously. Rear passengers were considered as well: footwells were built into the floorpan allowing a greater degree of comfort, although the 500D could still only be considered a 2 + 2.

By adopting the 499.5cc engine, the 500D achieved slightly higher performance with maximum output rated at 17.5bhp. This, coupled with the change to a Weber type 26 IMBI carburettor, meant the 500D was able to attain speeds of a little over 60mph (96kph), whereas 57mph (91.2kph) was the best *The Motor* could achieve with the previous model. Acceleration times, too, were improved although the car still took 30 seconds to reach 50mph (80kph) from a standing start. Fuel consumption was the victim of the extra power, but something like 46mpg (6 ltrs/100km) was still the norm.

If there was a single grumble with the 500 it must have been the rather odd pedal position which often gave rise to adverse comments in road tests. True, the pedals were in line with the front wheels and therefore were offset due to the intrusion of the wheelarches, but it was the geometry of the brake and clutch pedals that were of most concern. With the lever fulcrums set so low, continual clutch work on long journeys was the cause of some discomfort.

Left: A typical Sixties advertisement for the 500D: suicide doors were still a feature, a windscreen washer was fitted as standard and the courtesy light operated via the driver's door. The manufacturer's claim of brilliant performance, accleration and speed is a little optimistic! (Author's collection)

1961

In 1961 the 500D received a series of improvements. A windscreen washer was included as standard equipment; the interior light, incorporated with the interior rear-view mirror, was additionally controlled by a switch on the driver's door. There were also less obvious changes, too, such as mounting the ashtray in the centre of the fascia and moving the indicator warning lamp to the driver's side of the dashboard. The instrument pod remained virtually as before, the meagre information it supplied considered adequate enough for the 500. Even in the Sixties the car still lacked a fuel gauge which, for whatever reason, was deemed an unnecessary luxury.

Production steadily increased from the 20,900 500Ds built in 1960 to almost 87,000 in 1961; 1962 saw over 132,000 cars produced with an increase of 3000 the following year. In 1964, the last full year the 500D was built, almost 194,000 examples were manufactured: this was the car's most successful year, due in part to the fuel crisis when motorists grabbed hold of any car that could run on the smell of an oil rag. Production of the 500D continued until 1965, by which time some 640,000 cars had been built.

The 500D had an aptitude for finding fame: curiosity got the better of HRH Prince Phillip, Duke of Edinburgh, who tried it out in 1962. Although *Autocar* reported the event there was no indication of the Duke's opinion of the car. Economy runs were a favourite with the 500D: in July 1965 96.59mpg was recorded by W. Dembowski on a test run through the Cotswolds in England and in the same month Gordon Wilkins returned 124.32 mpg at Silverstone circuit. A 500D found service in the most hostile and remote part of the world – the South Pole: used by a New Zealand research team, the car, with only minor modifications and dubbed a snow-kitten, performed admirably as camp runabout.

The Nuova 500 era produced an increasing number of small economy cars which included mini-cars and micro-cars. Apart from the true micro-cars such as bubble cars, a whole range of low-priced utilities became very accessible. The late Fifties witnessed a move by the Japanese government to bring motoring within the means of the masses; with dramatically increased output and overhead costs decreased, there was a push towards the export market. Among the first of the miniatures to evolve in Japan was the Subaru 360, a diminutive 356cc two-stroke with its engine mounted vertically above the rear axle. The Subaru's design was not unlike that of the Fiat 500 Nuova – there was almost a family resemblance – its overall length was just an inch greater than the Nuova's but it had a fractionally shorter wheelbase. Although performance was on a par with the 500, the Subaru's economy was outstandingly better at 73mpg (4 ltr/100km).

After the Subaru came the Suzuki Suzulight 360, the Mitsubishi A10 and Minica and the Mazda R360. The Honda N360, with front-wheel-drive and an

air-cooled 354cc twin-cylinder engine, made some impact in Britain and Europe, as did the S600, an extremely pretty sportscar. Despite these innovative developments the Japanese were unable to imitate Fiat's art of providing so much interior space within such diminutive exterior proportions.

Nearer to Italy, Russia came up with the little Zaporozhet with its V4 748cc air-cooled, rear-mounted engine. At first glance the similarity between this Soviet "mini" and the Fiat 500 and 600 appeared quite remarkable. European manufacturers were also producing some interesting utility cars: from Germany the NSU Prince 11 was just a whisper larger than the Fiat 500 Nuova and with comparable performance provided by its air-cooled 583cc engine. The Netherlands produced the Daf 600 which was more in the league of the Fiat 600 with its 590cc front-mounted air-cooled twin and idiosyncratic belt transmission; from Citroën there appeared the Bijou, a strange contraption built from 2CV running gear and bodied in glass fibre, the design of which was meant to represent a mini DS. A product of Citroën's British factory, the Bijou was doomed to failure. Also from Britain a host of three-wheelers could not provide the same comfort or performance as the Fiat 500: cars like the Meadows Frisky was just too eccentric to be contemplated. The real threat from Britain was, of course, the Mini, one of the motor industry's greatest success stories.

From France came the Vespa 400, descendant of the motor scooter by Piaggio and basis of designs by Dante Giacosa. By 1959 it was selling well; 12,000 having been delivered in its first year of production. The Vespa was entrenched in the micro-car bracket due, no doubt, to its 393cc air-cooled 2-stroke engine and compact dimensions. It really was akin to both the Topolino and Nuova 500, as well as the Bianchina and NSU/Fiat Weinsberg variants which are discussed later. Just like the Topolino and Convertible 500, the Vespa had a full-length fabric folding roof, suicide doors, fixed windows (models exported to the USA had sliding windows) and room enough for just two adults and luggage on a rear platform. With performance on a par with that of the Fiat 500, the success of the Vespa was shortlived, even with a price equivalent to a little over £300. Both the Fiat and Citroën 2CV took the market away from this practical little car and, sadly, it lasted only until 1961.

500F

The demise of the popular and highly successful 500D signalled a process of metamorphosis for the baby Fiats. Since 1957 the Nuova – with remarkably little change from initial conception – had continued to delight hundreds of thousands of motorists worldwide. In

Dressed in white furs, these two elegant signorinas make a delightful twosome. The car is a 500F announced in March 1965; its most significant external feature was front-hinged doors. (Courtesy Jill Forde)

Left: The change to front-hinged doors resulted in thinner door pillars and a deeper windscreen, so providing greater visibility. Height of the 500F was raised by 0.39 inch (10mm). (Courtesy Fiat Auto (UK) & Fiat SPA Ltd)

Right: Other changes to affect the 500F were the sills, which were not so deep, and the shape of the front bonnet rear edge. Mechanically, modified driveshafts, a heavier duty clutch and revised carburation meant slightly improved performance and a weight increase of 44lb (20kg). (Courtesy Fiat (UK) & Fiat SPA Ltd)

Below: In 1968 the 500L (Lusso) appeared as an up-market alternative to the 500F, which remained in production. (Courtesy Fiat (UK) & Fiat SPA Ltd)

March 1965 the 500F was announced; at first glance it looked virtually the same as previous models, but a second look revealed a whole range of different features. Code-named 110F, the latest 500 retained the 499.5cc engine from its predecessor and a slight modification to the carburation provided a limited increase in power, uprating it to 18bhp. Fiat claimed a maximum speed of 59mph (95kph) and fuel consumption of 51mpg (5.5ltr/100km) yet *Motor*, in its tests, consistently bettered these figures, reaching 64mph (102kph) and returning 53.5mpg (8ltr/100km).

The most significant design change was the adoption of front-hinged doors which had been forced upon the car by Italian safety regulations. More or less at the same time a similar modification was made to the 600. By changing to rear-opening doors it was possible to

design a deeper windscreen and thinner door pillars which, apart from increasing the overall height of the car by 10mm, improved the field of vision. There were other changes, too: the sills were less deep and the rear edge of the front bonnet was a slightly different shape. The unladen weight was also increased by 44lb (20kg).

Along with the body changes there were several mechanical revisions. Modified driveshafts and a heavier duty clutch enhanced the car's durability. On right hand drive cars the windscreen wipers were at last repositioned to sweep a larger area, so rectifying a grievance owners had expressed about earlier cars. Internally, the 500F changed little over its predecessors; the position of the pedals was still an area of concern, but at least the car was quieter and a modified heater assembly prevented fumes from entering the car. *Motor* said of the 500F: "it's a small, small car"; "... it is the custom to drive small Fiats flat out in Italy and the car seems to be designed for this treatment."

In 1968 Fiat transferred production of the Giardiniera estate car to Autobianchi; from its introduction in 1960 over 161,000 cars had been built. This figure represented production up to 1965 as there were no cars built from then until Autobianchi took over. At just about 14% of all 500s built up to the end of 1965, sales of the Giardiniera were surprisingly low.

1968

1968 was another particularly significant year for the 500. In September, Fiat announced the 500L (Lusso) but not before 1,682,456 500s of all descriptions had been produced. Outwardly, there was little change between this and the 500F which continued in production. The give-away features were a smaller and re-designed front badge; a Fiat 500L motif on the engine compartment cover and the dropping of the "Nuova" designation. Bright plastic replaced aluminium for the rear number plate and nudge bars were adopted front and rear to provide extra protection when parking. The front protectors curved upwards from under the front valance, ahead of the bumpers and parallel with the bottom of the headlamps: rear bars gave added protection to the lamp clusters and rear wings but were designed so as not to interfere with opening of the engine compartment cover. The addition of the nudge bars increased the overall length of the car by some 50mm. Hub caps were re-designed and made slightly smaller than those for the 500F while the 500L was given radial-ply tyres as standard. Extra brightwork adorned the 500L: plastic imitation chrome trim was added to the rubber window surrounds and the same pseudo-chrome trim added to the roof gutters, so increasing overall appeal.

The majority of refinements lay within the car's interior. Whereas the 500F retained the pod-shaped speedometer, the "L" version sported an all-new cowled oblong unit, similar to that fitted to the 850 saloon, incorporating the luxury of a fuel gauge. Creature comforts were also catered for in the 500L: moquette-type carpets replaced rubber mats, re-designed seats in imitation leather reclined and a fully padded fascia gave a degree of opulence. Chrome window-winders from the 124, a re-designed steering wheel, and map pockets in the doors were all provided – at the expense of retaining the basic trim for the 500F. The extra refinement, however, incurred a price penalty. Whereas the 500F was listed at 475,000 Lire, the 500L sold for 525,000 Lire. Export markets, such as Britain, preferred the 500L to the 500F, the refined trim finding greater acceptability than the austerity of the cheaper model. Both versions of the 500 continued in production until 1972 and between them accounted for sales of some 2.2 million cars, an extraordinary achievement for any motor company. Overall, since manufacturing began fifteen years earlier, more than 3.25 million units have taken to the roads across the world.

1972 was the end of the line for the demure and diminutive 500. Progress and evolution is a necessity for every car manufacture and Fiat was no exception. Just as the Topolino had given way to the 600 in 1955 and the 500 Nuova made its somewhat shaky entrance in 1957, now the time had arrived for another model to continue the Fiat tradition as popular small economy car. So the 126, which is discussed in greater detail in the final chapter, made its debut. Alongside the 126, the ultimate version of the 500 continued in production, sharing some of the running gear of its descendant.

500R

The final series of the 500 was given an "R" designation and underwent a fur-

Identification features of the 500L include nudge bars front and rear. Mechanically similar to the 500F, an additional feature was the adoption of radial-ply tyres. (Courtesy Fiat Auto (UK) & Fiat SPA Ltd)

Interior of the 500L. Note the reclining seats and smart trim. Carpets replaced rubber mats and chrome window winders adorned the doors. Externally, the 500L benefited from brightwork around the window surrounds. (Courtesy Fiat Auto (UK) & Fiat SPA Ltd)

Externally similar in appearance to the 500F, the 500L was the penultimate model, the last being the 500R. This is a 500L which, apart from the additional protectors, has a revised front badge. A new logo also appeared on the engine cover. (Courtesy Claire Scott)

Rear styling of the 500L; note the rear protectors to aid parking. The Nuova designation was dropped and the 500L had a more luxurious interior which included a new instrument cowl that incorporated a fuel gauge. (Courtesy Claire Scott)

ther exercise in modification. The most important feature of the 500R was its engine, again a vertical air-cooled twin, but enlarged to 594cc, the unit which was also used for the 126. The floor pan, too, was that from the 126 and the last of the 500L models; instead of using the all-new gearbox, the infamous "crash" box from the 500F was installed. Wheel hubs from the 126 were fitted, but instead of the wider wheels, those from the 500L were used while radial-ply tyres were fitted only as an optional extra. The interior trim was more evocative of the 500F with its single round-pod speedometer, old-style dashboard, steering wheel and painted fascia. Seats no longer reclined, although such seats could be specified as an option, and the rear seat was of the non-folding type. Apart from its wheels, the 500R could be readily distinguished from the 500F by its new-type oblong Fiat badge on the front panel.

Naturally the 500R was more powerful than its predecessors: with power output at 23bhp, it was capable of well

A parade of 500s pose for the camera. The car second from left is a Fiat-Abarth 595; note the similar paint style to the 500 Sport. (Author's collection)

over 62mph (100kph). Also increased was the price, 660,000 Lire, a far cry from the 465,000 Lire of the original 500. The 500R never sold as well as earlier models; the 126 obviously captured a lot of the market and the newly-launched Panda created its own niche. In its first year, just 7255 500Rs were built, peaking at 51,755 in 1973.

The 500R, the last in a series of unique cars. Introduced in 1972 at the same time as the Fiat 126, the 500R was fitted with the 594cc engine but had less power than the 126. The constant mesh gearbox from previous 500 models was retained. External identification features of the 500R are the 126-type wheels and the rhomboid Fiat badge at the front. This three-quarter rear view shows the plain badge on the engine cover. The trim was more in the style of the 500F with a dashboard and single pod-type nacelle. A fuel gauge was considered unnecessary and the 'R' had a low-fuel warning lamp instead. (Courtesy Fiat Auto (UK) & Fiat SPA Ltd)

A pristine 500L without its nudge bars. A 650cc engine has been fitted in place of the original and a complete restoration undertaken to a very high standard. (Author's collection)

By 1974 numbers dropped to 47,373 before dipping to a little over 28,000 in its final year, 1975.

From the late Sixties there is little doubt sales of the 500 were being affected by competition from other

Special frontal treatment and extended wheelarches denote this as no ordinary 500L. With a conversion by Ital Corsa's Jimmy Di Carlo to include an 800cc engine, a mild mannered car has been turned into a snorting monster! (Author's collection)

Special-bodied Fiats came in no more eccentric guise than the Vignale Gamine with its dummy front radiator grille. Running gear is pure 500. (Author's collection)

manufacturer's ultra-economy cars such as the Renault 4, Citroën 2CV and Dyane. All three were genuine four-seaters with both the Renault 4 and Citroën Dyane sporting hatchback bodies capable of swallowing enormous loads. Not only was performance often better than the 500, fuel consumption was not sufficiently different to be of huge consequence either. For all their utilitarian flexibility, however, cars such as the Renault and Citroën were never intended as ultra-small cars, which is where the Fiat undeniably excelled.

If the 500's performance was considered lethargic, this shortcoming was more than compensated for by its sheer agility and nippiness about town. Some commentators hesitated to recommend the 500 for long distance driving; this certainly was not appreciated by its native Italians, nor by committed enthusiastic owners who would not have dreamt of tackling long journeys in any other car.

Coachbuilt variants

Just as the specialist coachbuilders had set to work on the 600, so the 500 was similarly dealt with. Giannini produced an enchanting workhorse in the style of a pick-up, the engine turned on its side under the floor in Giardiniera style. The same company was also responsible for a little monster capable of almost 90mph (140kph) whilst Ghia built, amongst other variants, a beach buggy. Viotti produced a tiny fixed-head coupé and Vignale designed a strange open 2-seater, complete with separate front wings, exposed headlamps and a huge dummy radiator grille in the form of the Gamine. Commonly and affectionately known as "Noddy's" car, the Gamine has found a number of enthusiastic owners around the world. There were offerings also from Rudolpho Bonetto with a pretty and sleek convertible, from Monterosa, Lombardi and Savio. Moretti, Pininfarina and Siata were also represented.

The running gear from the 500 was used in a number of experimental vehicles, often used within the Mirafiori works as well as other Fiat factories for evaluation purposes. Some were successful, others less so. From those

An impressive display of 500s set against the magnificence of London's Tower Bridge. The occasion was to celebrate the launch of the Cinquecento and 60 years of city car design. (Author's collection)

experiments evolved micro Jeep-like utilities such as the "Ranger" and "Cargo"; prototype lightweight folding transporters, powered by the 500's engine, could be dropped from aircraft and used by paratroopers, while the "Muletto," an excellent off-road machine which appeared in 1960 driven by the Giardiniera engine, could carry five passengers and 750lb (340kg) of equipment. With four-wheel drive, the Muletto weighed only 1278lb (580kg). Two highly unusual vans made their appearance: a four-wheeler with the 500 engine driving the front wheels, and an even stranger three-wheeler which was more in the style of a mechanical horse. Known as the "Pully," the latter was shown at the Frankfurt motor show in 1962.

On the sporting side Abarth and Steyr-Puch brought home the trophies. With all the might of Abarth engineering, cars based on the 500 were a force to be reckoned with: together with styling by Zagato, anything was possible. The sporting and competition 500s have played an important part in Fiat history and are covered in greater detail in the following chapter.

As Fiat opened manufacturing plants around Italy, so 500R production was transferred to SicilFiat in Sicily, where it continued until the last Fiat 500 was built in 1975. The last car left the assembly line on 1st August and represented the end of a chapter on one of the world's most popular and best-loved cars. Happily, enthusiasts of the 500 are globally united in keeping the soul and character of this tiny but big-hearted car very much alive.

VII

THE VARIANTS

Abarth and the sporting Fiats

The sign of the scorpion, the emblem which has adorned many a high performance and sporting Fiat as well as other revered Italian makes since 1949, is synonymous with the name of Carlo Abarth, founder of one of motorsport's most respected tuning and engineering companies.

Carlo Abarth was freed from a prisoner of war camp in 1946 and set up his business three years later. The intervening years were spent in the company of two famous motor industry names: Dr. Ferdinand Porsche and Cisitalia. Abarth's introduction to motorsport had been in the form of motorcycling until a near-fatal accident caused him to retire from racing and devote his time to modifying and tuning engines. Work for Carlo Scagliarini enabled Carlo Abarth to form his own company: Scagliarini, who had associations with Fiat and raced Cisitalias, asked Abarth to tune his racing team's cars. With an investment from Scagliarini, who became a leading shareholder in the new company, premises were established in Turin in April 1949. Abarth's free association with Fiat continued until 1971 when the Abarth company was purchased by Fiat and amalgamated into its vast empire.

Initially, Abarth concentrated on the manufacture of specialist exhaust systems mainly for racing cars, but later branched out into production of high performance camshafts and valve springs. Engine conversions for Fiat, Simca, Lancia, Alfa Romeo, Porsche and others followed but it is with Fiat that the name of Abarth is most associated. The connection with Fiat can be traced back to Cisitalia days when, in the mid 1940s, both Carlo Abarth and Dante Giacosa were involved with Piero Dusio in the design of the Cisitalia 1100. By 1949, through lack of funds, the Cisitalia company folded.

Abarth's first major success was to transform the standard Fiat 1100B with its 68mph (110kph) top speed into a 114mph (182kph) sports machine. Later, Abarth turned his attention to the Fiat 600 when it was introduced in 1955, but not before conversions were made available for the Topolino.

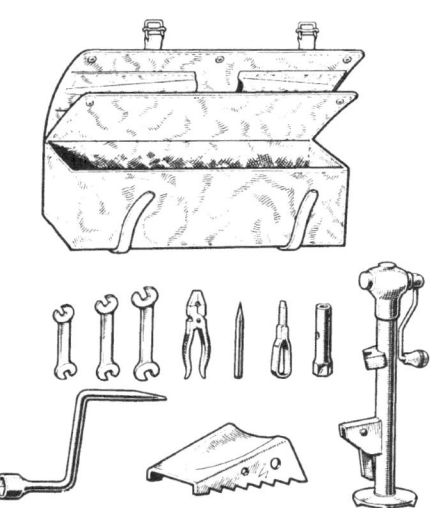

The loneliness of the long-distance rally driver ... A Fiat-Abarth, possibly an 850TC or 1000, storms out of the darkness. (Courtesy Haymarket)

Discussing the finer points. The centre of attention is this 1959 750 Fiat-Abarth Zagato "Double Bubble" built on the 600 floorpan. (Courtesy Tony Castle-Miller)

600 becomes Fiat Abarth 750

The first Fiat 600 was delivered to Abarth during the early days of 1956 and was the beginning of a long and fortuitous association with what, until the mid-Sixties, proved to be the company's best selling model. This first car, known as the Fiat Abarth 750, was transformed into a sporting machine capable of over 81mph (130kph) compared to the 58mph (93kph) of the standard 600. Included in the high performance package was a modified engine of 767cc which featured a completely new crankshaft, high compression pistons and a lighter flywheel: a larger capacity radiator provided the extra cooling required.

The 750 could sprint from 0-60mph (0-96kph) in under 20 seconds, whereas a production Fiat 600 took a leisurely 54 seconds. To go along with the increase in power, Abarth incorporated a number of other modifications, including a revised speedometer capable of recording higher speeds, a tachometer, an Abarth grille and wheel trims. Special red stripes along each side, together with a bonnet mascot, set the car apart visually from its standard sibling

Fiat Abarth 750 Zagato.

While potential customers were trying out the 750 (a number were made available to visitors to the 1956 Turin show), the highly revered and old-established Zagato concern was busy preparing for the new Italian racing season which traditionally started early in March. Due to make its first appearance at Monza was the Fiat Abarth 750 Zagato prototype, the forerunner of what would become a whole series of hugely successful GTs. Of course, the first Fiat Abarth Zagatos required further development and it was left to a 750 saloon to take the class trophy in the 1956 Mille Miglia. After the prototype car, the Zagato series I appeared with an aerodynamic lightweight aluminium body built with only minor modifications upon the standard 600 frame. With the same engine displacement as the 750 saloon, the coupé had a maximum speed in excess of 94mph (150kph).

Zagato Series II & III

By 1957 Abarth's Fiat-based Zagato

The business end of the "Double Bubble" 750 Fiat-Abarth Zagato. (Courtesy Tony Castle-Miller)

Right: Pininfarina's Fiat-Abarth 500 record breaking car. Bursting into service in 1958 it quickly set new records of endurance. Averaging speeds of over 72mph (115kph) for 10 days, the car went on to take even more records. It's now on display at Fiat's historical museum in Turin. (Courtesy Haymarket)

series II had put in an appearance and could be identified by its "double-bubble" roofline and rather sharply raked front bonnet. Headlamps, which on previous models were enclosed, were uncovered and rear lamps oval-shaped.

Series II cars achieved fame by winning their class event in the 1957 Mille Miglia, the last year of this prestigious road race. Series III cars quickly followed and although mechanical specification was almost identical to the previous model, changes were made to the styling. Front wings were re-designed to incorporate the headlamps behind plastic covers, and large bulbous overriders were fitted to the nose.

It is claimed that the now famous "double-bubble" styling was implemented to give Carlo Abarth, who was 6ft. 2in. (1.88m) tall, extra headroom.

Abarth and the Nuova 500

1957 was, of course, the year of the Nuova 500, a car that Abarth & Company associated themselves with from the beginning, having their version ready for the Turin Show in the Autumn. Capable of over 62mph (100kph) the Abarth was a world apart from the sluggish little 500 that had appeared in the Summer of that year. Orders for early deliveries were being taken for the Abarth car which, in addition to the scorpion emblem, had a distinctive two-tone paint finish.

In February 1958 both the Fiat 500 Nuova and Abarth achieved outstanding acclaim by accomplishing a marathon endeavour staged at the Monza circuit. Throughout the 7-day event the 500 completed over 11,000 miles (18,186km) at an average speed of 67.5mph (108kph). The record-breaking Monza 479cc Nuova 500 had been modified to achieve a maximum speed of 74mph (118kph) and was responsible for not only greatly promoting the car but establishing a firm relationship between Abarth and Fiat. There is no doubt the event helped popularize the Nuova after its calamitous start and wherever the car was exhibited it succeeded in attracting huge attention.

Zagato was by no means the only coachbuilder associated with Abarth's engine and tuning conversions: from 1949 on the company's engines could be found in Bertone-designed cars as well as Ghia, Boano, Viotti, Vignale and Pininfarina designs.

Record breakers

There were others, too. One of the most interesting designs was based upon the Fiat 600 with bodywork by Vignale in the style of a teardrop and with gull-wing doors, hence its goccia nickname. Only three Vignale prototypes were built and sadly this 94mph (150kph) machine never went into production.

Amongst the most fabulous variants must certainly be the Bertone and Pininfarina single seat cars designed to challenge speed and endurance records. Both the Fiat 500 and 600 formats were used in record-breaking attempts, the first being at Monza in June 1956. The superbly aerodynamic Bertone machine, complete with enclosed cockpit and wheelarches, windcheating front-end and rear tailfin, was altogether outstanding. Luckily, the car has been preserved and can be seen at Fiat's Turin Museum. The same 747cc engine that had first proved the Fiat Abarth 600 saloon pushed this speed trials car to an average of 98mph (156kph) over a distance of 2340 miles (3744km). Two months later the same car, but with a slightly larger 785cc engine, pushed the speed up to 105mph (168kph) over 2516 miles (4025km). The maximum speed the car attained was an amazing 120mph (192kph).

The following year it was the turn of Pininfarina to grab the honours with its aerodynamic car which more resembled a spacecraft than a motor vehicle, especially with its periscope air feed to the carburettor. This time the 747cc engine propelled the car to an astonishing maximum of 136mph (218kph), covering 7441 miles (11,906km) at an average of 103mph (165.37kph).

In September 1958 Abarth and Pininfarina attempted the 500cc class record with a 479cc engine car: after six days 12,500 miles (20,000km) had been covered at an average speed of almost 75mph (121kph), peaking to a maximum of 111mph (178kph). The same car later broke its own record, smashing through the 100mph barrier (160kph) for a 12-hour period.

Right: A Spanish Fiat-Abarth 1000 at Barcelona, 1968. Series II Berlina Corsa cars could achieve over 120mph (192kph) and were fitted with 4-wheel disc brakes. Many of these cars had 5-speed gearboxes. (Courtesy Tony Castle-Miller)

Pininfarina-bodied Fiat-Abarth 500, dressed to tackle endurance records. Note the periscope to aid air supply to the engine's intake system.
(Courtesy National Motor Museum)

A further development was the design of a mid-engined car. Using the 747cc unit, the engine and gearbox were turned 180 degrees within a Pininfarina steel box section chassis and resultant trials realised maximum speeds of 131mph (210kph).

Abarth TC

Whilst the special-bodied cars were making history, development and production continued with road-going 750 and 850 variants. Between 1960 and 1961, the first Abarth TC – Turisimo Competizione – 850, which was based on the Fiat 600D, made its appearance. With a displacement of 847cc, the 850TC was fitted with a Solex carburettor and reinforced suspension capable of handling the car's 52bhp and 92mph (147kph). In place of drum brakes as found on the standard 600D, Girling disc brakes were fitted to complement the car's extra power which rocketed it from 0-30mph (0-48kph) in 3.5 seconds and 0-60mph (96kph) in 12.4 seconds.

850TC Nürburgring Corsa

Raising the power to 68bhp and maximum speed to 93.75mph (150kph), the 850TC Nürburgring Corsa appeared from 1962 and was the first Fiat Abarth saloon to have an auxiliary radiator fitted to the front of the car. Further modifications pushed the maximum speed to over 112mph (180kph) making it one of the most spectacular saloon cars ever to race at the famous Nürburgring circuit.

Fiat Abarth 1000TC

In the meantime, on-going experiments used the 600 engine block to build a one-litre DOHC motor derived from the 750 unit which eventually resulted in the Fiat Abarth 1000TC being ready for 1961 with a displacement of 982cc. Built for road-going use rather than out-and-out competition work, the car had a top speed of 94mph (150kph) from its 68bhp. Competition-wise, however, the Fiat Abarth 750, 850 and 1000 models were a match for the Mini-Coopers which had been taking many of the trophies.

Fiat Abarth 1000TC series II cars started to appear from 1964. Increased

Right: 850TC Corsa series 1 cars of 1960 had maximum power of 52bhp at 5800rpm and were capable of speeds of 92mph (147kph). 850TCs eventually developed enough power to take them over 100mph (160kph), the 850TC Berlina Rally Monte Carlo attaining almost 110mph (176kph). (Courtesy Tony Castle-Miller)

Left: Possibly at the Nürburgring, a cluster of Fiat-Abarths prepare to do battle. (Courtesy Haymarket)

Below: Tony Castle-Miller at the Nürburgring in 1986 with his Fiat-Abarth 850TC. Note the front-mounted oil and water auxiliary radiator. (Courtesy Tony Castle-Miller)

cooling was a necessity and, as a result, a larger auxiliary radiator was mounted at the front of the car. Securing straps had to be fitted to the bonnet while engine cover supports held the rear lid rigidly open to assist cooling as well as helping with stability at speed. The 600-based variants were by this time using bodies with front-hinged doors which, apart from the safety angle, improved the car's aesthetics. Developing 76bhp at 7000rpm, it was possible

to wind the car up to a very respectable 118.75mph (190kph).

A year later in 1965, series III 1000TCs arrived and could be identified by their massive fibre-glass bumpers moulded into the front of the car which, by now, incorporated both auxiliary water and oil-cooling radiators. With power now up to 80bhp at 7400rpm and

Left: The Middle Barton 850TC Fiat-Abarth with Tony Castle-Miller at the wheel. Hockenheim, 1991. (Courtesy Tony Castle-Miller)

Nürburgring 1989 and Tony Castle-Miller vies for the lead with an Auto-Union. In pursuit are a Renault, Mini and Fiat 595SS. (Courtesy Tony Castle-Miller)

a maximum speed in excess of 120mph (192kmh), it was not long before a series IV car made its debut with 85bhp at 7600rpm and a staggering 122mph (195kph) capability.

1000TC Radiale

The ultimate Fiat 600-based saloon was the 1000TC Radiale. With

Thruxton, Easter Monday, 1968. Two Fiat-Abarth 1000 Berlinas wait to show what they can do on the circuit. It was nothing for these machines to roar up to speeds of over 125mph (200kph). (Courtesy Tony Castle-Miller)

two Weber 40 DCOE carburettors, five-speed gearbox and 106bhp, the 1966 series cars were enormously powerful with a top speed of 130mph (208kph). Later, in 1970, the performance was uprated still more by the fitting of modified carburettors. Maximum output increased to 112bhp at 8200rpm, so producing a tremendous top speed of 135mph (215kph).

The success of the Zagato 500 Nuova-based cars in the Liége-Brescia-Liége minicar rally has already been mentioned. It is important to note, however, that these cars soon engendered a lot of popularity in motorsport, especially with their 21bhp maximum power and top speed of 72mph (115kph), creating very close racing. Pininfarina, keen not to be left out of the scene, built a pretty

little streamlined car not too dissimilar to that of the rival Zagato. Pininfarina's Abarth model was faster than the Zagato and could achieve an honourable 90mph (145kph). Soon after the appearance of Abarth's Monza marathon 500 Nuova, Fiat launched its own Sport version of the 500, the power output of which was similar to the Abarth machine. Whilst there is no account of Carlo Abarth's

Fiat-Abarth 595SS. Note the special wheels and standard Abarth two-tone paintwork. (Courtesy Haymarket)

reaction there is some suggestion that he might have been aggrieved, which could account for why virtually no 500-based Abarth cars appeared until 1963 when the 595 made its debut.

Abarth 595

The first 595s were based on the 500D; modifications to the camshaft, pistons and carburettor increased the capacity to 594cc and 27bhp. Top speed of the series I cars was in excess of 75mph (120kph), a far cry from the original 500 Nuova. Abarth 595s could be easily identified by their scorpion emblem and Abarth badge in place of the usual Fiat mark, a fully equipped instrument panel and the 595 logo on the passenger side of the dashboard. Further modifications followed in the shape of the 595SS and Corsa, both of which received stronger suspension to complement the increased power.

Abarth 695

Entry into the 700cc motorsport category meant additional power was necessary for the twin-cylinder car: in 1964 Abarth introduced the 500-based 695 with its 689cc engine; output shot up to 38bhp at 5200rpm and the car was capable of around 88-90mph (141-144kph). When the Fiat 500F was introduced with its front-hinged doors, the Abarth car changed accordingly; in fact, specification was continually modified until 1966 when the 695SS Assetto Corsa III arrived. Complete with flared frontal arrangement, front-mounted oil-cooler and facility for raising the engine cover for extra stability and cooling, series III cars competed directly with the 750 and 850TC machines, having maximum speeds approaching 90mph (144kph).

Bertone and Boano Spyders, Viotti Coupé

Abarth used the Fiat 600-based engine for a number of experimental and exotic cars with styling by some of Italy's most revered designers. In 1956 the 747cc engine powered the Bertone 750 Spyder which was capable of over 100mph (160kph), while the 633cc engine graced the extremely pretty Boano Spyder. Viotti's 750 coupé, with its luxury trim and 94mph (150kph) plus capability, made its debut at the 1956 Geneva show and received much attention.

Bialbero and Monomille

The Fiat Abarth Bialbero was also rather special as it was the first competition car to have a front-mounted radiator. This 1960 sports coupé was fitted

Fiat 600 floorplan was used to good effect for this Abarth 1000 Bialbero. In front is another 1000 Bialbero, while to the left of it is a 600 conversion. (Courtesy Tony Castle-Miller)

With a 600 floorpan and aluminium body, this 1000 Monomille of 1963 poses a very pretty picture. This machine had a top speed of over 112mph (180kph). It is more than likely this car had bodywork built by Sibona and Basano. (Courtesy Tony Castle-Miller)

with the 982cc engine with two Weber carburettors, and pushed top speed to a little over the 125mph (200kph) mark.

In 1960 Abarth produced the 1000 Bialbero GT, the first all-Abarth designed body to appear. Again, the 982cc engine was used to propel the car to over 131mph (210kph). A power increase for 1962 resulted in the Bialbero World Champion car with an achievable 135mph (215kph). The 1000 Monomille GT arrived in time for 1963 with the 600D-based engine and front radiator. Over 112mph (180kph) was well within its reach and the road-going car boasted an interior as rich as its performance.

Abarth's standard conversions for the 500 and 600 road-going cars may not have had quite the same appeal as the true racing machines, but they did provide phenomenal performance and handling. Whereas the standard Fiat 600 could achieve a maximum of almost 60mph (96kph), the 750 was capable of 80mph (128kph) and took considerably fewer seconds reaching it. The road-going Zagato 750GT, with its low-drag shape and lightweight body, raised the maximum speed even further to 96.5mph (154.4kph). The Motor, summing up the 850TC with its 93.5mph (150kph) limit said: "one can love it or loathe it – but nobody could describe it as dull."

As for the 595, although much slower than its bigger relative, it managed outstanding performance for such a small car. With a maximum speed of almost 80mph (128kph) it was far quicker than comparable cars and demonstrated a true sporting quality. The 595 out-ac-celerated the Mini and knocked 20 seconds from the standard 500's 0-50mph (0-80kph) figure; in terms of maximum speed it was the most rapid of all the minis at the time. Fuel consumption suffered as a result but the 595 was not driven for out and out economy. Side by side, the differences between the 500 and the 595 could easily be determined: the 595 had lower suspension and the rear wheels adopted a distinct camber.

If you drive a 595, you'll find that all the charisma of the Abarth is there to experience and enjoy.

Steyr-Puch

The Austrian Steyr company was formed soon after the First World War. During the inter-war years at least two famous personalities were associated with the concern – Hans Ledwinka and Ferdinand Porsche. After the Second World

Steyr-Puch's volatile version of the the Fiat 500. This car is fitted with a solid roof and looks decidedly top heavy. Staid design belies the potency of the 650cc horizontally-opposed air-cooled twin shoe-horned into the tail. Twin fuel tanks were fitted into the front compartment and a second spare wheel (front and rear tyres were differently sized) was housed behind the driver's seat. (Courtesy Haymarket)

Insert pic: The answer to creating a 600-based estate car was forward control, moving everything frontward on the same wheelbase as that of the 600. Three versions of the Multipla were available, a 4/5 seater, 6-seater and, as illustrated, a taxi. (Courtesy Fiat Auto (UK) & Fiat SPA Ltd)

War Steyr assembled Fiat cars for the Austrian market, including the Topolino and, later, the 600 and Multipla.

It is the 500 for which the Steyr is most noted: in 1957 the Nuova was built under licence with Steyr's own 493cc engine, modified rear suspension and larger, more powerful brakes. Two further engines completed the power line-up: a 643cc unit which developed 20bhp, and a 660cc 27bhp which was the basis of the 650TR, the company's fastest production car. Instead of the vertical in-line twin-cylinder engine, Steyr used its own air-cooled horizontally opposed unit which provided incredible performance. Maximum speed of the 650TR was about 90mph (143kph), but it was the acceleration and speed through the gears that was most impressive.

Apart from the front badge and Steyr emblem, the 650TR outwardly appeared almost identical to the Nuova 500, although the Steyr was designed with a full length hood. The interior had a number of modifications including a revised dashboard and instrument binnacle. A second spare wheel lived behind the front seats as the front tyres were a smaller size than the rear. In the front compartment any spare room that had been available on the standard model was lost to a second fuel tank whilst, at the rear, the engine and its associated equipment appeared to be squeezed in with a shoehorn.

Autocar was very definite about the car's ability: "... once the clutch is fully home and the revs start climbing the little Steyr takes off like a rocket with a deafening scream from the gears." The Steyr was faster than the Mini-Cooper, knocking a good 15 seconds off the 0-80mph (0-128kph) figure at 35 seconds – and the Mini-Cooper with an engine of 997cc, too.

However agile and good a performer the Steyr was, its success was, unfortunately, shortlived.

600 Multipla

The first true variant of the 600, the Multipla, probably caused more dilemma and concern for Dante Giacosa than any other associated model. Whilst the 600 was nearing its final outlines of design, Giacosa was well aware that the success of the Belvedere and Giardiniera estate car versions of the Topolino was going to be a difficult act to follow when the 500 was eventually laid to rest. Also of concern was the question of how to design an estate car body around the running gear of the 600 with its vertical in-line rear-positioned engine.

In his autobiography, Giacosa admits that the prospect of finding a 600-derived replacement for the Belvedere was quite formidable and the cause of several sleepless nights; he further discloses that he hoped he would have found a solution to the conundrum before any of Fiat's senior management started asking for his ideas.

In retrospect, the "all-service" Multipla, as the Belvedere and Giardiniera replacement became known, was one of the most cleverly designed and ingenious cars in automobile history and certainly thirty years, or thereabouts, ahead of its time. Mounting the engine at the rear of the 600 made it difficult to

design a conventional estate-type vehicle as it was impossible to build a car with a low rear floor and full tailgate. The equivalent interior space of the Belvedere had therefore to be obtained ahead of the engine compartment. The solution that Giacosa eventually came up with was to move everything forward, including the driving position. Even then, the estate car would not have the traditional rear door. As an

In designing the Multipla, the main difficulty was to create an estate car out of the 600 with its rear-mounted engine. Giacosa admits to the loss of several nights' sleep in finding an answer to the problem. (Courtesy Fiat Auto (UK) & Fiat SPA Ltd)

exercise in forward control, the Multipla was without comparison and served as forerunner to the people-carrying concept vehicles that started to become popular in the 1970s.

Whilst ingenious in design, the Multipla was also one of the most idiosyncratic cars of its time. By adopting forward control it was possible to turn a vehicle of very modest dimensions into a full six-seater load carrier with three rows of seats. To put it succinctly, the Multipla was only 1 foot (305mm) longer, and 1 inch (25mm) wider than the baby Fiat Cinquecento of the 1990s.

Along with the engineering practicalities associated with the Multipla to accommodate three rows of seats, the most important issue was to preserve the car's identity. Bearing in mind that the structure of the vehicle was only 10 inches (254mm) longer than the 600, and that it retained the same wheelbase, the task was not an easy one.

By adopting forward control for the Multipla it was not possible to retain a frontal identity with the 600 saloon. The all-service variant of the 600 took on an oddly top heavy appearance, made all the more conspicuous by the raised headlamps and huge overriders. (Courtesy Fiat Auto (UK) & Fiat SPA Ltd)

As the frontal design was dictated by forward control, Giacosa decided that the rear styling should be left virtually identical to that of the saloon. Design detail of the Multipla – still referred to at this stage by its "100 Familiare" code name – was completed by the middle of 1953 with the intention that the vehicle be in production by no later than early 1955.

In the event the Multipla was not too far behind schedule, making its debut at the Brussels show in January 1956. A mixed reception greeted the Multipla: there was some anxiety over its peculiar and controversial styling and yet appreciation of its engineering solutions. The Multipla's true attributes were quickly understood and the car soon proved itself as a most adept all-purpose vehicle.

Due in part to the Multipla's unique and unconventional characteristics, the car took some getting used to. The suicide doors positioned immediately over the front wheels made entry to the front seats, which were unusually upright, less than easy. Once in the car there was a feeling of being very far forward, almost to the point of being remote from the rest of the vehicle. The driving position was

The rear styling of the Multipla retains much of the character of the 600 saloon in order to preserve a corporate identity between the two models. (Courtesy Fiat Auto (UK) & Fiat SPA Ltd)

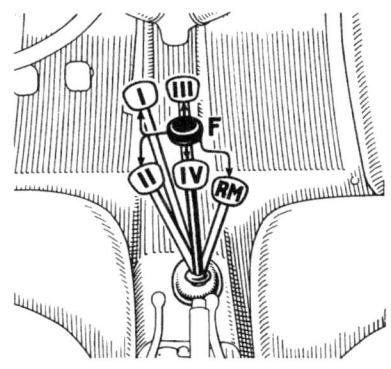

more akin to that of a van or small lorry. Front layout of the Multipla was strangely cumbersome: the steering shaft from the front axle to the universal joint mid-point on the steering column passed between the driver's legs. Equally inconvenient was the spare wheel, which stowed against the front bulkhead immediately ahead of the front passenger. On the credit side, the wide rear doors provided particularly easy access and the lack of a tailgate was hardly noticeable.

With the occasional seats in position, six people could be carried in comfort; folded down, almost limousine conditions prevailed. Used as a camper it was possible to recline both the front and rear seats to form a full-length bed, while as a load-carrier the rear seats folded into a flat luggage platform which could carry 7cwt (approximately 356kg).

In design, the Multipla changed little throughout its life span of some ten years, during which period 150,000 vehicles were built. At almost 8 inches (200mm) higher than the saloon it looked top-heavy, accentuated by the fact it used the same wheels as the 600. The prominent headlamps appeared to be positioned at an unusually high level and were made all the more conspicuous by the huge overriders attached to the bumper. Front windows, unlike those on earlier 600 saloons, were of the wind-down type with sliding windows fitted to the rear doors. As far as can be recorded a folding roof was never a factory option. Although the Multipla was marketed as a 4/5-seater, a 6-seater and taxi variant were also offered.

Mechanically, there was a general similarity between the Multipla and the 600 saloon: the same 633cc 4-cylinder water-cooled engine was used but the Multipla's 4-speed gearbox received a modified final drive ratio. The track was increased by 81mm at the front and, instead of utilising the 600's front suspension, coil springs and anti-roll bar from the Fiat 1100 coped with the extra weight.

On introduction of the 600D in 1960, the same mechanical modifications – which included the more powerful engine – were applied to the Multipla. When, however, Italian safety regulations dictated that front-hinged doors be fitted to all cars, the Multipla's design and construction prevented such compliance and, as a result, production came to a halt in 1966.

Performance from the Multipla was, as could be expected, a little torpid but it was possible to achieve a maximum speed of 55mph (90kph) with a healthy fuel economy in the region of 42mpg (6.7lt/100km). With the increase in power after 1960, 65mph (104kph) was feasible, but at a cost in fuel consumption.

A number of variants appeared, both under the Fiat badge and those offered by special coachbuilders. In taxi form the Multipla was especially popular, particularly in its native Italy. It also enjoyed a measure of success in Britain with fleets of vehicles operating in Central London and Watford. There was also a proposal to introduce it to Glasgow, Manchester, Birmingham, Leeds and Southampton.

In Italy the Multipla enjoyed a reputation as jack of all trades and could be found in useful service from ambulance to delivery van. Specialist coachbuilders were quick to respond and presented a whole series of attractive vehicles. Pininfarina showed a luxury 6-seater with the spare wheel cleverly incorporated on the front of the vehicle, while a whimsical open sun-cruiser with cutaway sides was more at home in sun-drenched climes. Vignale presented an eccentric space-age runabout more at home on a Hollywood film set than in Turin. Ghia, as well as producing a van with sliding slide panels, announced the Multipla Jolly which, in keeping with the 600 Jolly, featured wicker seats. Coriasco featured the Furgoncini, a delivery vehicle with a flat low-loading platform, accessible from both sides through wide-opening doors; also offered by Coriasco was the Pulmino, a 6-seat minibus. Moretti also produced a well-appointed minibus, but on the whole it was O.M., a sezione of Fiat, who produced the majority of commercial variants.

There were, quite naturally, the inevitable one-off and limited edition styling exercises, including variants with exaggerated rear wings and restyled coachwork. Few such examples were built but offerings from the like of Fissore and Scioneri survive.

It should be remembered that the Multipla was the first practical multi-purpose vehicle and, as such, displayed a daringly efficient and workable concept, successful beyond all doubt. Few Multiplas outside Italy have endured the ravages of time and

The Ghia Jolly in its Multipla-based form retained 6-seater capacity, albeit with wicker seats. Note that the two sets of rear seats are facing each other. (Author's collection)

climate but, happily, the relatively few that have remained are in enthusiastic hands.

Neckar and NSU-Fiat

NSU's history can be traced back to 1905. Fiat, however, took over the company's manufacturing plant at Heilbronn in 1930 to build vehicles for the German market. Amongst the cars produced was the Topolino 500 in coupé and sports 2-seater versions. Following

The Coriasco Furgoncini derivative of the Multipla was marketed with two, three or four wide-opening side doors. This is the Quadriporte. (Author's collection)

More of a mini bus than a station wagon, this Coriasco Pulmino 6-seater retains its Multipla identity at the front but resembles the Fiat 850T at the rear. Note this vehicle has 6 doors. (Author's collection)

the Second World War, the Heilbronn plant produced NSU-Fiats as well as special export vehicles based upon the Fiat 600 and 500 Nuova with Jagst and Neckar badges. Fiat-based cars for German consumption were also produced at Heilbronn and included the Bianchina and Autobianchi. Due to a legal dispute, NSU-Fiat changed its name to Neckar in 1959, so recalling the earlier company name of Neckarsulmer.

The Fiat 600 was built by NSU-Fiat as the Jagst 770 from 1960. These were fitted with the 600D's 767cc engine, although initial cars had the earlier-style 600 body. Later Jagst 770s received the updated body and from June 1964 the Jagst 2 appeared complete with front-hinged doors. In almost every other respect Jagst models represented current Fiat design and in 1967 the NSU-Fiat badge and Jagst logos were dropped. Thereafter cars were sold as Fiats, but not before more than 150,000 Jagsts had been produced.

For a short period while the changeover in company name was in progress, both NSU-Fiat and Neckar names were used on cars from Heilbronn. In this period Neckar presented the Jagst 770 Coupé and Spyder with coachwork by Vignale. Known as the 'Riviera' both variants were well-equipped and finished to a high standard.

Also from Heilbronn, the Weinsberg 500 Limousette and Coupé appeared, both of which were loosely based upon the Nuova 500. Running gear was pure Fiat 500 although the coachwork had little in common other than general dimensions. Quite distinct in character, the Weinsberg cars were built in small numbers, only 6190 were produced between 1959 and 1963. With perhaps some greater similarity to the NSU Prinz, the Weinsberg 500 sported two-tone coachwork, a wrap-around rear window on the coupé version and hooded headlamp brows.

The Heilbronn-produced mini-vans

The 600D was marketed by NSU-Fiat as the Jagst 770 in two versions: limousine and limousine mit schiebedach (sunroof model). The Jagst was fitted with a sliding fabric roof that extended almost as far back as the rear window. (Author's collection)

Two versions of the 500 were built by NSU-Fiat at Heilbronn and were known as the Weinsberg 500. This is the Limousette with perhaps a hint of the styling of the NSU Prinz. The Coupé is shown in the colour section. (Courtesy National Motor Museum)

using Fiat 500 Giardiniera mechanical components have already been discussed. However, the research department was responsible for a number of experimental vehicles, some of which got no further than prototype models. These included a 500 automatic variant using a belt system not unlike the Daf, and a 500-based electric car. As to the latter, Moretti tried unsuccessfully to produce a 500 Nuova electric runabout.

Autobianchi

Formed from a joint venture in 1955 between Bianchi, Fiat and Pirelli, the new combine centred its production at Desio. The Bianchina – largely based upon the Fiat 500 – was the first car from the new union. Produced in two versions, the standard 500-based car appeared in September 1957; eleven months later the Bianchina Speciale with the 500 Sport platform made its entrance. In 1961, the range was further extended by the arrival of the 110DB Coupé and Convertible, based upon the Fiat 500D, while the Panoramica estate car used the Giardiniera as its base. At the same time, a van version appeared which shared the running gear of both the Panoramica and Giardiniera. Bianchina variants were marketed with a 20% premium which allowed for greater comfort, two-tone paintwork, redesigned fascia and more effective soundproofing. Whilst running gear was from the 500 Nuova, body pressings were entirely different and suspension modified to give less roll in cornering.

The coupé and convertible models are highly sought after although very rare: as for right hand drive cars it is thought only six were built and that two have survived, although the current whereabouts of one of them is unknown.

The Stellina, a convertible variant using the 600 platform, was marketed in 1964 without much success. A number of other versions of Fiat-based cars

Right, top: Autobianchi marketed a small van as well as the Giardiniera, saloon and coupé. The frontal appearance resembles the Bianchina but the van was mechanically similar to the estate car: its engine lying flat under the rear floor. The rear door hinged at the top whereas the Giardiniera version had a side-hinged door. (Author's collection)

Autobianchi's Bianchina Special Coupé. Based on Fiat 500 running gear the Bianchina was fitted with luxury trim and the car had lowered suspension, too. Priced between the Fiat 500 and 600, the Bianchina enjoyed only moderate success. (Courtesy Haymarket)

Below: The Bianchina van made an ideal delivery runabout and its load capacity was surprisingly generous at 35cu.ft. (Author's collection)

Vignale - Fiat Gamine

Top left: In convertible form the Bianchina is a desirable and lovable variant of the 500. It's now very rare; even more so in right hand drive form. (Author's collection)

Left: The Gamine, a charming but tiny tourer based on the 500 with bodywork by Vignale. Looking more like a toy car, the Gamine attempted to recreate an association with the Balilla 508S. The radiator grille at the front is, of course, a dummy; the air-cooled twin is situated in the tail. (Author's collection)

Above: The cheeky lines of the Gamine. Despite the grille at the front the engine is installed at the rear in normal Fiat 500 fashion. (Author's collection)

Left: The 500 Jolly, an open fun car with cutaway doors. This version is based on an early series 500. Note the giveaway ventilation louvres in the front panel. (Author's collection)

The Jolly's interior, complete with very uncomfortable wicker seats. (Courtesy Andrew Minney)

appeared and, in general, Autobianchi was used as a test department for Fiat ideas. In 1969 all Giardiniera production was transferred to Desio and from then on the Fiat 500 estate car was sold with Autobianchi's badge and unique frontal styling. Although Italian regulations demanded that all cars had to have front-hinged doors from the mid-1960s, the Giardiniera continued with its suicide doors until the 1970s.

Although the Autobianchi name lived on, the company was taken over in its entirety by Fiat in 1968 and became Fiat SPA. Due to Fiat's policy of empire building and establishing filials world-

A charming and atmospheric brochure illustration for the Ghia Jolly. In the same brochure were also details of the 600 and Multipla versions. (Courtesy National Motor Museum)

wide, a number of variants appeared from time to time; others were produced by specialist coachbuilders using either Fiat Nuova 500 or 600 platforms and running gear but very few examples still exist.

Vignale
While producing an attractive coupé with Abarth modifications, Vignale also offered the Gamine mentioned earlier. This demure 2-seater was inspired by the Fiat Balilla sports car of the 1930s but, although very charming, did not sell in huge numbers. The dummy front radiator grille contrived to recall the splendour of the 508S. Under the Vignale coachwork existed the ubiquitous Fiat 499.5cc air-cooled vertical twin mounted in the tail. Undeniably alluring, the Gamine has become something of a cult car and is either loved or hated by 500 devotees. A number of right hand drive cars were imported to Britain by Demetriou and Sons but, at £700, were vastly over-priced.

Ghia
As well as producing special-bodied 600 saloons, Ghia also produced the 500, 600 and Multipla "Jolly" which was intended as a fun car and beach buggy. For fine weather only, the cars were fitted with special bodies with cutaway sides and wicker seats, the only protection from the elements being the windscreen and an optional sunshade. The Ghia fun cars were designed without the sophistication of windscreen wipers, although the Multipla version, for some reason, was so equipped.

Fiat 600s were amongst the first to be produced under licence by this Yugoslavian company. Here, a model based on the 600D is seen in rural surroundings. Note the Zastava badges on the front panel. (Courtesy Haymarket)

The Spring was the last of the Siatas, a company perhaps better known for producing engine modifications for the Topolino. Based on the running gear of the 850, the Spring represented a return to the trend of producing rather attractive derivazioni of Fiat models. (Courtesy National Motor Museum)

The 600 was produced by SEAT at Barcelona from 1957 until, eventually, all export models were transferred to the Spanish works after production ceased in Italy. This 4-door model appears rather stretched, especially with the addition of rear quarterlights. (Courtesy Haymarket)

SEAT

Established in 1953 at Barcelona, the SEAT organisation based car production almost entirely on Fiat designs. SEAT's version of the 600 was produced from 1959 and in 1964 alone some 76,000 cars were assembled. As has been detailed elsewhere, all export production of 600Ds was eventually transferred to Barcelona. A specially-designed 4-door variant was also produced: with suicide doors and a rear quarterlight the saloon on a stretched platform looked decidedly ungainly.

Siata

Prior to the Topolino, Siata mainly traded in customized versions of Fiat cars. When the 500 was announced in 1936, the company produced an overhead valve conversion for the normal side-valve engine. Later, when the Fiat 600 was introduced, a few Siata convertible versions appeared with 735cc engines, but only until 1960 when Abarth took an interest in the company and produced the Siata Abarth Berlina.

Zastava

The Yugoslavian plant at Kragujevac was established a year after Seat's factory at Barcelona. Amongst the first cars to be produced was a Fiat 600-derived model. An enlarged factory was completed in 1964 with the capacity for building 82,000 cars a year. The new plant initially concentrated on the Fiat 600D before continuing with the Zastava 750S, which was generally similar but equipped with a modified fascia and instrument cowl. Although the bodywork was identical to the Fiat, it lost much of its brightwork and embellishment.

Motor Holdings, New Zealand

Fiat 500 Nuovas were also produced in New Zealand by Motor Holdings of Auckland. Traditionally builders of British orientated variants, it was a measure of some success for Fiat to gain a foothold in New Zealand's motor industry. The price for producing Fiat-based cars was a fair percentage of locally-produced components such as brake hoses and cables, paints and solvents, exhaust systems, batteries, wiring looms, speedometer cables, air filters and interior trim. Almost 5000 Nuova 500s were sent to New Zealand in kit form for local assembly before the plant was upgraded to build Fiat 850-based cars.

The numerous versions and variants of the 600 and 500 Nuova, some more successful than others, serve to illustrate the soundness and versatility of the basic design of both cars and how automobile history is all the richer for their existence.

Three variations on a theme: on the left is a 500 Jolly all dressed up for the beach; centre is a 500F for 1968 and in fighting mood is the Autobianchi Giardiniera. (Courtesy Haymarket)

FIAT 500 & 600

VIII

THE END OF AN ERA

Enter the 850

The Fiat 600D had been on the market four years with annual production in excess of a quarter of a million cars when the "all-new" 850 saloon made its debut in May 1964. The family resemblance of the two models is immediately recognizable, the basic character of the 850 being directly inherited from the 600. Even the type designation 100 was retained, although with the suffix letter 'G', presumably for grande, translated as meaning large or long.

Appreciating the success of the 600, Fiat had been anxious to extend its small to medium size model range as early as the late 1950s with the intention that the newcomer would eventually take over from the 600. Dante Giacosa had already established some provisional ideas on future development which included front-wheel-drive and engine sizes of one litre capacity. It is therefore a little curious that the 850 with its obvious ancestry was chosen as the future breadwinner.

Without delving into the vast depths of Fiat history, politics and intrigue, it is sufficient to note that a number of designs and prototypes were contemplated, which included completely new body styles and front-wheel-drive. Fiat's researches were channelled in a three-dimensional pattern: Simca developed the 1000, Autobianchi the Primula and Fiat the 850. Of all of these the most significant was the Autobianchi with its three-door hatchback styling, transverse engine and front-wheel-drive.

The principles of the 600 were retained in the 850: engine layout was practically the same with its in-line 4-cylinder water-cooled unit mounted at the rear with the radiator positioned alongside; suspension was generally similar although an anti-roll bar was fitted at the front in addition to the transverse leaf spring. Despite the

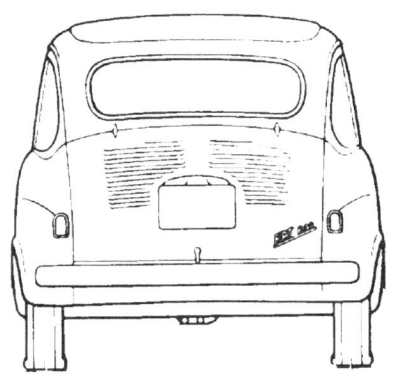

A final series 600D side by side with the car originally intended to supersede it. The 850 was introduced in 1964 and subsequently received modifications in 1968 to appear as the 850 Special. (Author's collection)

From this angle, the family likeness between the 600, on the left, and the 850 is clearly seen. (Author's collection)

family likeness and unitary construction, the body pressings were different to those of the 600 and a few inches were added to the overall dimensions. In essence, the "all-new" 850 was not quite so new. Successful beyond all doubt, it was, nevertheless, a stop-gap while research continued on formulating a new corporate model range. Whilst Giacosa recognized the route of future development, the appearance of a new model retaining a rear engine when other manufacturers relentlessly surged ahead with front-wheel-drive was, in the least, odd.

The development of the 850 had been fraught with difficulties: Fiat senior management had bypassed and overridden Giacosa to implement changes to specification and, in the final days of the car's design and testing, a major decision was taken by Oscar Montabone to alter its rear shape from that of a fastback to a notchback. All the while Giacosa contended with such meddling in affairs, he was already smarting from being up-staged by Issigonis' clever development of the Mini.

There were several design differences between the 600 and 850. The fuel tank, instead of being located under the front bonnet, was relocated between the rear seat and the engine compartment; the length of the car was increased by 14.17 inches (360mm), width by 1.77 inches (45mm) and the wheelbase lengthened by 1.06 inches (27mm). The increased dimensions safely placed the 850 into the 4/5 seater category although much of the spartan nature of the 600 remained. Power was also increased – with the 767cc engine bored out to 843cc the top speed was given a 10mph (16kph) boost, raising the maximum to around 76mph (122kph). Most noticeable was the difference to the rear styling which incorporated an extension to the engine housing. Apart from adding to the aesthetics, Montabone's reason for modifying the car at a late stage was to increase the car's overall performance.

Further developments led to the

850 Special being put through its paces. The 'Special' designation denoted a revised trim and mechanical changes which included disc brakes on the front wheels. (Courtesy Haymarket)

A trio of 850s. On the left a saloon, flanked on the right by the Coupé, a Fiat design department product. In the background is the Bertone Spyder which mainly found its market in America. (Courtesy Haymarket)

850 Super which squeezed another couple of miles per hour from the engine. Two years after the 850's launch the Idroconvert arrived, a semi-automatic version which did away with the clutch pedal but retained manual gearchange by use of a torque converter. A further two years on, in 1968, the 850 Special with revised trim and frontal styling appeared. The 843cc engine was made to deliver a maximum of 52bhp and 84mph (134kph) but to effectively control the new-found power, disc brakes were fitted to the front wheels which received larger section tyres. The trim of the Special was accordingly updated with a sports steering wheel and revised seating.

Three variants appeared: the 850T, a modified version of the Multipla based upon the O.M. station wagon; the 850 Coupé and the Spyder. The Coupé, an extremely pretty machine and obviously a development of the 850 saloon, was the product of Fiat's own styling department; the Spyder, however, was the inspiration of Bertone by whom it was built. Both sports versions used the 843cc engine with power increased from 42bhp to 52bhp for the Coupé and 54bhp for the Spyder. The speed of the Coupé matched that of the Special saloon, whilst the Spyder achieved 90mph (144kph). Naturally, disc brakes were fitted

Abarth also turned its attention to the 850. Early modifications produced the 130 and 150 – the model designation serving to indicate the maximum speed in kilometres per hour – which received only the mildest of tuning. It was left to the Abarth 1000 to provide the real performance and with engine capacity of up to 982cc and 54bhp, it was good for speeds in excess of 94mph (150kph). Then arrived the 1600, its 1592cc engine shoe-horned into the tail; speed shot up to 135mph (216kph) although it is claimed 150mph (240kph) was possible. The real demon was the 2000 Berlina "Mostra" which had a claimed maximum speed of 160mph (256kph). A one-off car, the Mostra was acclaimed for its fearful performance. Needless to say, Abarth also modified the 850 Coupé and Spyder variants with some success and transformed what were mild-mannered sporting cars into mighty performers in true Italian tradition.

The 600D remained in production in Italy until 1969 and from then on continued to be built long after in Fiat factories around the world. After the hype and furore of the 850 as the car to continue Fiat's fortunes, it lasted just a little over a year longer than its predecessor. Total production accounted for some 1.78 million saloons. The Coupé and Spyder remained in production until 1973 with a little over million cars built, most of the Spyders, however, were exported to the USA. Only the 850T, dubbed the Familiare, saw a prolonged production period and served as a highly versatile and rugged competitor to Volkswagen's campervan.

Fiat 127 and Panda

The real successors to the 600 were the Fiat 127, launched in 1971, and the Panda, which was introduced in 1980. Styled by Pio Manzu, the 127 made its debut without him seeing the fruits of his efforts: on the day the car was to be officially accepted by Fiat's Presidential Committee, Manzu was killed on his way

The Fiat 127 is a direct successor to the 600. Styled by Pio Manzu, the main ingredients were front-wheel-drive and a transverse engine. (Courtesy Fiat Auto (UK) & Fiat SPA Ltd)

to Turin from Rome in his 500. Apart from its modern hatchback styling, the 127 was most significant for its front-wheel-drive and transverse engine. The Panda also carried two-box construction and front-wheel-drive but in a package extremely angular in shape.

As if clutching at a past legacy, the Panda was initially offered with an optional twin-cylinder 652cc engine for home sales, while export models were fitted with an 843cc motor or the 903cc unit that had originally seen service in the 127. Eventually a four-wheel drive version became available. Utility was the Panda's key word and it could be forgiven because the car was competing directly with the like of Citroën's Dyane and Renault's 4L with its fold-back roof, tubular deck chair seats and a fabric fascia which doubled as a parcel shelf.

The other direct descendant of the 600 is the Panda. When first introduced it was thoroughly utilitarian and could be specified with the twin-cylinder 652cc engine for home market orders. The car pictured here is the CLX with full-length sunroof. (Courtesy Fiat (UK) & Fiat SPA Ltd)

Fiat 126

Appearing less than two years after the 127, the 126 reversed Fiat's trend

The 500's replacement, the 126. For a time Fiat marketed the 500R which shared the 126 platform, engine and wheels. Rather more angular than the 500, there is a hint of 127 styling at the rear but generally the 500's cheeky character has remained. (Courtesy Claire Scott)

of adopting front-wheel-drive, sharing its rear-positioned, air-cooled twin with the 500R. The 126 was the 500's true successor, assuming a slightly larger body and bigger engine at 594cc. Although Fiat 500 enthusiasts would have it otherwise, much of the Nuova's appeal can also be found in the 126, although there is a hint of the 127's styling, especially at the rear. It was originally intended that the 126 – in the form of a slightly re-designed Nuova to enable it to be a 4-seater rather than a 2+2 – share a great deal more of the 500's character. This concept would have allowed the costs to be kept to an absolute minimum whilst giving new life to a proven and greatly admired principle. In all respects, history was seen to be repeating itself when Giacosa returned to some of the original sketches he had considered for the 500 in its development stages. Prototype cars, slightly larger but distinctly reminiscent of the 500, were seen to include extra cooling vents above the rear wings. Giacosa's views for the 500's replacement were rejected out of hand with the consequence that he paid less attention to the project, leaving Paolo Boano to carry on the search for a suitable solution. By 1970 the stage had been reached whereby serious consideration could be given to a specific design.

The car that was announced on 22nd October 1972 was, in all fairness, surprisingly akin to the concept of the 500. With a more boxy, less curvaceous appearance and slightly larger dimensions, the 126 really was still only a 2+2. Differences in size were minimal: the wheelbase remained virtually the same, within a millimetre or so of the 500, the 126 was less than 4 inches (100mm) longer and 2 inches (50mm) wider, while the roof line saved 2 inches (50mm) in height. Larger wheels, 13 inch (330mm), ensured that the 126 was well-shod. The new bodyshell and increased engine power assisted in achieving a respectable 65mph (105kph), made all the easier by a synchromesh gearbox. Extra interior space provided greater comfort and, by placing the fuel tank under the rear seat, more luggage space became available under the front bonnet. As for interior styling, not much had changed from the 500: choke and starter controls remained at floor level and the dashboard supported a single pod-shaped nacelle which incorporated both speedometer and fuel gauge. No longer was a sunroof supplied as standard equipment, which was certainly a minus for the 126; there was, however, some compensation from improved heating and ventilation which was capable of mixing both warm and cool air.

Variations of the original 126 soon began to appear and at the beginning of 1974 the 126L – which included a sunroof as standard – made its debut. At the end of 1976, the de Ville arrived with an engine capacity increase to 652cc; the special edition de Ville boasted the luxury of velour cloth seats, carpets and cloth trim on the lower part of the doors. More powerful brakes, sound-proofing, a heated rear window and an alternator all added to driving pleasure.

The most significant change to affect the 126 occurred with the announcement of the Bis in September 1987. Billed as an encore, the Bis received far more than just skin-deep treatment. With a production move to FSM in Poland, the 126 received a smart new cloth-trimmed interior, an instrument panel that could be called comprehensive (certainly by 500 and 126 standards) and a rear seat that folded down to increase luggage space. Further improvements included provision of a rear wash-wipe and the disappearance of the heating control valve beneath the rear seat. By far the most dramatic change, however, was the transformation of the 126 into a three-door hatchback made possible by a new engine laid on its side.

In order to provide a tailgate the 126 underwent a fundamental mechanical change. The robust and reliable air-cooled vertical twin, the origin of

Engine size on the 126 eventually increased to 652cc which helped propel the car with a little less effort. This version of the 126 is shown with side protectors. (Courtesy Claire Scott)

Hatchback versatility arrived with the 126 Bis. By adopting a water-cooled engine and turning it on its side, it was possible to conceal it under the rear floor. (Courtesy Fiat Auto [UK] & Fiat SPA Ltd)

Front three-quarter view of the 126 BIS hatchback – a very practical small car. (Courtesy Fiat Auto [UK] & Fiat Spa Ltd).

As well as building the 126 Bis, FSM also produced their own convertible. The doors are redesigned to give extra strength and rigidity to the bodyshell. Close inspection shows the conversion to be rather crude, however. (Author's collection)

With a sturdy panel concealing the engine it was possible to not only have a rear luggage boot of almost generous proportions but, by folding the back seat, allow a flat loading platform, so converting the 126 into a load carrier with easy access through the full-height tailgate.

In hatchback form, the 126 swallowed vast amounts of luggage for a car of such tiny dimensions: for town and country alike it proved an ideal vehicle, the ultimate in a long succession of baby Fiats.

Cinquecento

Progression of technology dictated a completely new direction for Fiat's small car 35 years after the Nuova first appeared. As successor to the Topolino, 600, Nuova 500 and 126, the 500 was born again as the Cinquecento.

The development of the Cinquecento goes back to the late 1970s and was the responsibility of Mario Maioli who,

Despite the Cinquecento's diminutive proportions, it nevertheless set new standards in aerodynamics with a Cd figure of just 0.33. The interior layout enabled tall drivers to be accommodated in complete comfort, although Fiat's claim that the car was a five-seater suggests cramped conditions if all were adults. (Courtesy Fiat Auto [UK] & Fiat SPA Ltd.)

which could be traced back to the very first Nuova of 1957 and beyond, was superseded by a brand new engine. Still of two cylinders, water replaced air for cooling and the unit turned flat so that it nestled down neatly behind the rear wheels, almost similar in concept to the Giardiniera. Rear side air-intakes, increased in size in order to dispense with the grilles on the rear panel, together with a side-positioned radiator and electric fan, provided adequate cooling. Another 52cc pushed the capacity to 704cc and top speed to a fraction over 70mph (112kph) which was out of all proportion to the Topolino and original 500 Nuova.

until his retirement in the mid-1990s, was head of Fiat's own design centre Centro Stile and architect of such models as the Fiat Panda and Uno; the latter being voted "Car of the Year in 1984." Whereas Fiat's other small cars, the 126 and 127, had a sloping C-pillar which compromised rear passenger headroom, Maioli began to reverse this trend, firstly with the Panda, then the Uno and, to greater effect, with the Lancia Y10. By adopting a steeply raked rear design it was possible, with the Cinquecento's introduction, to devote as much as 58% of the car's volume to containing passengers and luggage. Using clever design principles, Fiat's engineers managed to pack a lot into a small area and, at just 10ft 7in (3,227mm) long, the Cinquecento can seat five people (not all adults!) in considerable comfort.

Careful attention to the car's styling and aerodynamic efficiency was necessary to ensure reasonable performance. The Cinquecento's surprisingly low Cd figure of 0.33 was made possible by adopting features incorporated into the design of the Uno and Tipo, such as an aerodynamic profile, together with a narrow roof line and 'clamshell' doors which wrap around the windscreen pillar and flow smoothly into the roof panel (dispensing with the need for protruding rain gutters). One result of the Cinquecento's efficient styling proved to be its low level of wind noise, a particularly welcome feature on long motorway journeys.

Mario Maioli's insistence that, above all, the Cinquecento needed to be a highly practical car, resulted in a high level of passenger protection. Exceeding EEC crash test legislation at the time of its launch, side-impact reinforcement provided additional passenger safety, a factor Fiat considered crucial in view of the vehicle's 'city car' role making it particularly vulnerable to side-on mishaps in urban traffic conditions. Protecting the passenger zone as a 'safety cell,' the front and rear structures of the car were designed to deform in the event of a major accident. The stringent US safety regulations were met, the Cinquecento featuring a strengthened floor with large transverse reinforcements and a transverse strut fitted between the two windscreen pillars in addition to a braced central B-pillar. In the case of an impact, therefore, the car conformed to roof section strength requirements. Front and rear bumpers were made from recyclable polypropylene; the doors were notably large and had a wide opening to ensure accessibility.

Interior accommodation proved particularly generous, with ample shoulder and headroom. Adequate leg and foot room was available because the passenger side of the facia was curved, and the undersides of the front seats were specially shaped so that rear occupants had good foot clearance. A large window area added to the Cinquecento's practicality and the good all-round visibility was furthered by the simple but elegant instrument binnacle.

The Cinquecento's comparatively long wheelbase (86.6in/2,200mm) allowed not only a comfortable driving position for a person over 6ft tall, but optimised the car's stability and handling characteristics, features enhanced by the use of full-size 13 inch wheels. Safety, of course, was paramount and the 9.5in/240mm front disc and rear drum brakes were designed to provide exceptional stopping power; servo-assistance was added for consistently light pedal pressures, and a load proportioning valve reduced the possibility of premature wheel lock-up under heavy braking conditions. A turning circle of a tight 28.9ft/8.8m was made possible by adoption of rack and pinion steering and MacPherson strut front suspension. Rear suspension comprised a trailing arm design (as used on the Fiat Tipo) and anti-dive under braking suspension geometry characteristics were also employed.

Corrosion problems blighted many car manufacturers during the 'seventies and 'eighties and experience in preventive techniques resulted in protection designed for long-term effectiveness. All external body parts manufactured from steel had the benefit of being zinc-coated on both sides, with extra synthetic protection applied to the front wheelarches. Additionally, rear suspension arms were manufactured from aluminium-coated steel.

Longevity and reliability were the key issues of the Cinquecento's design and, from the outset, servicing intervals, at 9,000 miles (14,400km), were designed to be as minimal as possible. Intensively tested before the car was presented to the motoring public, 750 prototypes covered 5 million gruelling miles (8 million km) to iron-out potential weaknesses. Fuel consumption was obviously an important criteria and, alongside the ultra-economy of the 2-cylinder water-cooled engine, even the the 4-cylinder power unit proved it could return well in excess of 40mpg (7lt/100km), even when being driven particularly hard.

Fiat unveiled the Cinquecento in Rome during December 1991. The intention was not merely to offer a successor to those cars produced between the '30s and '80s, but to serve a traffic-conscious society with a new generation vehicle which was as environmentally friendly as possible. In concept and technology the Cinquecento led the field in small car design: diminutive external measurements belied its internal dimensions and accommodation. When sitting at the wheel of the Cinquecento and experiencing the amount of usable space, it's almost impossible to believe the car is only fractionally longer than a Mini.

The specification of the Cinquecento at its introduction included the option of the in-line 704cc 2-cylinder water-cooled engine, as installed in the 126Bis, or a transverse 903cc 4-cylinder catalytic unit which originally powered the Fiat 127 and Autobianchi A112. There was nothing out of the ordinary about the 4-cylinder engine; a four-in-line unit with a cast iron block, light alloy cylinder head and in-line valves operated by pushrods with hydraulic tappets. A third option was also available, an electric car, the Cinquecento Elettra, intended for use in large towns and cities, and guaranteed to produce zero emissions. Designed to be plugged into any 220 volt mains socket to recharge

Fiat revised its Cinquecento range in 1995, having already modified the 4-cylinder engine in 1993 from a capacity of 903cc to 899cc to comply favourably with taxation arrangements in a number of countries. The model range comprised four versions, S, SX, Suite and Soleil (for some markets the Suite was unavailable and the 2-cylinder engine was also withdrawn from the catalogue. Although surprisingly well-equipped, the S was the base model; the SX offering a greater degree of sophistication. Air conditioning was standard with the Suite, but offering an element of fun was the Soleil which, apart from its full-length electrically operated fabric roof, had the same refinements as the SX. (Courtesy Fiat Auto [UK] & Fiat SPA Ltd.)

Available in mainland Europe in 1994, and the UK in 1995, the Sporting version of the Cinquecento offered real panache. The 1108cc, 54bhp engine from the Fiat Punto was shoe-horned under the bonnet, resulting in stunning performance and a top speed of around 150kph/93mph. (Courtesy Fiat Auto [UK] & Fiat SPA Ltd.)

the batteries, the Elettra could only be supplied as a 2-seater, the rear seats having been removed to make room for the battery pack.

In 1993 the 903cc push-rod engine, which was produced in the former Yugoslavia at the Yugo car plant at Kragujevac by Zastava, was replaced by an almost identical unit, but with a displacement of 899cc to comply favourably with vehicle taxation laws in a number of countries.

A high performance Cinquecento became available in 1994 with introduction of the Sporting version which used Fiat's 54bhp 1,108cc Fire engine.

Crisp styling immediately created a sports image and the car was clearly identifiable by the asymmetrical air intake, body-coloured rear-view mirrors and bumpers (the latter with a black central strip) and the four-spoke alloy wheels with low profile tyres. At the rear an oval exhaust pipe added a distinctive visual element. A closer look at the car revealed lowered suspension (20mm) although the car's stiffer shock absorbers and front anti-roll bar were unseen.

The Sporting was treated to an all-new interior trim which included anatomically-shaped seats with red seat belts, leather-trimmed steering wheel and gearlever, a redesigned instrument panel to include a rev counter, and the addition of a perforated metal accelerator pedal to further the sporty image. The facia, steering column housing, door pockets and rear panels were finished in charcoal grey, while the contrasting dark grey seat upholstery had a multicolour stripe pattern in distinctive shades to compliment the dramatic external finishes, Sporting Red, Broom Yellow and Black. Further features included electrically operated front windows, central locking, athermic glazing and halogen headlamps.

The Cinquecento Sporting's performance was stunning compared to

Sporting versions were available in a range of paint finishes as bright as the car's performance potential. Colour-coded bumpers and mirrors, plus an asymmetrical air intake added to the car's bold styling treatment. Alloy wheels and low profile tyres were all part of the package, as well as lowered suspension and an oval exhaust tailpipe. (Courtesy Fiat Auto [UK] & Fiat SPA Ltd.)

the standard Cinquecento, the Fiat Punto derived engine and gearbox permitting a maximum speed of over 93mph/150kph. Refinements in engine design, which included modifying the shape and thickness of the engine block as well as the addition a crankshaft damper to the front pulley, resulted in later Sporting models being less noisy than earlier cars.

Early in 1996 Fiat announced a range of special accessories – marketed under the Abarth banner – for the Sporting models. Included was an even lower suspension set-up, five-spoke alloy wheels, aerodynamic bumpers, spoiler and side skirts. Mechanically, multi-point fuel injection raised the car's power output to 90bhp; brakes developed from those used on the Uno Turbo were also specified.

During the Summer of 1995 Fiat overhauled the Cinquecento model range; four engine options (including the Elettra model) were available (the 704cc 2-cylinder unit was dropped in some markets). In 900 guise, three models were offered, the S, SX and Suite, the latter being top-of-the range with air-conditioning as standard. All were powered by the 899cc 4-cylinder unit, while the Sporting continued to use the 1100 Fire engine. In the Spring of 1996 the Soleil version was added to the range; apart from an electrically-operated double-layer fabric roof and a dedicated metallic paint finish range as well as white, the specification was comparable with that of the SX.

The S became the base model with the 900 engine and was offered with basic trim: the SX was more elabo-

Special interior trim and extra instrumentation identified the Sporting from the rest of the Cinquecento range. Equipment levels, which were impressive, included electric windows, central locking and halogen headlamps. (Courtesy Fiat Auto [UK] & Fiat SPA Ltd.)

rate and featured side rubbing strips, a glass pop-up sunroof, central locking and electric front windows, a driver's airbag, front seat belt pre-tensioners (both optional on the S), metallic paint and colour co-ordinated bumpers completed the package. The Suite embodied all of the SX's features but additionally had air-conditioning and body-coloured door handles, rear-view mirrors and bumpers. The Suite was not available in the UK but the Soleil was; marketed more as a fun car, the vehicle had certain appeal with its electrically operated wide-opening fabric roof and attractively patterned seats.

Production of the Cinquecento ceased in early 1998 and, during the car's seven year history, some 50,000 units were built.

Out-performing almost every other car of its size, the Sporting's underbonnet equipment was shared with the Fiat Punto. Refinements appeared in later production models - a redesigned engine block and a crankshaft damper on the front pulley, resulting in lower noise levels. (Courtesy Fiat Auto [UK] & Fiat SPA Ltd.)

Seicento

The arrival of Fiat's new baby car in March 1998, the Seicento (or 600), took the small-car concept, so ably designed by Dante Giacosa in the 1930s, into the 21st Century. Slightly larger than the Cinquecento, the Seicento is designed as a city car with a refinement that makes it eminently suitable for longer journeys. The Seicento's styling, which is softer and more curvaceous than that of its predecessor, belies the fact the car is smaller than its rivals.

As small as it is, the Seicento has a surprisingly roomy interior, large enough to accommodate five people. It is remarkably similar to the formula originally considered by Fiat for a baby car; a minimal car with a water-cooled engine and front-wheel drive. With evolution, the fundamental concept has not been forgotten.

Successor to the Cinquecento, the Seicento which was launched throughout mainland Europe in the Spring of 1998. Fiat's objective was to reinterpret the design and engineering features typical of a compact car. Although smaller than its major rivals (3.32 metres long and 1.5 metres wide), the Seicento is marginally larger than its predecessor. A softer styling trend has been adopted with the result that it looks bigger than it actually is. The Seicento boasts a roomy interior and is approved as a 5-seater. The new baby Fiat is therefore the ideal city car, but with the refinement and comfort necessary for longer and more demanding journeys.
The Seicento was launched with two engine options, 900cc and 1100c, and both offer excellent fuel economy – a feature of all baby Fiats – as well as good performance. The Citymatic version has an automatic clutch, and the Seicento Elettra has sufficiently small batteries to allow accommodation for four people. The Polish plant at Tychy produces the Seicento and, like all Fiat's production facilities throughout the world, features state-of-the-art technology to ensure the highest standards of product quality. (Courtesy Fiat Auto (UK) and Fiat SPA Ltd.)

IX

LIVING WITH A BABY FIAT

Ask any motoring historian to name the most outstanding cars ever designed and, somewhere near the top of the list, along with the Austin Seven, Ford Model T, Morris Minor, VW Beetle and Citroën 2CV, will be the Fiat 500. The tiny Italian contender is considered an icon in motor car design for very good reason: for over sixty years it has proved that the best things are wrapped in the smallest parcels.

Almost every driver in Italy has at some time owned a baby Fiat. The car is to the Italians what the 2CV is to the French, the Beetle to the Germans and the Morris Minor and Mini to the British. If 'Fiat is Italy,' as was once said, then the fun-loving 500 mirrors the nation's youth. Italy, and the world, fell in love with the 500 with the debut of the Topolino in 1936: the adoration continued with the 600 and 500 Nuova in the 'fifties. Now, in the 'nineties, the Cinquecento, and its successor the Seicento, is providing motorists everywhere with a car which is both

As demure as it is, the Fiat Topolino has immense charm – particularly in original 500A guise – and is keenly sought after by enthusiasts who recognise the car's relative rarity. Despite its size and tiny engine, the 500 was blessed with spirited performance, a factor appreciated by its devotees which included the fifth Lord Howe, who was President of the British Racing Drivers' Club and the ERA Club. Only a handful of Topolinos (all types) have survived in the UK and even less are in roadworthy condition, although greater numbers exist in mainland Europe, namely Italy, Holland, Germany and Switzerland. (Courtesy Fiat Auto [UK] & Fiat SPA Ltd.)

The Siata Special was one of a number of models based on the Fiat Topolino offered by specialist coachbuilders. The car's sporting aptitude is shown to good effect here in this evocative, if rather damaged, photograph taken while the car was competing in the 1939 RAC Rally. In the driving seat is A.C.Westwood, who's getting to grips with an uphill section along an unmade woodland track. (Author's collection)

accommodating and seriously fun-loving. Nothing fundamental has changed in sixty years.

Topolino

Although built in relatively large numbers – over half a million were produced (without counting those vehicles manufactured in France as the Simca Cinq) – the car is now something of a rarity, especially right hand drive versions.

The 500A is the most sought-after model because of its styling originality, the exposed headlamps giving the little car a cheeky appearance worthy of its 'Topolino' nickname. Marque devotees are, however, always on the lookout for the elusive 500B which, sharing the same basic shape as the 500A, was fitted with an overhead valve engine instead of the earlier side valve affair. Produced for one year only, a mere 21,623 500Bs were built before the 500C made its appearance in 1949. Retaining the 569cc ohv engine, the 500C featured full-width frontal styling and a reshaped tail which concealed the spare wheel in a compartment beneath the boot floor. Despite its restyling the 500C, fortunately, lost none of the original lovable image for which the Topolino was admired. Over twice as many 500Cs were built as the 500A and 500B combined and, as a result, today's values for these cars tend to be slightly lower than the earlier series.

For the Topolino, values are somewhat academic as few cars have survived in the UK compared to the rest of Europe. Those enthusiasts fortunate enough to find a car in concours condition will have to pay rather more for

The Topolino was a familiar competitor in all types of motoring events and, despite is diminutive size, was particularly agile. This appears to be a navigation run. (Author's collection)

a 500B than a 500A or 500C. A good condition 500B can command prices of ₤12,500-£15,000, while a similar 500A will command around £11,000. A pristine 500C will attract values of £7000-£10,000 while a structurally-sound example requiring mechanical attention and some trim refurbishment will cost in the region of £4000-£5500. For this amount the purchaser would expect the car to be complete, free of rust and rot and running.

Replacement parts can be difficult to source; the French specialist Depanoto

The Topolino was built in France as the Simca Cinq and parts for these cars are still available through recognised specialists. Values of the Simcas are similar to those for the Italian models, but estate and van versions, as depicted here, are at a premium due to their rarity. This Simca was pictured at the 1997 Beaulieu Autojumble. (Author's collection)

at Nogent Le Retrou, near Le Mans, keeps a good stock (they also supply parts for Simca, Peugeot, Renault and Citroën) otherwise it will mean contacting specialists in Holland, Switzerland or Italy. Both the Fiat 500 Club and the Fiat Register have contacts throughout Europe. Trim parts are specially difficult to source, particularly such items as the smart wing top direction indicators fitted to the 500C models. There is no need to panic over tyres, though: Michelin's skinny 125x15s will fit and are in plentiful supply because they also fit some types of Renault 4 and Citroën's 2CV and derivatives.

Areas of a Topolino to check include the chassis, which should be free of corrosion; the cabin floor, which can corrode at the scuttle point, and the boot floor. Doors should open and close easily, the locks should operate and the sliding glass should be intact. Make sure that the window locks work and that the window channels are free from corrosion. Also lift up the battery compartment behind the seats (rear seats were never fitted except for 400 British-built Topolinos) to check that no leakage is apparent and that the base is not corroded. On 500C models 12-volt electrics are provided which ensures easier starting. Under the bonnet everything appears very cramped and mechanical work can be impeded due to the sheer lack of space. The fuel tank, which is located under the bonnet and sits just above the driver's and passenger's knees, should be checked for leaks, especially the breather hose and overflow. It has been known for excess petrol to drip into the cabin with potentially disastrous results. Check the roof, too: most examples of Topolino have a simple fabric folding affair which should be draught-free and watertight; make sure the folding mechanism works and the hood fits correctly.

Both engine types are perfectly straightforward and, with proper maintenance, provide longevity. The four-speed gearbox is, like the engine, very durable but can be prone to some whine, especially in second gear. If the noise develops to any great extent it will be necessary to remove the gearbox to fully investigate the problem. Do not be cajoled into believing that a thick gear oil will cure the noise; the whine might disappear for a while, but the underlying problem will remain.

Some play in the steering mechanism will often be encountered and, to cure this the king pins may have to be replaced. On cars which have a very high mileage, or have been mechanically neglected, wear in the steering assembly might mean removal and restoration of the complete system. Cars that have been standing for any length of time will possibly suffer from seized brake cylinders. Replacements are available but it might be prudent to overhaul the entire braking system to include brake shoes and brake pipes.

Inside the car all the controls and instruments, few as they are, should be operational. The ignition key operates the lights as well as the ignition; awkward to use, the key, when half-inserted, switches on the car's electrics and, when pushed fully home, activates the lights. A built-in indicator warns of insufficient battery charging. A simple flick-switch in the centre of the facia immediately below the windscreen works the direction indicators – flashers on the 500C but semaphores on the 500A and 500B. It is essential that the indicators operate properly because making hand signals in a Topolino is almost impossible; the efforts of a contortionist are needed to get an arm through the sliding windows. For such a small car the facia appears surprisingly well appointed and incorporates a central panel comprising two circular dials. In front of the driver is the speedometer and odometer and a similar dial in front of the passenger houses the fuel level and oil pressure gauges. Three push/pull controls operate the starter, choke and hand throttle and two other smaller switches activate the single speed windscreen wipers (which seem to move interminably slowly) and the control panel back light. The horn push button is situated in the centre of the steering wheel and the interior light

Successor to the 500A and B was the 500C. Despite the car's full-width frontal styling and reshaped tail, this, the last of the Topolino models, shared many of the earlier cars' characteristics. Although built in larger numbers than was the 500A, the 500C is relatively scarce and cars in good condition are not easy to find. The 569cc engine is responsive and provides spirited performance, the top speed being a little under 60mph/96kph. Here, the author's own car keeps good company with a 500L at a Fiat enthusiasts' event. (Author's collection)

is incorporated within the interior rear-view mirror.

The seats in such a tiny car are, understandably, narrow and, according to an occupant's size, accommodation tends to be somewhat cramped, although leg room is reasonable. Visibility is poor compared to today's standards; the plastic window in the hood is hardly transparent and the small windscreen and side glasses restrict all-round vision. Soundproofing is minimal, but for all its shortcomings the car is a delight to drive, the controls being remarkably light. There is a lot of play in the long gearlever but gearchanging, once the narrow gate is mastered, is as slick as a hot knife through butter. The handbrake is very positive and, instead of mechanically operating the rear brakes shoes, locks the transmission.

On the road, the Topolino is definitely fun. In good weather it is far better to have the hood down if only to relieve the effects of claustrophobia. Remember that the Topolino is a 2-seater and, despite Fiat's publicity claims when the car was first introduced, it really is unsuited for accommodating two children sitting on cushions on the rear platform! Considering the Topolino's minute proportions, together with its challenged muscle power, performance is very respectable up to 45mph (72kph), which is near the car's maximum speed.

As when considering the purchase of any classic car, do take careful advice when buying a Topolino; the outlay for having a specialist check the vehicle before purchase may seem an unwarranted expense, but a modest sum could save serious expenditure later. Likewise servicing: unless an owner is a competent mechanic it might be best to leave maintenance and repairs to a specialist. Any of the enthusiasts' clubs would be able to supply a list of recommended garages or mechanics, the services of which will enhance a car's driving and ownership pleasures.

The 600 and Multipla

As the spiritual successor to the Topolino, the Fiat 600 and its charming derivative, the Multipla, were amongst the most innovative cars of the mid-fifties. The compact design and, for the era, generous accommodation, ensured lasting popularity. Thanks to the car's introduction at a time when a reasonable purchase price and low running costs were essential, the healthy sales figures, both in Britain and the rest of Europe, have resulted in a greater than expected survival rate for the saloon. The Multipla, however, has faired less well and no more than a handful exist throughout the UK.

The advantage of the 600 over the

Introduced in 1955 (the car illustrated is a later model), the Fiat 600 was originally intended as the Topolino's replacement. Clamouring for something rather smaller, Italian motorists were rewarded with the 500 Nuova. Values of the 600 are not high even though good examples are hard to find. There are fewer surviving 600s than 500 Nuovas. Problem areas, as far as the enthusiast is concerned, are similar to those associated with the 500. (Courtesy Fiat Auto [UK] and Fiat SPA Ltd.)

Few Multiplas in this condition remain, so this example is a credit to its owner. Having the dimensions of the 600 Saloon, the Multipla, amazingly, could seat six and was a forerunner of the many MPVs which are popular today. (Courtesy Haymarket)

Topolino is that the car was designed as a genuine four-seater, the positioning of the engine above and behind the rear axle allowing the maximum amount of interior space to be utilised for passenger accommodation. A truly postwar car, the 600 shared little with its ancestor in the way of design and thus belonged to a whole new generation of models which, of course, included the 500 Nuova. The close relationship between the 600 and its smaller cousin, together with the fact that well over 2 million examples were produced, has meant that replacement parts are also generally more readily available than for the Topolino.

As regards ownership of a 600, the car has much in common with the 500 Nuova, despite the latter's lesser dimensions and different engine design. Information concerning the 600, therefore, is generally appropriate to its smaller relation, more of which follows later in this chapter. Of the remarkable six-seater – cum-camping-car derivative, the Multipla, which helped pioneer the entire concept of the multi-purpose vehicle – there is only a slight styling resemblance between the two models although they share the same running gear.

Values for the 600, like those of the Topolino, are somewhat academic, despite even this model's now relative rarity. The cult factor which surrounds the 500 Nuova is gradually extending to the 600 and prices of these cars are rising quite rapidly. Both Simon Lynes of Autotoys and Tony Castle-Miller of Middle Barton Garage recognise growing interest and are receiving an increasing number of enquiries.

Despite its distinctiveness and rarity, the Multipla, with its uniquely refreshing design, is now condemned to the category of time-forgotten cars. A few years ago it was incapable of raising more than modest prices, even for an example which had been well restored or was in good original condition. Things are different now; the Multipla has found new appeal and stirs the passions of many an enthusiast. Whenever a Multipla appears for sale it succeeds in attracting surprisingly high values, but it would need a dedicated devotee to take on a restoration project. Whilst the labours of renovation will certainly be repaid by the pleasures of owning and driving such a vehicle, the likelihood of ever recovering the expense in terms of both material costs and man-hours is slim. Ironically, it is over forty years since the Multipla was so successfully created, yet car designers have difficulty in devising a small car which is equally innovative or practical.

Mechanically, the 600 models are fairly straightforward; the bodyshell, with its integrated construction, can be the cause of problems to the extent that serious corrosion may preclude any satisfactory restoration, therefore committing the vehicle to be broken for spares.

Mechanical components and body panels (Multipla excepting) are available from specialist suppliers although demand for parts is somewhat limited compared to the 500 Nuova models. In many instances specialists rely upon obtaining supplies direct from Italy and the fact that some components are interchangeable with the Fiat 850 ensures that availability is good for the time being at least.

At the time of writing one of the most worrying issues as far as the enthusiast is concerned is the availability of leaded four-star petrol, which is scheduled to be discontinued by the year 2000 in Europe. In an attempt to provide customers with the opportunity to continue using their cars, marque specialists are anxiously devising engine conversions or modifications which will allow unleaded fuel to be used. The problem, of course, is not confined to Fiat owners but to all owners of classic, vintage and veteran cars which require leaded fuel.

When contemplating the purchase of a 600, several factors need to be considered. The price is obviously important but, with values as they are, the would-be purchaser should be prepared to pay a premium in order to acquire a car in the best condition. The compactness of the 600, together with

The 600 is vulnerable to decay around headlamps and along leading edges of front wings. Notice how rust has spread along the seams – the result of water penetration. (Courtesy Anthony Taylor)

When buying a 600 look for evidence of rust around the front wheelarches and rear section of front wings. This is a classic example of how decay can form on these cars. The floor pan must also be checked for signs of rust. (Courtesy Anthony Taylor)

its modest running costs, does make this the ideal vehicle for an enthusiast buying his or her first classic car. The fact that baby Fiats as a whole enjoy a wide following, and that an industry exists to cater for enthusiasts, makes ownership all the more enjoyable.

It is easy to fall in love with the first 600 you see, especially if it is polished, has clean windows and gleaming brightwork. All that glitters is not gold, however, and the unwary can be caught out by what cannot be immediately seen. A fresh coat of paint can often hide a multitude of sins and it is often best to have the car examined by an independent specialist who can determine its true condition. A car without any history should be treated with caution, but a vehicle which is known within club or enthusiasts' circles may prove to be a more reliable prospect.

Depending upon a purchaser's level of experience and mechanical abilities, a car costing considerably less than one that is pristine, and in a corresponding condition, may appeal, especially if a full restoration project is the intention. For a person without mechanical or engineering skills, attempting such a task will almost certainly result in disaster, leading to both disillusionment and a bank-breaking experience. The advice, therefore, is to purchase a car through a reputable and recognised specialist, even if the initial cost is a little higher than at first envisaged. The enjoyment of the car will last appreciably longer than any initial concern over its extra cost.

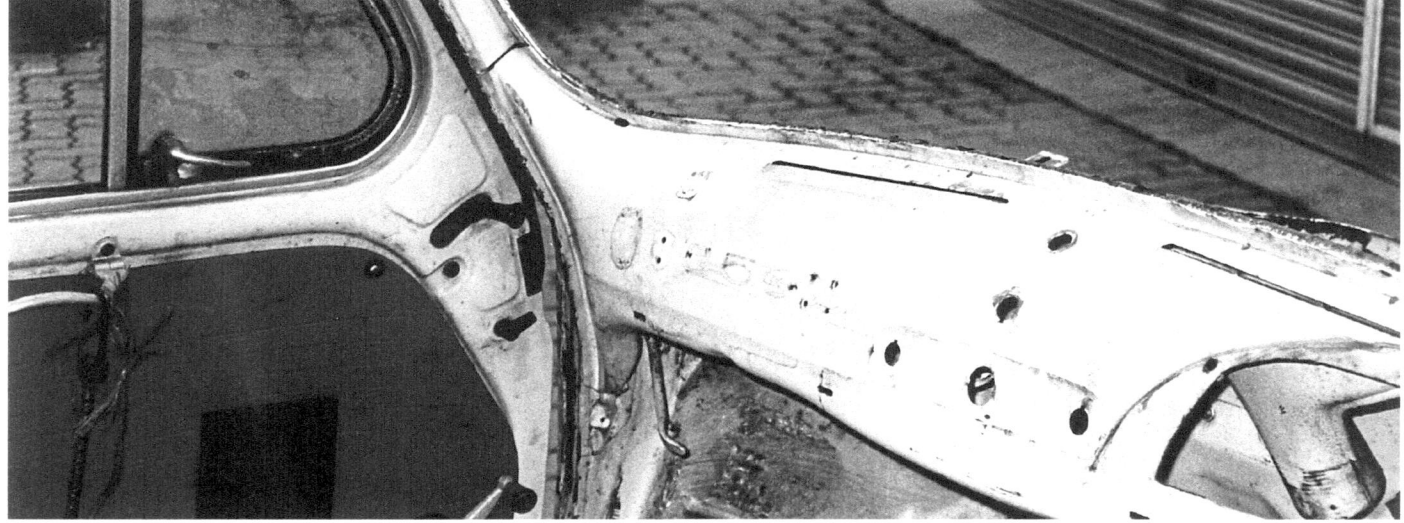

A Fiat 600 in Abarth guise undergoing early stages of restoration at Middle Barton Garage. There are signs of rust around the windscreen, heater vents and scuttle. (Courtesy Anthony Taylor)

Anthony Taylor's Fiat Abarth following restoration. Interest in the 600 range is generally increasing and having an affect on values, which are rising quite rapidly. It is not only Abarth conversions which are popular, but standard models, too. (Courtesy Anthony Taylor)

Anthony Taylor's resplendent 850cc Fiat Abarth in company with other racing Fiats. (Courtesy Anthony Taylor)

For those enthusiasts contemplating buying a 600 which has been subjected to tuning modifications, some caution must be exercised to determine that the conversion has been correctly carried out. Likewise, an enthusiast buying a 600 with the intention of preparing it to rallying or racing standards is well advised to consult the leading specialists in this field, such as Middle Barton Garage, at Middle Barton in Oxfordshire, Autotoys, or Radbourne Racing of Wimbledon in south west London. A number of other specialist firms around the world will prepare cars, and the enthusiast is advised to check with local clubs and the listings in this book's appendices.

The 600's successor, the 850, is unlikely to command anything other than rock bottom prices. The Coupé and

Early 500 Nuova's are difficult to find; despite this, values are seldom high. Performance of the very early models was dire, but improved with the introduction of the Normale. The specification of the first Nuova, the Economica, was very limited and, not surprisingly, sales were poor. Even in Italy, parts for the first generation cars are difficult to source. This illustration is a publicity photograph dating from the car's introduction in 1957. (Courtesy Fiat Auto [UK] and Fiat SPA Ltd.)

Spider versions fare a little better (top prices for a 850 Spider can be double that of a saloon and yet still fall short of £2500 at the time of writing), however, but, on the whole, apart from dedicated Fiat enthusiasts, the classic car fraternity have yet to recognise these attractive cars. As the running gear is similar to that of the 600 there is little to add to that already written, except to say that corrosion can present a severe problem. Happily, finding replacement parts is not too much of a problem and those specialists serving 600 owners will normally be able to help.

The Fiat 127, which is not really within the brief of this book, has yet to be accepted as a classic vehicle although, when introduced, its styling was largely responsible for it being voted Car Of The Year. Like many other cars of its era, the 127 suffered from chronic corrosion.

500 Nuova

Everyone recognises the little Fiat 500; its lovable and chubby styling is equally admired in Britain, America, Australia and beyond, as well as its native Italy. Its fan club is the classic car fraternity throughout the entire world and, happily, the 500's survival rate is excellent, thanks to a production record of well over 3 million units. A tribute to the car's designer, Dante Giacosa, the Fiat 500 – arguably the greatest little car ever produced – is very much alive and well.

The production demise of the Fiat 500 was mourned by its devotees everywhere; as soon as it was no longer available, everyone who had never experienced this legend of a motor car, wanted one. Accepted in society equally with a Ferrari, the successor to Italy's Little Mouse had simplicity of design to thank for its success and popularity.

As with all cars, the demure 500 has its plus and minus points. The minuses, such as limited accommodation, virtual absence of luggage carrying space and almost non-existence performance, are out-balanced by the plusses. Design simplicity, mechanical and build quality, reliability, an ability to go anywhere, longevity, economy and its sheer delightfulness to drive, not to mention its quirky charm, are its enduring strengths.

Notwithstanding the car's tiny proportions, inside and out, how a family of four Italians with their accoutrements ever managed to squeeze into its confines remains a mystery, despite the clever shoe-horning of the drivetrain into the tail. They did, however, and many a family photograph album has snapshots to prove it.

The demand for the 500 is commensurate with the model's commercial success; early types are now virtually impossible to find outside Italy, and even in the car's native land these are sourced with some difficulty – especially well-preserved examples. The original Nuova, the Economica, ultra-basic and

The 500D, which was introduced in 1960, is particularly sought-after amongst Fiat enthusiasts for its styling features which included 'suicide' doors and attractive trim detailing. The availability of parts for this, the final generation of early Nuova models, can be a problem outside Italy. (Author's collection)

far too slow for modern conditions, is very rare and, because the condition of an unrestored car is likely to be poor because parts simply do not exist, values are not high. Only a restored car in nothing less than pristine condition can attract 'collector's car' prices. With the introduction of the Normale, performance become close to acceptable, but even these cars are now virtually unobtainable.

The 500D, which was introduced in 1960, retained the original type of rear-hinged suicide doors and external trim detailing, which is so much a feature of these cars. This model, too, is now a rarity and parts, in similar vein to earlier models, can be exceptionally difficult to trace, Italian specialists mostly being the sole source. The most readily available models are, therefore, the later Nuovas, introduced in 1965, the 500F and 500L, which can readily be identified by having front-hinged doors.

Both the 500F and 500L versions were built until 1972, but it is the first-mentioned pre-1971 cars with metal facias, two-tone seats, a simple instrument pod and aluminium door push catches that are most sought after. Even these cars are getting more difficult to find and, by comparison, the 500L, with its 'luxury' trim and plastic facia, is quite common. The use of plastic on the 'Lusso' extends even to the trim around the guttering and is often a source of corrosion.

Values vary according to a car's condition rather than age, although very early cars in a restored and prime condition may attract higher than average prices. At the time of writing it is generally difficult to find a decent car offered as a private sale for under £4000, although MoT failures and those in need of complete renovation can be obtained for as little as £1500. Such examples should, of course, be treated with extreme caution as the amount of work required to restore a car to its original specification will be both time consuming and expensive. At the opposite extreme, a car in concours condition, or specialist-built, will command as much as £10,000. However, it should be possible to find a vehicle

Over two million post-1965 500 Nuovas were built and, thanks to the car's build and engineering quality, a large number have survived. A great many can still be seen in daily use throughout Europe, especially in Italy, Holland and Switzerland, where this 500L was photographed, in Zürich City Centre. (Courtesy Maria Cairnie)

Fiat 500 specialists exist throughout Europe; some only sell these cars, whilst others supply full service and restoration facilities. The cars for sale at this specialist near Horgen, in Switzerland, are all 500Ls. Some enthusiasts, however, prefer the 500F with its distinct interior styling. (Courtesy Maria Cairnie)

A severe case of decay, this 500 awaiting restoration illustrates some of those areas of a Fiat 500 Nuova which are vulnerable to rust. The wheelarches have all but disappeared and rot has extended to the bonnet edges. Rust has also formed in the weld seams, and around the headlamps. (Author's collection courtesy Jim and Sheila Ellis)

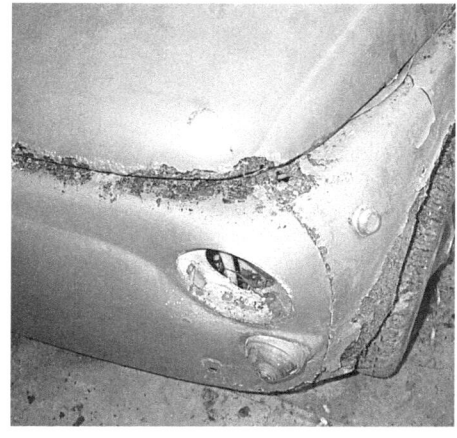

Rust has eaten through the tops of the wings, and the metal around the top of the front compartment is very thin. Luckily, replacement panels are available through Fiat specialists. (Author's collection courtesy Jim and Sheila Ellis)

which is in good original condition, has low mileage and is offered by a marque specialist for around £7500. The cars most popular with enthusiasts are usually those costing between £5000 and £6000.

Two less obvious factors can have an affect on the availability of good 500s: on average, because of the car's attractiveness and reasonable running costs, baby Fiats tend to have a lower ownership turnover than many other classic cars. A vehicle's colour can drag a price down; Fiat produced some awful colour schemes during the era of the 500 Nuova and it is not everybody that wants a dirty orange or lime-green coloured car!

No mention as yet has been made of the 500R, or the Giardiniera, for the reason that, outside mainland Europe, both are a rarity. The 500R was never imported to Britain, for example, but that does not mean that a prospective buyer will not stumble across a car which has been personally imported. Build numbers of the 500R were 334,000, half the total of 500Ds produced. Values of the 500R may be somewhat less than the 500L if only because, in true Fiat chronology, it had more to do with the 500 Nuova's successor, the Fiat 126. The Giardiniera is of such rarity that the already stated values may not necessarily apply, although too high a premium over the asking price for a saloon may be inappropriate. Although mechanically similar to the saloon, the Giardiniera has a slightly different drivetrain layout due to the engine being turned on its side to lay under the rear compartment floor. Body panels rear of the doors are different to those of the saloon and could be difficult to replace. A few van versions, based on the Giardiniera, were sold and have an interest value among dedicated enthusiasts.

Having decided life can no longer be sustained without a baby Fiat in the family, there shouldn't be any question as to whether it will fit in the garage. The car's diminutive size could even possibly allow several to be accommodated, depending upon available space. The investment is hardly likely to break the bank; running costs are very reasonable and insurance costs will mostly fall within the lower categories. Before committing to the purchase of a car though, there are a number of factors to be considered, not least of which is having some idea of what to expect from a particular vehicle in order to judge its overall condition; also the model's strengths and weaknesses as a whole. Regular maintenance is important; the chosen car, which may well be in pristine condition when purchased, will quickly show signs of wear and tear if neglected.

Seeking an honest vehicle in good condition, a prospective purchaser should generally avoid a poor 'do-it-yourself' rebuild. Cars having sub-standard paintwork should be treated with extreme caution; the surface of the car is a good indicator to the vehicle's general condition and a cheap respray will inevitably hide a multitude of horrors which will be expensive to rectify.

Check, initially, the car's exterior and look for any corrosion around the seams between the front panel and wings. Normally rust traps, the channels should be clean and clear; look for signs of previous repairs as water can penetrate body filler. The front panel itself is vulnerable to stone chipping

There is precious little luggage space in the Nuova's front compartment. The floor is vulnerable to rot and extensive rusting is evident in this instance. Care should always be taken when filling the petrol tank as access is restricted; some owners carry a funnel to avoid fuel spillage. (Author's collection courtesy Jim and Sheila Ellis)

Rust can form along the bottom of the windscreen, and at the rear of the wheelarches. (Author's collection courtesy Jim and Sheila Ellis)

Top – The new owner of this very tatty 500L is a glutton for punishment! There is virtually no part of the car which is not rotten due to neglect and abuse and Daniel Hammond looks somewhat concerned as his restoration project is delivered from a scrap dealer. Although it is unusual for a car to be in such an advanced state of decay, the extent of corrosion does, however, aptly illustrate the potential problem areas associated with 500 model range. Sills, door bottoms, floor pans and wheelarches are all vulnerable. Water can seep into the front compartment and settle into the well holding the spare wheel and in a short time rust can form; rot around the rear wheelarches can spread into the engine compartment to weaken the rear suspension, thus making repairs quite difficult. The engine cover, and the vent above it, is also susceptible to decay. Above – A happy ending. Following restoration, Daniel Hammond's 500L reflects the number of hours spent in carefully returning the car to its original condition. When attempting a restoration project such as this, it is worthwhile replacing the engine and gearbox, if badly worn, with a unit from the Fiat 126, which was the Nuova's successor. The increase in power will not only be appreciated but will also enhance the car's value. (Courtesy Daniel Hammond)

which, if not properly treated, can result in large patches of rust forming. By lifting the bonnet and removing the spare wheel, any signs of corrosion at the bottom of the well, caused by water getting past the rubber seals, will be immediately evident.

Wheelarches are prone to corrosion; the lips may look clean but, only by feeling the surface, which should be smooth, will you determine whether a paint covering or poor repair is masking something sinister. A particularly vulnerable area is the lower rear section of the front wheelarch where plating is often found to have been welded into place. Corrosion may also be found at the bottom of the leading edge of the rear arch, signifying that decay may have spread to the inner sills. The inner flitch panels should not be overlooked and, in cases where rust is very prevalent, the suspension could be in danger of collapse. Do not forget to ensure that the inner rear wheelarches are sound: if there are signs of corrosion here, further checks inside the engine bay will be necessary; rust in this area should be avoided at all costs as repairs will be extensive.

Giardinieras suffer the same problems as saloons, but an additional difficulty is the virtual non-existence of replacement body panels. This example has rusted around both front and rear wheelarches, and along door bottoms; the engine cover has completely rotted away. Engine vents, which are missing on this car, are susceptible to rot; so is the roof area at the top of the rear door. (Author's collection courtesy Jim and Sheila Ellis)

The doors on the 500 can be a problem; the lower edges are particularly vulnerable to rot, often from the effect of water seeping through perished window seals and collecting in the door bottoms. Even if there is no evidence of decay, the use of filler can be detected by simply feeling along the door's underside. The upper edges are also susceptible to corrosion and a finger-tip test will readily indicate any repairs. The main door panels should be sound, but look for evidence of minor side impact damage, such as parking knocks. Also look for any signs of rusting around the rear quarterlights, which could be difficult to make good. Care should be taken to inspect the fabric roof and its folding mechanism to ensure it has not been abused by incorrect use and that the material has not been marked or torn.

A specific area to check is the floorpan where rust can form around the drain holes, seat runners and footwells. In serious cases, it may be possible to see right through. As the floorpan is relatively easy to replace any temporary repair is a false economy and cars which have patches on the underside are best avoided. An immediate clue to problems in this area can be gained from within the car itself; damp carpets or floor covering and a musty smell is usually an indication of a rotten floorpan.

While examining a car's interior, any soiling of seats and door fabrics should be spotted. Mostly hard-wearing, torn and unkept seating is, nevertheless, unsightly and, if evident, can be an indication that the car has been mechanically neglected, too.

Some restoration work has commenced on this Giardiniera; the front wings have been rebuilt but the doors and sills show signs of extensive decay. On a car such as this, expect the worst and look for a rotten floor pan, too. (Author's collection courtesy Jim and Sheila Ellis)

Sills and floor pan of this Giardiniera look very precarious. Always check for rust around the seat runners and footwells; in extreme cases it's possible to see through the floor. The seats do not look particularly comfortable for long journeys but are, in fact, surprisingly supportive. (Author's collection courtesy Jim and Sheila Ellis)

The engine compartment should be viewed critically as the panel above the cover – the vent area – can rust badly. Although easily replaced, a corroded panel could indicate further neglect, especially in the engine compartment. The mechanical aspect of the car is one of the 500's strongest points.

The vertical twin cylinder air-cooled engine is very robust and, with careful maintenance, should provide many thousands of miles of trouble-free motoring. A common problem is the result of over-filling the engine with oil so that it leaks through the rocker cover and gaskets to form an unsightly mess. The condition of the cooling system is obviously very important and a

The lack of instruments is one of the 500's charming features. Unless the chosen car is a restoration project, it's advisable to check that everything works. Remember that only on the 500L was a fuel gauge fitted; other models were equipped with a low-fuel warning indicator on the facia. (Author's collection courtesy Jim and Sheila Ellis)

Rear wheelarches are vulnerable on the Nuova and, if the rot is very extensive, as illustrated here, expect to see an engine compartment which is rust-ridden, too. (Author's collection courtesy Jim and Sheila Ellis)

check to ensure that both the fan and thermostat are operating properly is essential. A rattling fan is a sign of impending trouble and under-cooling could lead to engine seizure. Air-cooled engines are inherently noisy, but if a clonking sound can be heard, suspect worn engine mountings or crankshaft. Unless certain of the problem, it may be advisable to take specialist advice. Having only two cylinders, the condition of the sparkplugs is critical; the plugs are awkwardly placed and care is needed not to drop them in the engine casing when changing them.

Removal of the engine and gearbox as a whole is straightforward and experts claim it is possible to do this in under an hour. Usually very reliable, the 'crash' gearbox can, however, be prone to failure of bottom gear and reverse, detectable by a tendency for the car to jump out of gear very easily. With the engine and gearbox removed from the vehicle, it is simple enough to remove the top cover of the box to carry out a thorough inspection.

Some enthusiasts prefer to install the engine and gearbox from the air-cooled 126, successor to the 500 Nuova, which fits into place with virtually no modification being required. At 23bhp at 4800rpm, the 126 engine is slightly more powerful than the 500's 22bhp unit and provides a wel-

Engine covers, and the vents above, often give cause for concern. Although some decay is evident here, replacement is straightforward. (Author's collection courtesy Jim and Sheila Ellis)

come increase in performance as well as having the benefit of electronic ignition. Fitting the larger engine, which has a cubic capacity of 594cc compared to the 500's 499cc, tends to improve the value of the car despite the break with originality. At the same time as the 126 was introduced, Fiat also unveiled the 500R, which shared the 126's de-tuned engine providing only 18bhp. Instead of receiving the 126's transmission, the gearbox from the 500 was used complete with its constant mesh gears. There is little point, therefore, in attempting to transplant running gear from a 500R if a donor car is found.

The extent of rot inside the engine compartment of this Giardiniera is clearly visible. In such cases the rear suspension can easily collapse. (Author's collection courtesy Jim and Sheila Ellis)

A car which has been restored can be an attractive proposition to an enthusiast either new to the marque or not wanting to spend time and money having renovation work carried out. It is advisable to check on a car's history and, if unsure that it has been well cared for, the vehicle should be independently inspected prior to purchase. In this example of a 500L, a total rebuild has been carried out and the white wall tyres give it the finishing touch. (Author's collection)

The 500's suspension is rugged and designed for longevity but this does not mean it will not require attention at some time, especially on those cars subjected to very high mileages and unsympathetic handling. Although problems are seldom encountered with the rear coil springs, the front transverse leaf spring can lose tension. Tell-tale signs are easy to detect as the ride will be poor and the spring itself will lack its usual concave appearance but, instead, will be straight, and thus requiring replacement.

The 500 is no different to other cars when it comes to niggling foibles. In the case of the diminutive Fiat, weaknesses include the starter cable, which stretches or becomes crimped, and the bonnet release mechanism which is also cable-operated. Those cars fitted with 126 engines will not be affected by starter cable problems as pre-engaged starters were fitted. To overcome the bonnet release mechanism failure, it is preferable to be double-jointed as it will be necessary to lean inside the car and push down on the release button while pulling up the bonnet from the outside!

Driveshafts have a habit of coming adrift, always at the worst possible moment, of course, but are relatively inexpensive and easy to replace. Fuel pumps have a tendency to fail and to try to effect a repair is not economical as complete replacements are readily obtainable. The same applies to the carburettor as, rather than repair, it is simpler to fit an exchange or rebuilt unit; starting and fuel economy will both be dramatically improved. Rear lamp units are prone to failure, espe-

Pictured at a classic car show, this 500 Nuova is in good all-round original condition. Such cars are eagerly sought-after and can provide many thousands of miles of enjoyable motoring. When considering purchasing a 500, first impressions are always important; a careful appraisal of a car's external condition may reveal poor paintwork or repairs which could be hiding all sorts of unwanted problems. The condition of the car's interior is also important as scuffed or torn seats will possibly indicate neglect in other areas, including the engine compartment. (Author's collection)

cially on the 500L which often suffers from poor earthing. Much time can be spent in making repairs when a new lamp cluster can be readily obtained at a very reasonable price.

Having accepted the 500's foibles, the baby Fiat is both practical and fun to own, a bonus being its miserly running costs. There is a tremendous camaraderie amongst enthusiasts and it is usual to receive a friendly wave from other owners. Far from sharing many of the shortcomings normally attributed to microcars and bubble cars,

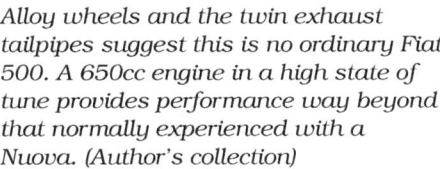

Alloy wheels and the twin exhaust tailpipes suggest this is no ordinary Fiat 500. A 650cc engine in a high state of tune provides performance way beyond that normally experienced with a Nuova. (Author's collection)

Customising techniques can vary from distinctive paint finishes, as depicted here, to full-scale body and engine conversions. The purchase of a customised car should be approached with caution as handling will almost certainly be very different to those of an original production model. (Author's collection)

such as poor performance and doubtful handling, the 500 is a fully-fledged production saloon in miniature with a fine pedigree. Motorway driving over long distances can be tedious, but it is on the open road where the 500 really comes into its own. It has little difficulty in keeping up with the flow of traffic, although it is unlikely to set a scorching pace, unless it has an Abarth or Radbourne conversion. The air-cooled twin buzzes competently away in the tail and, because that is where most of the car's weight is, the handling is light but precise. For its size and performance potential, therefore, acceleration (apart from very early models) is adequate although top speed is well inside most national speed limits. Braking, too, is efficient but commensurate with the car's age and limited performance. Possibly one of the greatest hazards is not with the car or the 500 owner, but with other road users who perceive the tiny Fiat to have a tortoise-like speed. A common frustration is that drivers of larger and faster cars tend to pull out in front of the Fiat assuming, mistakenly, that by giving way they will be held up. That a vehicle appears to other road users to be travelling more slowly than it actually is, is a problem often encountered by drivers of small or elderly cars.

For those new to the pleasures of the baby Fiat, the cabin may seem dreadfully spartan, especially those of the 500F and earlier types which were fitted with the microscopic tear-drop speedometer pod ahead of the steering wheel. The seats feel narrow and lacking in support compared to those fitted to larger cars, whilst the cacophony from the 'boot' can at first be unsettling: a few miles at the wheel, though, is usually all that is necessary to confirm that this is a most able and spirited machine. Some enthusiasts consider the 500L, with its 'luxury' trim and sophisticated facia, to have digressed from the original concept of a minimalist car, but that is a matter of personal opinion.

The 500 Nuova's shape and character make the car an ideal contender for customising. While many enthusiasts do not support such practices, preferring instead to concentrate on originality, there is agreement, nevertheless, that it is better for a car to be customised than scrapped, which may otherwise be the only alternative. From the outset of production, Fiat itself embarked on a form of customising by offering the 500 in rally guise and by association with

Successor to the 500 Nuova was the 126. Early air-cooled models can be identified by the vents in the engine cover. Later 126 models, such as the car on the right, which is a 126 Bis, were water-cooled and the rear hatchback door (never a feature on air-cooled models) was without ventilation panels. Air-cooled 126s proved very reliable but the water-cooled Bis model, with the engine laid on its side under the rear floor, was less so. (Author's collection)

Abarth. Even such models as the Jolly were in essence the product of customising techniques, although marketed as derivatives of the saloon.

Different levels of customising exist, from elaborate paint finishes to reworked body panels; adoption of flared wings and wide-section tyres, more powerful engines, some water-cooled. A particular practice amongst performance enthusiasts is the adoption of the Reliant engine which was normally fitted to that company's three-wheel vehicles. When considering the purchase of a customised car, great care must be taken to ensure the vehicle complies with current legislation and that it is indeed roadworthy. When attempting customising techniques it is important that all work is expertly carried out and that safety is not compromised.

Routine maintenance is essential to keep the 500 in good running order and, as a brief guide, the following procedures should be carried out. Do not forget to check for any variances in the instructions for individual models.

Every 1500 miles (2400km): change engine oil (on later models this need be attended to at 3000 miles or 4800km intervals); lubricate king pins and check battery condition.

Every 3000 miles (4800km): clean air cleaner filter; check and top up brake fluid reservoir; top up level of steering box oil; check gearbox and differential oil level; inspect fan belt and sparkplugs, replace if necessary, and check distributor.

Every 6000 miles (9600km): lubricate distributor, renew air cleaner filter element and check shock absorbers and steering mechanism.

Every 12,000 miles (19,200km): drain (when hot) gearbox/differential oil and refill; lubricate starter motor and generator end bearing; grease front wheel bearings. Check and adjust, if necessary, valve clearances.

Every 18,000 miles (28,800km) grease rear wheel bearings.

Fiat 126

A most able and worthy car, the 126 largely failed to achieve the same popularity as its predecessor due to a boxy design which, although functionable and modern-looking, lacked the curvaceous and cheeky appeal which had become the 500 Nuova's hallmark. New standards of performance came from a more powerful engine and redesigned gearbox, but even the layout, improved by relocating the fuel tank from the luggage compartment to beneath the rear seat, could not compensate for the Nuova's uniqueness. Although a four seater, the angular shape of the 126 really could not accommodate a payload of adults without discomfort.

Values of the 126 are, at the time of writing, very low, which makes purchase of a well maintained example desirable even if the intention is to transfer its power train. The 126, which has a healthy survival rate, is prone to rusting in most of the places mentioned for the 500, and neglected cars will show signs of severe corrosion on the front panel and valance, the door bottoms and engine cover.

The main departure from original baby Fiat design arrived with the introduction of the 126 Bis in 1987. A water-cooled 704cc engine, turned on its side and laid under the floor, allowed a true hatchback design which revolutionised the model. By laying the rear seat flat the luggage space was vastly improved and, even with the seat in place, a respectable amount of rear boot space was available, which was never the case with the air-cooled car. Even the tailgate and a heavily modified facia could not hide the car's origins although, compared to the early designs, the equipment level was impressive. At 26bhp, performance – in contrast to the 500 and early 126 models – was positively spirited and a maximum of a little above 70mph (112kph) was possible with a tail wind and good road surface.

The 126 Bis, too, has its foibles: neglect of the engine compartment and failure to keep it clean will result in a surfeit of messy oil on the upper surface of the engine which, when hot, wafts smelly fumes into the passenger cabin. It has been known for the engine dipstick to work loose, due to vibration, with the result that oil is sprayed all over the engine compartment. Vibration can also be responsible for the loosening of engine hose, air filter and electrical connections, the consequence

Neatly designed, the 126 Bis, with its hatchback styling, was capable of carrying greater loads than the previous model, especially with the rear seat laid flat. The water-cooled 704cc engine was quieter than its air-cooled predecessor but, unfortunately, proved not so reliable. Oil seals were a continual problem and vibration of the engine could cause the dipstick to work loose, allowing oil to spurt into the engine compartment. (Author's collection)

being poor starting and rough running. Cylinder head gasket problems can also prove troublesome, something seldom experienced with previous models. For all its shortcomings, the twin-cylinder water-cooled engine is robust and capable of running at high revs over long distances. Even with hard use oil consumption should remain low and, as far as petrol consumption is concerned, the car should virtually run on the smell of an oil rag. Engine noise is intrusive as the power plant is positioned behind the rear seat and virtually within the passenger cabin, concealed only by an opening panel in the load compartment floor.

At the front of the car, the seals around the bonnet lid perish easily due to water becoming trapped within the folds of the rubber. Water gets past the seals and drips onto luggage before seeping down to the well where the spare wheel is carried and, if not mopped up, corrosion will quickly start. The front panel is vulnerable to stone chippings which, if not repaired, will allow rust to form.

The water-cooled 126 Bis marked the final stage of rear-engine development for Fiat's baby cars; new models, spearheaded by the Cinquecento, were designed with a front-positioned engine and front-wheel-drive. The fact that the 126 Bis is the last generation of rear-engined Fiats may just be enough, in years to come, to make it something of a novelty, if not a classic.

The Cinquecento

Announced at the end of 1991, Fiat baptised its new baby car Cinquecento to continue a tradition which spanned 55 years and revive memories of the most well-known of all small Fiats, the 'Topolino.'

Cinquecento, unsurprisingly, became the accepted leader in small car design and, while evocative of a past era, proved a truly modern and able competitor in a huge and ever-growing automotive market sector. Whereas the Nuova, and to a great extent the 126, was essentially a 2+2, the Cinquecento was a family car with the claim, by Fiat, that it could accommodate five people. Cinquecento, too, proved to be an able performer, a criteria more than achieved with the Sporting version. It should be recognised that the Sporting was, for its size, a highly capable car with a formidable performance potential. It is likely that previous owners will have used the car's athletic abilities to the full and, therefore, a prospective purchase might need to be considered in this light.

When contemplating buying a used Cinquecento, the prospective owner should obviously note the car's service history; the model is relatively recent as far as baby Fiats are concerned and a down-at-heel vehicle should be avoided, as should one which has not been regularly maintained. Pointers to a car's overall condition will be any broken or repaired paintwork, which might conceal accidental damage; soiled or torn seats will indicate unsympathetic ownership but look in the boot for evidence of scuff marks and heavy use. Fiat dealers will certainly be a source of used cars and, while their prices may carry a premium, it can be expected that these cars will be ideally presented and valeted; they may well carry a manufacturer's warranty as well as any guarantee provided by the dealer. It is unusual to find high mileage cars as the typical owner, in the UK at any rate, used the Cinquecento as a second car or family runabout over short distances.

The original Cinquecento models, those with the 704cc and 903cc engines, were discontinued and replaced by three models, the S, SX and Soleil, as well as the Sporting. A purchaser might well wish to pay a higher price for a more recent car with updated trim specification.

The Cinquecento was popular with hire-car companies, and an opportunity to purchase a relatively young Cinquecento may therefore arise as fleets are replaced. Such cars do not necessarily have high mileages and mostly are regularly serviced and maintained. The car's reasonable price made it attractive as a courtesy vehicle and a number of accident repair companies ran small fleets for the convenience of their customers. It is unlikely that a Cinquecento will have been used as a company car.

Having been on the market since late 1991 (1993 in the UK), the Cinquecento was replaced by a new model, the Seicento, in Spring 1998, the European launch taking place at

The Cinquecento suffered relatively few vices. Phased out in 1998, there are plentiful supplies of good low-mileage cars, including the Sporting version, which is illustrated here. It would be prudent to check a car's service history and also to ensure there is no evidence of accident damage. Tell-tale signs of potential, but hidden, trouble can be poor paintwork or a down-at heel appearance. (Courtesy Fiat Auto [UK] and Fiat SPA Ltd.)

Turin on the 18th March. Intended, obviously, to revive memories of another icon, the 600, this is a further development of the small but highly efficient family car for which Fiat is so acclaimed.

APPENDICES

DIRECTORY OF CLUBS, SUPPLIERS & SPECIALISTS

Australian clubs
Fiat Club of the A.C.T.
Membership Secretary: Clive W. Roach, PO Box 1119, Canberra City, A.C.T. 2601, Australia. Website www.fiatclubact.org.

Belgian clubs
Fiat Club Belgio
Website www.fiatclubbelgio.be.

Club Fiat 500 Belgium
Website www.clu500-belgium.net.

Club Fiat 500 Brussels
Website www.clubfiat500brussels.com.

British clubs
Abarth Cars UK
Website www.abarthcars.co.uk.

Abarth Register
All owners of Fiat Abarth 500 and 600 models are welcome.
Tony Castle-Miller, Middle Barton Garage, Troy, Ardley Road, Somerton, Bicester, Oxon OX25 6NG.
Tel 01869 345766, fax 01869 356581, email carsandparts@middlebartongarage.com, website www.middlebartongarage.com.

Fiat 500 Club
Established 1992 to cater for all the needs of the 500 owner and enthusiast. In addition to a close association with other European Fiat 500 clubs, the club enjoys a full events and social calendar with meetings held nationally. Members receive a quality bi-monthly A4 newsletter which is well-illustrated and contains a wide range of articles and features.
The Membership Secretary is: Sheridan Bowie, email membership@fiat500enthusiasts.co.uk.

Fiat Motor Club (GB)
All Fiat models are catered for with separate registers for 500, 126 and Cinquecento; 600 and 850; Multipla; Abarth; 500A, 500B and 500C Topolino. Eleven magazines are published each year together with a year book. The main event of the year is the Fiat National Weekend held during the summer months.
Email enquiries@fiatmotorclubgb.com.

Fiat Register
Membership is restricted to pre-war Fiats, but includes the Topolino up to 1955. Regular newsletter contains information of interest to owners of Fiat models up to 1955.
Richard Pattern, Sounion, South Street, Maidstone, Kent ME16 9WY.
Email richardpattern@blueyonder.co.uk.

Other British clubs/registers
127, 128 Register
Website www.fiatforum.com.

600, 850 Register
Clifford Peters, Auto Rossa, 3 Hightown Industrial Estate, Crow Arch Lane, Ringwood, Hants BH24 1NZ, England. Website www.fiatforum.com (see also Auto Rossa).

850T, 900E Caravanette Register
Website www.fiatforum.com.

Club 126 UK
Website www.club126.co.uk.

Multipla Register
Website www.fiatforum.com.

Panda Register
Website www.fiatforum.com.

Racing Register
See Abarth Cars and Abarth Register.

Topolino Register
Fred Watts, Bignores Cottage, Darenth Road, Dartford, Kent DA1 1LZ, England.

British suppliers & specialists
Auto Rossa
3 High Town Industrial Estate, Crow Arch Lane, Ringwood, Hampshire BH24 1NZ, England.
Tel: 01425 478648, fax: 01425 474297, email info@autorossa.com. website www.autorossa.com.
Sales, service and repairs as well as Fiat specialists for 500/126/600/850/X19.

D.P. Motors
13-15 Sutton Road, St Albans Herts AL1 5JQ.
Tel 01727 53923, website www.dpmotors.com.
Fiat 500 specialist, also Alfa Romeo and Lancia. Parts, sales and service including full restorations.

Fancy Spares
Court Farm Business Park, Buckland Newton, Dorchester, Dorset, DT2 7BT, England.
Tel: 01300 345577
Contact: Malcolm Fancy. Stockist of obsolete Fiat parts.

Ital Corsa
11 Fairmile, Fleet, Hampshire, GU13 9UT, England. Tel: 01252 613335.
Servicing, repairs and parts for all baby Fiats as well as complete restorations.

Middle Barton Garage
Troy, Ardley Road, Somerton, Bicester, Oxon OX25 6NG.
Tel 01869 345766, fax 01869 356581, email carsandparts@middlebartongarage.com, ebsite www.middlebartongarage.com.
Abarth specialist and supplier of classic Fiat parts as well as Abarth parts, new or remanufactured. Services include general servicing, engine, transmission and chassis rebuilding, including also race preparation.

Radbourne Racing
213-217 The Broadway,
Wimbledon, London SW19 1NL,
England. Tel: 0181 540 9991. Fax:
0181 543 2994
High performance conversions,
restorations, etc.

Ricambio International
11 Manor Road, Wallington,
Surrey SM6 0BW. Tel 0208 669
3800, fax 0208 669 3803, email
enquiries@ricambio.co.uk, web
www.ricambio.co.uk.

Dutch clubs & specialists
Autobedrijf Dick Baas
Energiestraat 10, 1411 AT
Naarden, Holland. Tel 035-
6947936. (See also www.
amklassiek.nl.)

Fiat 500 Club Nederland
PO box 68, 3970 AB Driebergen-
Rijsenburg, The Netherlands.
Tel 0031 343 414262; www.
fiat500club.nl.

Fiat 600 Club Holland
Website www.fiat600nl.

Fiat Topolino Club Holland
Website www.topolino-club.nl.

Henk Poortinga
Stationsstaat 43, 3881 La Putten,
Holland. Tel 0341 353130.

Finnish clubs
Fiat Club Finland
Website www.gruppofiat.
finlandia.fi.

French clubs & specialists
Club Fiat de France
Website www.clubfiatdefrance.
free.fr.

Club Fiat 500
Visit www.club-fiat-500.com

Depanoto et Cie
4 Rue de la Malerie, 28400
Nogent-le-Rotrou, France. Tel +33
(0)2 37 52 43 25, website www.
depanoto-boutique.com
Simca Cinq parts.

Fiat 500 et derivées
Visit www.club500.free.fr.

German clubs & specialists
Abarth I.G. Deutschland
Contact: Klaus Kleber,
Hochbendweg 40, D-4150 Krefeld,
Germany. Tel 0215/316792, email
abarthCoppalMille@aol.com

Erster Fiat 600 Club
Visit www.oldtimer.net.

Fiat 126 Club Sud
Visit www.fiat126clubsued.de.

Fiat 126 Forum de Maluch
Visit www.maluch-forum.de

Fiat 500 Exclusiv Club Kiel
Ute.Sasse-Schulz, Süderstr.13
24802 Emkendorf ,Tel 04330 522,
visit www.fiat500kiel.weebly.com.

Fiat Club 600 Deutschland
SchwarzbachstraBe 36, 67716
Heltersberg. Tel 06333 602 778,
www.duo-soft.de

Fiat 500-Forum Deutschland
Visit www.500forum.de

Holtmann & Niedergerke
Amoberen Field 4, 32758
Detmold. Tel 05231 61790, email
info@holtmann-niedergerke.de.

Topolino Freunde Deutschland
Contact: Wolfgang Hildebrand,
Isardamm 3, 8192 Geretsried 1,
Germany. Tel 08171/8418, email
wolfgang.hildebrand@hotmail.de.

Italian clubs
Abarth Classiche.com
Via Plava 80, 10135 Torino.
Website www.abarthclassiche.
com.

Piave Jolly Club
Contact: Patrizia Capuzzo, Piazza
Giustiniani 14, 31100 Treviso,
Italy.

Registro Fiat Italiano
Contact: Antonio Amaldelli, Via
Cesare Battisti, 2, 10123, Torino.
Website www.registofiat.it.

New Zealand clubs
Fiat Owners Club New Zealand
Visit www.fiatnz.co.nz. Email
info@fiatnz.co.nz.

South African clubs
Auto Italiana.
Visit www.autoitaliana.co.za

Fiat Club Africa
Contact: Ian Huntly, PO Box
47120, Parklands 2121, South
Africa.

Fiat Club South Africa
Visit www.fiatclub.co.za.

Swiss clubs
Fiat 500 Club Schweiz
Visit www.fiat500club.ch.

Topolino Club Zurich
Contact: 8000 Zurich. Website
www.topolinoclubzuerich.ch.

USA clubs & specialists
Fiat Club America
Visit www.fluforum.
italiancarclub.com and www.
fiatclubamerica.com/chapters/

Fiat Lancia Unlimited
Contact: Jon Logan, 3258
Scioto Farms Drive, Hillard
OH 43026. Website www.
grassrootsmotorsports.com.

Fiat Plus
2131 Delaware Ave # D, Santa
Cruz, CA 95060, USA. Website
www.fiatplus.com.

Fiat Rear Engine Cars Club
Contact: Merkel Weiss, PO Box
682, Sun Valley, CA 91353-0682,
USA. Tel 818-768-3552.

International Auto Parts,
4351 Seminole Trail,
Charlottesville, VA 22911 USA.
Tel +1 800-953-0813, website
www.internationalautopartsfl.
com.

Midwest-Bayless Italian Auto
1333 Kingry St, Columbus, Ohio
USA 43211. Tel 614-784-8870,
website www.midwest-byless.com.

Current information and advice on enthusiast clubs and parts suppliers around the world can be updated by consulting the listings on the internet.

PRODUCTION FIGURES

Model	Years	Units built
Topolino		
500A	1936-48	122,213
500B	1948-49	21,623
500C	1949-55	376,371
600		
Saloon	1955-60	891,107
Multipla	1956-60	76,871
600D Saloon	1960-69	1,561,000
600D Multipla	1960-66	83,389
850		
All versions	1964-71	2,297,521
500		
Nuova 500	1957-60	181,036
500D	1960-65	640,520
500F & L	1965-72	2,272,092
500R	1972-75	334,000
126		
126	1973-92	80,868
Cinquecento		
Cinquecento	1992-6.97	45,789

SPECIFICATIONS

Topolino 500A
Engine: Type 500; front-mounted; 4 cylinders in-line; side valves; 569cc. Bore and stroke: 52 x 67mm; compression ratio: 6.5:1; maximum power 13bhp @ 4000rpm; ignition: coil and distributor.
Cooling: Water; thermosiphon; capacity: 8 pints (4.5 litres).
Fuel: Tank capacity: 4.84 galls (22 litres); carburettor and gravity feed.
Lubrication: Pressure 25psi (1.8kg/sq.cm).
Transmission: Rear drive via prop shaft; helical spur final drive; 4 speeds and reverse with synchromesh on 3rd and 4th. Central lever. Single dry plate clutch.
Suspension: Independent front by wishbones and transverse leaf spring with telescopic shock absorbers. Rear by rigid axle; early cars had quarter-elliptic springs, radius arms and hydraulic shock absorbers. Second series cars had semi-elliptic springs.
Brakes: Drums, hydraulic all-round with transmission parking brake.
Tyres: 4.00 x 15.
Steering: Worm and sector, 28.5ft (8.7m) turning circle.
Electrical: 12V, 75W dynamo, 30 a/h battery.
Dimensions: Wheelbase: 6.56ft (2000mm); track: 3.65ft (1114mm) front, 3.55ft (1083mm) rear; length: 10.55ft (3215mm); width: 4.18ft (1275mm); height: 4.52ft (1377mm); ground clearance: 5.67in (144mm).
Weight: 1179lbs (535kg) unladen; 1642lbs (745kg) laden.

Cinquecento 700
Engine: Type 170A.000; front-mounted, 2 cylinders in-line; ohv; 704cc. Bore and stroke: 80 x 70mm; compression ratio: 9:1; maximum power 31bhp @ 5000rpm; ignition: electronic.
Cooling: Water, pump, thermostat and booster fan. Capacity: 0.88 gall (4 litres).
Fuel: Tank capacity 7.7 galls (35 litres); carburettor and pump.
Lubrication: Pressure, sump 5.7lbs (2.6kg).
Transmission: Front drive, 4 speeds and reverse, all synchromesh, central lever, single dry plate clutch.
Suspension: Independent all-round, transverse arms, coil springs at front and longitudunal arms with coil springs at rear. Hydraulic shock absorbers all-round.
Brakes: Hydraulic, discs at front, drums at rear. Handbrake operating on rear wheels.
Tyres: 135/70 SR 13.
Steering: Rack and pinion, 29ft (8.8m) turning circle.
Electrical: 12V, 55A alternator and 32 a/h battery.
Dimensions: Wheelbase: 7.22ft (2200mm); track: 4.17ft (1270mm) front, 4.16ft (1268mm) rear; length: 10.59ft (3227mm); width: 4.88ft (1487mm); height: 4.71ft (1435mm).
Weight: 1487lbs (675kg) unladen; 2445lbs (1110kg) laden.
Performance: Maximum speed 79mph (127kph).
Average fuel consumption: 47mpg (6.1 lts/100km).

Topolino 500B
Engine: Type 500B; front-mounted; 4 cylinders in line; ohv; 569cc. Bore and stroke: 52 x 67mm; compression ratio: 6.45:1; maximum power 16.5bhp @ 4400rpm; ignition: coil and distributor.
Cooling: Water; thermosiphon; capacity: 8 pints (4.5 litres).
Fuel: Tank capacity: 4.73 galls (21.5 litres); carburettor and gravity feed.
Lubrication: Pressure 28psi (2kg/sq.cm).
Transmission: Rear drive via prop shaft; helical spur final drive; 4 speeds and reverse with synchro-mesh on 3rd and 4th. Central lever. Single dry plate clutch.
Suspension: Independent front by wishbones and transverse leaf spring with telescopic shock absorbers. Rear by rigid axle; semi-elliptic springs, hydraulic shock absorbers and anti-roll bar.
Brakes: Drums, hydraulic all-round with transmission parking brake.
Tyres: 4.25 x 15.
Steering: Worm and sector, 28.5ft (8.7m) turning circle.
Electrical: 12V, 95W dynamo, 38 a/h battery.
Dimensions: Wheelbase: 6.56ft (2000mm); track: 3.66ft (1116mm) front, 3.55ft (1083mm) rear; length: 10.53ft (3210mm); width: 4.18ft (1273mm); height: 4.51ft (1375mm); ground clearance: 5.70in (145mm).
Weight: 1322lbs (600kg) unladen; 1742lbs (790kg) laden.
Performance: Maximum speed 59mph (95kph).
Average fuel consumption: 56mpg (5 lts/100km).

Note: 500B Giardiniera differed as follows: length: 11.02ft (3360mm); height: 4.69ft (1430mm); fully laden weight: 2050lbs (930kg). Maximum speed 56mph (90kph) and fuel consumption: 53mpg (6.5 lts/100km).

Topolino 500C
Engine: Type 500B; front-mounted; 4 cylinders in line; ohv; 569cc. Bore and stroke: 52 x 67mm; compression ratio: 6.45:1; maximum power 16.5bhp @ 4400rpm; ignition: coil and distributor.
Cooling: Water; thermosiphon; capacity: 8 pints (4.5 litres).
Fuel: Tank capacity: 4.73 galls (21.5 litres); carburettor and gravity feed.
Lubrication: Pressure 28psi (2kg/sq.cm).
Transmission: Rear drive via prop shaft; spiral bevel final drive; 4 speeds and reverse with synchromesh on 3rd and 4th. Central lever. Single dry plate clutch.
Suspension: Wishbones and transverse leaf spring at front, rigid axle at rear with semi-elliptic springs and anti-roll bar. Telescopic shock absorbers all-round.
Brakes: Hydraulic all-round with transmission parking brake.
Tyres: 4.25 x 15.
Steering: Worm and sector, 28.5ft (8.7m) turning circle.
Electrical: 12V,130W dynamo, 38 a/h battery.
Dimensions: Wheelbase 6.56ft (2000mm); track: 3.66ft (1116mm) front, 3.55ft (1083mm) rear; length: 10.53ft (3210mm); width: 4.23ft (1288mm); height: 4.51ft (1375mm); ground clearance: 5.70in (145mm).
Weight: 1344lbs (610kg) unladen; 1763lbs (800kg) laden.
Performance: Maximum speed 59mph (95kph).
Average fuel consumption: 56mpg (5 lts/100km).

Note: Giardiniera and Belvedere versions differed as follows: length: 10.86ft (3310mm); height: 4.59ft (1400mm); fully laden weight inc 4 passengers and 110lbs (50kg) luggage: 1 ton. Maximum speed: 56mph (90kph) and fuel consumption: 48mpg (5.8 lts/100km).

Fiat 600
Engine: Type 100.00; rear-mounted 4 cylinders in line, ohv, 633cc. Bore and stroke: 60 x 56mm; compression ratio: 7.5:1; maximum power 22bhp @ 4600rpm; ignition: coil and distributor.
Cooling: Water; pump; capacity: 7.5 pints (4.3 litres).
Fuel: Tank capacity: 5.9 galls (27 litres); carburettor and pump.
Lubrication: Pressure: 38 psi (2.7 kg/sq.cm).
Transmission: Rear drive, gearbox and final drive combined 4 speeds and reverse with synchromesh on 2nd, 3rd and 4th. Central lever. Single dry plate clutch.
Suspension: Independent front and rear with telescopic shock absorbers; wishbones and transverse leaf at front, semi trailing arms and coil springs at rear.
Brakes: Drums, hydraulic on all four wheels with transmission hand brake.
Tyres: 5.20 x 12.
Steering: Worm and sector, 28.5ft (8.7m.) turning circle.
Electrical: 12V, 180W dynamo; 28 a/h battery.
Dimensions: Wheelbase: 6.56ft (2000mm); track: 3.75ft (1144mm) front, 3.79ft (1154mm) rear; length: 10.55ft (3215mm); width: 4.53ft (1380mm); height: 4.61ft (1405mm); ground clearance: 6.29in (160mm).
Weight: 1289lbs (585kg) unladen, 1972lbs (895kg) laden.
Performance: Maximum speed 62mph (100kph).
Average fuel consumption: 49mpg(5.7lts/100km).

Fiat 600D
Engine: Type 100D.000; rear-mounted 4 cylinders in line, ohv., 767cc. Bore and stroke: 62 x 63.5mm; compression ratio 7.5:1; maximum power 29bhp @ 4800rpm; ignition: coil and distributor.
Cooling: Water; pump; capacity: 8 pints (4.5 litres).
Fuel: Tank capacity: 5.9 galls (27 litres); carburettor and pump.
Lubrication: Pressure: 38 psi (2.68 kg/sq.cm).
Transmission: Rear drive, gearbox and final drive combined; 4 speeds and reverse with synchromesh on 2nd, 3rd and 4th. Central lever. Single dry plate clutch.
Suspension: Independent front and rear with telescopic shock absorbers; wishbones and transverse leaf at front, semi trailing arms and coil springs at rear.
Brakes: Drums, hydraulic on all four wheels with handbrake operating on rear wheels.
Steering: Worm and roller, 28.5ft (8.7m) turning circle.
Electrical: 12V, 230W dynamo; 32a/h battery.
Dimensions: Wheelbase 6.56ft (2000mm); track: 3.77ft (1150mm) front, 3.81ft (1160mm) rear; length: 10.81ft (3295mm); width: 4.52ft (1378mm); height: 4.61ft (1405mm); ground clearance: 5.71in (145mm).
Weight: 1333lbs (605kg) unladen, 2038lbs (925kg) laden.
Performance: Maximum speed 68mph (110kmph).
Average fuel consumption: 48mpg (5.8 lts/100km).

Note: From chassis number 2,035,001 (1965) the fuel tank was increased in size to 6.8 galls (31 litres).

600 Multipla
Engine: Type 100; rear-mounted 4 cylinders in line, ohv, 633cc. Bore and stroke: 60 x 56mm; compression ratio: 7:1; maximum power 21.5bhp @ 4600rpm; ignition: coil and distributor.
Cooling: Water; pump; capacity 10.5 pints (6 litres).
Fuel: Tank capacity 6.5 galls (30 litres); carburettorand pump.
Lubrication: 38psi (2.78 kg/sq.cm)
Transmission: Rear drive, gearbox and final drive combined; 4 speeds and reverse with synchromesh on 2nd, 3rd and 4th. Central lever, single dry plate clutch.
Suspension: Independent front and rear with telescopic shock absorbers; coil and wishbone with anti-roll torsion bar at front and coil springs with diagonal swinging arms at rear.
Brakes: Drums, hydraulic on all four wheels with transmission hand brake.
Tyres: 5.20 x 12.
Steering: Worm and roller, 28.5ft (8.7m) turning circle.

Electrical: 12V, 180W dynamo; 28 a/h battery.
Dimensions: Wheelbase: 6.56ft (2000mm); track 4.04ft (1230mm) front, 3.80ft (1157mm) rear; length: 11.61ft (3540mm); width: 4.76in (1450mm); height: 5.18ft (1580mm); ground clearance: 6.30in (160mm).
Weight: 1610lbs (730kg) unladen, 1959lbs (889kg) laden.
Performance: Maximum speed 57.1mph (91.36 kph).
Average fuel consumption: 38.5mpg (7.5 lts/100km).

600D Multipla

Engine: Type 100D.008; rear-mounted 4 cylinders in line, ohv., 767cc. Bore and stroke 62 x 63.5mm; compression ratio: 7.5:1; maximum power 29bhp @ 4800rpm. Ignition: coil and distributor.
Cooling: Water; pump; capacity 12 pints (6.7 litres)
Fuel: Tank capacity 6.4 galls (29 litres); carburettor and pump.
Lubrication: 35.5-42.6 psi. (2.5-3 kg/sq.cm.)
Transmission: Rear drive, gearbox and final drive combined; 4 speeds and reverse with synchromesh on 2nd, 3rd and 4th. Central lever. Single dry plate clutch.
Suspension: Independent front and rear with telescopic shock absorbers; wishbones and transverse leaf at front, semi trailing arms and coil springs at rear.
Brakes: Drums, hydraulic on all four wheels with handbrake operating on rear wheels.
Steering: Worm and roller, 28ft10in (8.80m) turning circle.
Electrical: 12V, 230W dynamo; 36 a/h battery.
Dimensions: Wheelbase 6.56ft (2000mm); track 4.03ft (1230mm) front, 3.80ft (1157mm) rear; length: 11.63ft (3545mm); width: 4.74ft (1445mm); height: 5.18ft (1580mm); ground clearance: 6.30in (160mm).
Weight: 1654lbs (750kg) unladen, n/a laden.
Performance: Maximum speed 65mph (105kph).
Average fuel consumption: 33mpg (9 lts/100km).

Note: Taxi version unladen weight increased to 1697lbs (770kg).

Nuova 500

Engine: Type 110.000; rear-mounted 2 cylinders in line, ohv., 479cc. Bore and stroke 66 x 70mm; compression ratio: 6.55:1; maximum power 13bhp @ 4000rpm; ignition: coil and distributor.
Cooling: Air.
Fuel: Tank capacity 4.6 galls (21 litres); carburettor and pump.
Lubrication: Pressure 27lbs psi (1.9 kg/sq.cm.)
Transmission: Rear drive, gearbox and final drive combined; 4 speeds and reverse, constant mesh on 2nd, 3rd and 4th. Central lever. Single dry plate clutch.
Suspension: Independent front and rear with telescopic shock absorbers; wishbones and transverse leaf spring at front, semi trailing arms and coil springs at rear.
Brakes: Drums, hydraulic on all four wheels, hand brake operating on rear wheels.
Tyres: 125 x 12.
Steering: Worm and sector, 28ft (8.6m) turning circle.
Electrical: 12V, 180W dynamo, 32 a/h battery.
Dimensions: Wheelbase: 6.04ft (1840mm); track: front 3.68ft (1121mm), 3.72ft (1135mm) rear length: 9.74ft (2970mm); width: 4.33ft (1320mm); height: 4.35ft (1325mm); ground clearance: 5.11in (130mm).
Weight: 1035lbs (470kg) unladen, 1498lbs (680kg) laden.
Performance: Maximum speed 53mph (85kph).
Average fuel consumption: 65mpg (4.5 lts/100km).

Note: Sport version performance as follows: Maximum speed 65mph (105kph); average fuel consumption 58mpg (4.8lts00km). Engine capacity increased to 499.5cc and 21bhp.

Nuova 500D

Engine: Type 110 D 000; rear-mounted 2 cylinders in line, ohv., 499.5cc. Bore and stroke 67.4 x 70mm; compression ratio 7.1:1; maximum power 17.5bhp @ 4000rpm; ignition: coil and distributor.
Cooling: Air.
Fuel: Tank capacity 4.6 galls (21 litres); carburettor and pump.
Lubrication: Pressure 25psi. (1.75 kg/sq.cm.)
Transmission: Rear drive, gearbox and final drive combined; 4 speeds and reverse, constant mesh on 2nd, 3rd and 4th. Central lever. Single dry plate clutch.
Suspension: Independent front and rear with telescopic shock absorbers; wishbones and transverse leaf spring at front, semi trailing arms and coil springs at rear.
Brakes: Drums, hydraulic on all four wheels, handbrake operating on rear wheels.
Tyres: 125 x 12.
Steering: Worm and sector, 28ft (8.6m) turning circle.
Electrical: 12V, 230W dynamo, 32 a/h battery.
Dimensions: Wheelbase: 6.04ft (1840mm); track: front 3.68ft (1121mm), 372ft (1135mm) rear; length: 9.74ft (2970mm); width: 4.33ft (1320mm); height: 4.35ft (1325mm); ground clearance: 4.92in (125mm).
Weight: 1102lbs (500kg) unladen, 1807lbs (820kg) laden.
Performance: Maximum speed 59mph (95kph).
Average fuel consumption: 58mpg (.48 lts/100km).

500 Giardiniera

Specifications of the Giardiniera are almost identical to the 500D, except for the following:
Engine: Type 120.000; maximum power 17.5bhp @ 4600rpm; oil pressure 24 psi.(1.7 kg/sq.cm).
Dimensions: Wheelbase: 6.36ft (1940mm); rear track: 3.71 (1131mm); length: 10.45ft (3185mm); width 4.34ft (1323mm); height: 4.44ft (1354mm); ground clearance 5.31in (135mm).
Weight: 1223lbs (555kg) unladen, 1928lbs (875kg) laden.
Performance: Maximum speed 59mph (95kph).
Average fuel consumption: 54mpg (5.2 lts/100km).

Nuova 500F and 500L

Engine : Type 110 F 000; rear-mounted 2 cylinders in line, ohv.
499.5cc. Bore and stroke 67.4 x 70mm; compression ratio: 7.1:1; maximum power 22bhp @ 4400rpm; ignition: coil and distributor.
Cooling: Air.
Fuel: Tank capacity 4.75 galls (22 litres); carburettor and pump.
Lubrication: Pressure: 34psi (2.4 kg/sq.cm).
Transmission: Rear drive, gearbox and final drive combined, 4 speeds and reverse, constant mesh on 2nd, 3rd and 4th. Central lever. Single dry plate clutch.
Suspension: Independent front and rear with telescopic shock absorbers; wishbones and transverse leaf spring at front, semi trailing arms and coil springs at rear.
Brakes: Drums, hydraulic on all four wheels, handbrake operating on rear wheels.
Tyres: 125 x 12.
Steering: Worm and helical sector, 28ft (8.6m) turning circle.
Electrical: 12V, 230W dynamo, 32 a/h battery.
Dimensions: Wheelbase 6.04ft (1840mm); track: front 3.68ft (1121mm), 3.72ft (1135mm) rear; length: 9.74ft (2970mm); width: 4.33ft (1320mm); height: 4.38ft (1335mm); ground clearance: 4.92in (125mm).
Weight: 1146lbs (520kg) unladen, 1851lbs (840kg) laden.
Performance: Maximum speed 95kph (59mph).
Average fuel consumption: 51mpg (5.5 lts/100km).

Note: Average fuel consumption of 500L: 53mpg (5.3lts/100km).

500R

Almost identical to the 500F, the following main specifications differ as follows:
Engine: 594cc (as Fiat 126) producing 18bhp instead of 23bhp.
Performance: Maximum speed 62mph (100kph).

126

Engine: Type 126 A.000, rear mounted 2 cylinders in line; ohv, 594cc. Bore and stroke 73.5 x 70mm; compression ratio 7.5:1; maximum power 23bhp @ 4800rpm; ignition: coil and distributor.
Cooling: Air.
Fuel: Tank capacity 4.5 galls (21 litres); carburettor and pump.
Lubrication: Forced.
Transmission: Rear drive, swing axle with half shafts; 4 speeds and reverse with synchromesh on 2nd, 3rd and 4th. Central lever; single dry plate clutch.
Suspension: Independent front and rear with telescopic shock absorbers; wishbones and transverse leaf spring at front and semi trailing arms and coil springs at rear.
Brakes: Drums, hydraulic on all four wheels with handbrake operating on rear wheels.
Tyres: 135SR x 12.
Steering: Worm and helical section.
Electrical: 12V, 230W dynamo, 34 a/h battery.
Dimensions: Wheelbase: 6.04ft (1840mm); track: 3.74ft (1140mm) front and 3.95ft (1203mm) rear; length: 10.02ft (3054mm); width: 4.52ft (1377mm); height: 4.38ft (1335mm) ground clearance: 5.51in (140mm).
Weight: 1270lbs (580kg) unladen, 1984lbs (900kg) laden.
Performance: Maximum speed: over 65mph (over105 kph).
Average fuel consumption: 54mpg (5.2 lts/100km).

126 Bis

Engine: Type 126 A2.000, rear-mounted, 2 cylinders in-line, ohv, 704cc. Bore and stroke: 80 x 70mm; compression ratio: 8.6:1; maximum power 26bhp @ 4500rpm; ignition: coil and distributor.
Cooling: Water with pump and booster fan.
Fuel: Tank capacity: 4.63 galls (21 litres); twin choke carburettor and pump.
Lubrication: Pressure, sump: 5.5lbs (2.5kg).
Transmission: Rear drive, 4 speeds and reverse, central lever and single dry plate clutch.
Suspension: Independent front and rear with telescopic shock absorbers; wishbones and transverse leaf spring at front with transverse arms and coil springs at rear.
Brakes:Drums, hydraulic on all four wheels with handbrake operating on rear wheels.
Tyres:135/70 SR 13.
Steering: Rack and pinion, 28.2ft (8.6m) turning circle.
Electrical: 12V, 45 A alternator, 34 a/h battery.
Dimensions: Wheelbase: 6.04ft (1840mm); track: 3.72ft (1134mm) front and 3.84ft (1169) rear; length: 10.19ft (3107mm).

width: 4.52ft (1377mm); height: 4.41ft (1343mm); ground clearance: 5.51in (140mm).
Weight: 1366lbs (620kg) unladen, 1531lbs (695kg) laden.
Performance: Maximum speed 72mph (116kph).
Average fuel consumption: 55.64mpg (5.1 lts/100km).

850

Engine: Type 100G. 000, rear-mounted 4 cylinders in line; ohv, 843cc, bore and stroke 65 x 63.5mm;compression ratio: 8.1:1; maximum power 40-42bhp @ 5300rpm. Ignition: coil and distributor.
Cooling: Water; pump; capacity 10.5 pints (6 litres).
Fuel: Tank capacity: 6.5 galls (30 litres); carburettor and pump.
Lubrication: Pressure 47psi. (3.3 kg/sq.cm).
Transmission: Rear drive, gearbox and final drive combined, 4 speeds, all synchromesh, and reverse. Central lever and single dry plate clutch.
Suspension: Independent front and rear; transverse leaf spring, wishbones and anti-roll bar at front, semi trailing arms, coil springs and anti-roll bar at rear.
Brakes: Drums, hydraulic on all four wheels, handbrake operating on rear wheels.
Tyres: 5.50 x 12.
Steering: Worm and helical sector,29ft (8.9m) turning circle.
Electrical: 12V, 230W dynamo, 36 a/h battery.
Dimensions: Wheelbase: 6.65ft (2027mm); track: 3.76ft (1146mm) front, 3.97ft (1211mm) rear; length: 11.73ft (3575mm); width: 4.68ft (1425mm); height:4.54ft (1385mm); ground clearance: 4.72in (120mm).
Weight: 1476lbs (670kg) unladen, 2358lbs (1070kg) laden.
Performance: Maximum speed 75-77mph (120-125kph).
Average fuel consumption: 44-46mpg (6.0-6.3 lts/100km).

Note: Two models of 850 saloon available, Standard and Super; Super models received the 42bhp engine. Semi-automatic transmission available from 1966. Coupé and Spider models available 1965 with 52bhp engines. Dimensions differ as follows: track: 3.80ft (1158mm) f, 3.98ft (1212mm) r, 11.84ft (3608mm); w:4.92ft (1500mm); gc: 5.31in (135mm). Max.sp. 84mph (135kph); a.f.c: 40mpg (7l/100km).

Cinquecento 700

Engine: Type 170A.000; front-mounted, 2 cylinders in line; ohv; 704cc. Bore and stroke: 80 x 70mm; compression ratio: 9:1; maximum power 31bhp @ 5000rpm; ignition: electronic.
Cooling: Water, pump, thermostat and booster fan. Capacity: 0.88 gall (4 litres).
Fuel: Tank capacity 7.7 galls (35 litres); carburettor and pump.
Lubrication: Pressure, sump 5.7lbs (2.6kg).
Transmission: Front drive, 4 speeds and reverse, all synchromesh, central lever, single dry plate clutch.
Suspension: Independent all-round, transverse arms, coil springs at front and longitudunal arms with coil springs at rear. Hydraulic shock absorbers all-round.
Brakes: Hydraulic, discs at front, drums at rear. Handbrake operating on rear wheels.
Tyres: 135/70 SR 13.
Steering: Rack and pinion, 29ft (8.8m) turning circle.
Electrical: 12V, 55A alternator and 32 a/h battery.
Dimensions: Wheelbase: 7.22ft (2200mm); track: 4.17ft (1270mm) front; 4.16ft (1268mm) rear; length: 10.59ft (3227mm); width: 4.88ft (1487mm); height: 4.71ft (1435mm).
Weight: 1487lbs (675kg) unladen; 2445lbs (1110kg) laden.
Performance: Maximum speed 79mph (127kph).

Average fuel consumption: 47mpg (6.1 lts/100km).

Cinquecento 900i cat

Engine: Type 170A1.046; transverse front-mounted, 4 cylinders in-line; ohv; 903cc. Bore and stroke: 65 x 68mm; compression ratio: 9.2:1; maximum power 41bhp @ 5500rpm; ignition: electronic.
Cooling: Water, pump, thermostat and booster fan. Capacity: 1.06 gall (4.8 litres).
Fuel: Tank capacity 7.7 galls (35 litres); electronic ignition.
Lubrication: Pressure, sump 8.26lbs (3.75kg).
Transmission: Front drive, 5 speeds and reverse, all synchromesh, central lever, single dry plate clutch.
Suspension: Independent all-round, transverse arms, coil springs at front and longitudunal arms with coil springs at rear. Telescopic shock absorbers all-round.
Brakes: Hydraulic, discs at front, drums at rear, Handbrake operating on rear wheels.
Tyres: 145/70 SR 13.
Steering: Rack and pinion, 29ft (8.8m) turning circle.
Electrical: 12V, 55A alternator and 40 a/h battery.
Dimensions: Wheelbase: 7.22ft (2200mm); track: 4.17ft (1270mm) front; 4.16ft (1268mm) rear; length: 10.59ft (3227mm); width: 4.88ft (1487mm); height: 4.71ft (1435mm).
Weight: 1564lbs (710kg) unladen, 2533lbs (1150kg) laden.
Performance: Maximum speed 87mph (140kph).
Average fuel consumption: 45mpg (6.7 lts/100km).

Cinquecento 900 (from mid-1995)

Engine: Type 1170 A1. 046; transverse front-mounted, 4 cylinders in-line; ohv; 899cc. Bore and stroke : 65 x 67.70mm; compression ratio: 8.8:1; maximum power 39bhp @ 3,000rpm; ignition electronic.
Other specification as 900i cat except:
Tyres: 145/70 R 13 (S); 155/65 R 13 (SX, Suite & Soleil).
Electrical: 12V; 64A Alternator / 32 Ah battery.
Dimensions: Track: rear, 1276mm.
Weight: 750kg (suite) unladen; 1150kg fully laden.

Cinquecento Sporting

Engine: Type 176 B2.000, transverse, front-mounted. 4 cylinders in-line; ohv; 1108cc. Bore and stroke: 70 x 72mm; compression ratio: 9.6:1; maximum power 54bhp @ 5500rpm; ignition: electronic.
Cooling: Pressurised liquid cooling; thermostatic electric fan. Capacity: 4.6 litres.
Fuel: Tank capacity: 7.7 gals (35 litres).
Lubrication: Pump; sump capacity: 0.77gal (3.5 litres).
Transmission: Front drive, 5 speeds and reverse, all synchromesh, central gear lever; single dry plate clutch.
Suspension: Independent all round; MacPherson struts with transverse arm at front with coil springs and anti-roll bar; trailing arms and coil springs at rear; hydraulic telescopic shock absorbers all-round.
Brakes: Hydraulic circuit with fixed pressure regulating valve on rear axle; front discs, rear drums, power-assisted. Handbrake operates on rear wheels.
Tyres: 155/65 SR 13; since May 1995 165/55 HR 13.
Steering: Rack and pinion; 29ft (8.8m) turning circle.
Electrical: 12V 64A alternator; 32 Ah battery. (UK specification 40Ah battery).
Dimensions: Wheelbase: 7.22ft (2200mm); track: 4.17ft (1270mm) front; 4.19ft (1276mm) rear; length: 10.59ft (3227mm); width: 4.88ft (1487mm); height: 4.71ft (1435mm).
Weight: unladen 1620lbs (735kg); fully laden 2535 lbs (1150kg).
Performance: Maximum speed 94mph (150km/h).
Average fuel consumption: 45.6mpg (6.2 lts/100km).

Seicento

(Only brief details of the Seicento were available at the time of publication)
Engine: Transverse, front-mounted. 4 cylinders in-line; ohv; 899cc or 1108cc.
Transmission: Front drive, 5 speeds and reverse, all synchromesh, central gear lever; single dry plate clutch.
Dimensions: length: 10.89ft (3320mm); width: 4.92ft (1500mm).
Performance: Maximum speed 53mph (85kph).
Average fuel consumption:46.8mpg (6 lts/100km).

BIBLIOGRAPHY

Abarth Guide – Alfred S. Consentino, published by Alfred Consentino Books.
All The Fiats – Giancenzo Madaro, published by Domus books.
Fiat – Michael Sedgwick, published by Batsford.
"Fiat" A Fifty Years Record – Arnoldo Mondadori Editore.
Fiat Cinquecento – Enrico Benzing, published by Automobilia.
Fiat, Races and Sports cars – Ferruccio Bernabo, published by Libreria dell' Automobile.
Fiat Sports Cars From 1945 to the X1/9 – Graham Robson, published by Osprey.
Fiat, Toute L'Histoire – Dominique P. Dubarry, published by E.P.A.
Fiat 500 Topolino – Marco Bossi, published by Giorgio Nada Editore.
Fiat 500 – Elvio Geganello, published by Giorgio Nada Editore.
Fiat 500/600 – 1936-69 by Walter Zeichner, published by Schrader Verlag.
Fiat 600 – Giancenzo Madaro, published by Giorgio Nada Editore.

Forty Years of Design with Fiat – Dante Giacosa, published by Automobilia.
Great Marques of Italy – Jonathon Wood, published by Viscount books.
Illustrated Abarth Buyers Guide – Peter Vack, published by Motorbooks International.

Other Fiat titles:
Automobili Fiat by Angelo Anselmi, published by Giorgio Nada Editore.
Fiat & Abarth 124 Spider & Coupé by John Tipler, published by Veloce Publishing.
Fiat Balilla New Edition by Antonio Amadelli, published by Giorgio Nada Editore.
Fiat 1100 by Brizio Pignacca, published by Giorgio Nada Editore.
Le Zagato. Fiat 8VZ, Alfa Romeo 1900 SSZ by Michele Marchiano, published by Giorgio Nada Editore.

INDEX

Abarth 31, 37-8, 40-2, 44, 58-9, 88, 103-110, 111, 128
Abarth, Carlo 104, 106, 109
Abarth & Fiat-Abarth:
  130 128
  150 128
  595 110-11
  595 Corsa 110
  595 SS 109-10
  600 106
  695 110
  695 Assetto Corsa 110
  750 105, 107, 110
  750 Zagato 105-6
  1000 109, 128
  1000TC & Radiale 107-9
  1600 128
  2000 Mostra 128
  Bilabero 110-11
  Monomille 110-11
  Nürburgring Corsa 107
Agnelli family 11
Agnelli, Giovanni 11, 13, 15, 21, 23
Alberti 73
Alfa Romeo 10, 54, 104
Allemeno (coachbuilder) 40
Austin 20, 34, 39, 54
Austin Seven 16
Autobianchi 73, 76-7, 93, 96, 98, 117-8, 121, 125, 126, 133
Auto Union, DKW 54

Bauhof 63
Bertone 41-2, 106, 110, 128
Bianchi 118
BMC 10, 20, 54, 57
BMC, Mini & Mini-Cooper 20, 54, 58, 96, 107, 109, 111, 117, 127
BMW 10, 78, 85, 87
Boano (coachbuilder) 40-1, 106, 110, 130

Boddy, Bill 86
Bond 10, 61
Bonelli, Piero 62-3
Bonetto, Rudolpho 102
Bono, Gaudenzio 26, 73, 76
Borgward 10

Borsattino, Vergilio 5
Bricherasio, Count di 11
British Motor Corporation - see BMC
Budd 26

Canta (coachbuilder) 40
Cavalli 13
Ceirano, Giovanni Battista 11-12
Chrysler 26, 44
Cisitalia 23, 104
Citroën 13, 34, 40, 54
  Bijou 96
  Dyane 102, 129
  Traction Avant 15, 21
  2CV 9, 19-20, 22-3, 35, 39, 54, 84-5, 96
  5CV 9
Coriasco 115-16

DAF 54, 96
D'Ascanio, Corradino 61-2
Dembowski, W. 95
Demetrious & Sons 122
DKW - see Auto Union
Dusio, Piero 104

Eldridge, Ernest 13
Enrico, Giovanni 12-13

Faccioli, Aristide 11-13
Fessia, Dr Antonio 15, 20, 28, 62, 133
Fiat 10-14, 54
Fiat-Concord 57
Fiat (models)
  Tipo A 12
  6hp 12-13
  8hp 13
  12hp 13
  126 73, 98-9, 129-131, 152-3
  126 Bis 91, 130-33, 152-3
  127 128-130, 133
  400 prototype 20-22, 60, 63, 76, 78
  500 Belvedere 9, 16, 18-19, 23, 27, 33, 46-7
  500 Giardiniera 18, 23, 27, 33, 46-7
  500 project 13
  500 Sport 88-90, 93, 109, 118
  500 Topolino 9-10, 14-20, 22-5, 62
  501 13, 42
  503 42
  509 13
  509A 13
  509S 13
  514 13, 42
  515 13
  522 13
  600 140-4
  700 prototype 20-2
  850 37-8, 44, 49, 56-7, 98, 124, 126-28, 137-40
  1200 50
  1500 14-15
  Balilla 14, 17, 20, 22, 42, 121-22
  Belvedere 93, 112
  Cargo 102
  Cinquecento 16, 113, 131-7, 153-4
  Giardiniera 90-3, 98, 103, 112, 118, 146-52
  Mephistopheles 13
  Muletto 103
  Multipla 27, 38, 46-7, 49, 51, 73, 91, 112-15, 122, 128, 141-52
  Nuova 23, 31, 41-2, 44, 53, 143-52
  Type 1 Taxi 13
  Panda 100, 128-29, 133
  Pully 103
  Punto 135
  Ranger 102
  Seicento 136-7
  Tipo 500 15

Topolino 82, 93, 96, 98, 105-12, 117, 124, 132
Uno 133
Fiat Spa 121
Fiorelli, Amando 28, 73
Fissore 115
Ford 10, 20, 34, 39-40, 54
Frisky (Meadows) 34, 78, 96
FSM 53, 130, 132
Fuldamobil 61

Gamine - see Vignale
Genero, Allessandro 28
Ghia 40-41, 102, 106, 115, 122
Giacosa, Dante 7, 8, 15-16, 20-27, 39, 49-50, 54-55, 59, 60-4, 73, 75-80, 88-96, 104, 112, 114, 127-27, 130, 133, 144
Giannini 102
Goggomobil 10, 34, 54, 85
Goliath 10, 78
Gregoire, J.A. 23

Heilbronn (NSU-Fiat works) 61-3
Heinkel 10, 69, 78, 85
Hillman 54
Hitler, Adolf 9
Honda 95-96

Ilo 71
Isetta (see also BMW) 10, 61, 78, 85
Issigonis, Sir Alex 54, 127

Jagst 117

Lancia 10, 104, 133
Lancia, Gianni 72
Lancia, Vincenzo 13
Lardone, Oreste 15
Ledwink, Hans 111
Lefauchaux, Pierre 9
Lloyd 10
Lombardi (coachbuilder) 49, 102

Maioli, Mario 132-3
Manzu, Pio 128-29
Marchesi, Enrico 11
Mazda 95
Meadows (Frisky) 96
Mercedes 42
Messerschmitt 10, 61
Michelotti 78
Mille Miglia 41, 58
Mini & Mini-Cooper - see BMC
Minica 95
Mitsubishi 95
Montebone, Oscar 73, 75-6, 127
Monterosa (coachbuilder) 40-1, 102
Moretti 102, 115, 118
Morris 20, 34, 39, 54
Moss, Stirling 42
Mosso 64
Motor Holdings, New Zealand 124
MPG & H (tuning specialists) 58
Mulliner (coachbuilder) 13
Mussolini 21

Nazzaro, Felice 13
Neckar 116-17
NSU & NSU-Fiat 34, 54, 57, 61-2, 73, 96, 116 17
NSU Prince 96, 117

O.M. 115, 128
Opel 21

Page (coachbuilder) 13
Panhard 23, 54

Panoramica Estate car 118
Piaggio 61-2, 96
Pininfarina (coachbuilder) 40, 54, 58, 102, 106-107, 109, 115
Pirelli 16, 34, 118
Porsche, Ferdinand 9, 104, 111
Pratt, Wally 58-59
Prince Phillip, HRH Duke of Edinburgh 95

Reliant 10, 61
Renault 9, 102, 109, 129
  4CV 9, 19-20, 27, 34-5, 38-40, 44
  4 & 4L 46, 54
  Dauphine 44, 46, 48, 54
  Riviera - see Jagst
Rootes Group 10, 54
Rudge Cycles 11
Ruffia, Count Roberto Biscaretti, di 11

Salamano, Carlo 25-8, 62, 78,
Savio 102
Scagliarni, Carlo 104
Scaglione, Franco 41-2
Scarfiotti, Ludovico 11
Schaeffer, Rudolfo 115
Scioneri 115
SEAT 57-58, 124
Short of Rochester (coachbuilder) 13
Siata 40-41, 58, 102, 122-23, 138
Siata-Abarth 124
Sibona & Basano 111
SicilFiat 103
Simca 17, 19, 23, 50, 54, 104, 126, 138-9
S.P.A. 15
Standard 20, 39
Standard-Triumph 54
Stellina 118
Steyr 57
Steyr-Puch 103, 111-12
Subaru 95
Suzuki 95

Trojan 61
Torazza, Giovanni 64

Valletta, Vittorio 23, 26-7, 73, 76
Vespa 61-2, 96
Vestidello, Luigi 78
Vignale (coachbuilder) 40-1, 78, 102, 106, 115, 117, 121-22
Viotti (coachbuilder) 40, 102, 106, 110
Volkswagen 9, 20, 27, 35, 39-40, 44, 54, 74, 128

Ward (coachbuilder) 13
Weinsberg (Fiat coachwork division) 62-3
Weinsberg 500 117
Wilkins, Gordon 95
Willys-Overland 54

Young's of Bromley (coachbuilder) 13
Yugo 134

Zagato (coachbuilder) 40-1, 58, 88, 103, 105-6, 108-9, 111
Zastava 57, 123-24, 134
Zaporozhet 96
Zundapp 61